Sobering

Melissa Rice

Sobering

Lessons Learnt the Hard Way on Drinking, Thinking and Quitting

1 3 5 7 9 10 8 6 4 2

First published in 2021 by September Publishing

Copyright © Melissa Rice 2021

The right of Melissa Rice to be identified as the author of this work has been asserted
by her in accordance with the Copyright Designs and Patents Act 1988.

Typeset by RefineCatch Limited. www.refinecatch.com

Printed in Denmark on paper from responsibly managed, sustainable sources
by Nørhaven

ISBN 978-1-912836-67-3

September Publishing
www.septemberpublishing.org

For The Rices

And, because having one of anything has always been a problem, including book dedications ...

For everyone feeling frightened, alone and hopeless about their drinking, I get it, I really do. I hope you find the happiness and freedom you so deserve.

Contents

Author's note

I didn't intend on being an alcoholic – who does? On the list of things I wanted to experience and achieve by the time I was thirty-two, I had never thought alcohol dependency, losing my marbles and my career as a teacher, getting locked in the family home for months on end, going to rehab, falling in love with recovery, sharing it all on a BBC podcast *Hooked: The Unexpected Addicts* and now writing a book would make the cut, but there we have it.

Please believe me when I say that I have no intention of convincing you that you are an alcoholic, and I am certainly not going to profess to have the answers on how best to get sober. I'm just a regular girl who swan dived from grace and hit every shameful branch along the way. I am *not* a professional in this stuff. I am a professional fuck-up at times, yes, but I am far from qualified to give you the answers. To be honest, I couldn't think of a more ill-suited person if I tried. I *just* about have the capacity to deal with my own problems, and there are still days when getting a wash and changing my knickers is seen as a huge success. So please, if you are struggling with either your mental health or your drinking, do make an appointment with your GP or seek professional help (resources can be found at the back of the book). I wish I had taken those courageous steps sooner.

Your head may tell you you're the first (and worst): you're not. You won't be the first or the worst and you certainly won't be the last. Addiction and mental health problems do not discriminate.

Finding yourself reliant on alcohol (or any substance) can be frightening and really bloody isolating. The personal shame, fear of being judged and anxieties around life without it brings just as much heartache as alcohol does. If these worries ring true for you, I get it, I really do. If this book helps just one person feel less alone, then – you know what? – it was worth reliving my darkest days and painfully cringing each time. There may be parts of this book that are a bit too close for home or trigger intense emotion and, if that is the case, I hope you have the safe space to process it and someone you trust to talk to.

I have learnt lessons the painful and shameful way, and I am sharing them with you for you to take what you can and leave the rest. My recovery is about connection and accepting that I can't do this alone, and to capture this you will also hear of experiences and insights of others: counsellors, professors, my family, my friends and, of course, people in recovery.

Early in my sobriety a fellow recovering alcoholic suggested that I should 'look for the similarities' and not the differences. It never dawned on me that I had been going through life only looking for reasons that made me and my circumstances different to everyone else's. So, I would ask (if I'm allowed to) that throughout these pages you look for those similarities and forget about our differences.

Sure, addiction dragged me to dark and dangerous places but recovery has brought out the best in life – and, dare I say it, it has brought out the best in me and the friends in recovery who feature in this book. I hope you are able to see that quitting the booze isn't the end, it's just the beginning. People do recover and there is a way out.

Introduction

Straight to it, no messing about and no pussyfooting around, we have to talk about mental health and alcohol. (I can hear my mum's thoughts already: 'Oh god, why is she starting this book with her mental health? She'll never find a husband now.') I was trying to think of a lighter subject to begin with, but when I think about my story, the fact is that the one constant that has stuck with me through thick and thin is my (poor) mental health; whether that be good old anxiety, bouts of depression, intrusive thoughts, self-destructive behaviours or self-defeating coping strategies – they all matter, and contributed to my reliance, and then dependence, on booze.

I don't separate my mental health issues from my addiction, and I don't favour or prioritise one over the other, because I can't. They are two co-existing, nightmarish bedfellows: when one kicks off, the other rears its ugly head; they are a loyal tag-team who, if left to their own devices, would have me locked in the family home like Bertha Mason in *Jane Eyre*, pickled and batshit. To manage my mental health is to manage my addiction and, let me tell you, when there is the infrequent moment that I feel like I have a good grasp of both it is pure bliss.

We are fortunate to live in an age where mental illness and

prioritising your head and well-being is commonplace – I'm pretty certain that if I had been born in the nineteenth century I would have been living the rest of my life in an asylum. (It still shocks me to the core what those suffering were subjected to in the name of 'treatments'.) Society has progressed and evolved with respect to mental health. We are more aware, are becoming more tolerant, and people are less likely to change the subject when they hear words like 'depression', 'anxiety', 'borderline personality disorder', 'bi-polar' and 'antidepressants' (to name a few). Some workplaces have well-thought-out mental health and well-being policies and in-house counselling services, while Instagram is packed full of mental health accounts. There are podcasts upon podcasts on 'how to cope', multiple national campaigns to spread awareness, while phrases such as 'It's OK to not be OK' are all the rage. I'm here for it all – the destigmatising of the mental health movement is a good thing. It is a *great* thing. I wish these resources and this level of human understanding had been around a decade ago when I was tying myself in knots, paralysed with fear, thinking I was the only person who thought and felt the way I did.

But as wonderful as this shift has been for us all, when I think about where addiction is placed in this well-being uprising, I feel somewhat dejected. Stigma around the topic, and unhealthy stereotypes, create a wall of shame, a barrier to seeking help, and form (perfectly 'valid') reasoning for keeping your struggle and even your success hidden until the time feels right and you feel safe enough to share your truth. During the height of my harmful drinking days, and even in my early days of sobriety, finding someone or something that really embraced addiction as part of the 'mental health' family was a struggle, and to a large part continues to be. The way I see it is that addiction is considered to be that embarrassing uncle at the wedding, the one you don't want the new in-laws or guests to see. He is of course family, and by principle he should be attending the do, but he is not representative of your family and, by god, you don't want pics of him in the wedding album. This may seem a little harsh but, believe me, I'm not the type to upset the apple cart or ruffle feathers (if anything, I'm the type of person who would go to any lengths to keep all the apples perfectly placed and those feathers silky smooth), but I know I'm not a lone ranger with this feeling that addiction is not considered, perceived or received like other mental illness 'relatives'.

Living in a 'recovery house' for two years – a block of flats for women who are leaving rehab and in early recovery – meant that I had a focus group to hand. I asked the girls their opinions on addiction being detached from 'mental health', and all eight women shared their thoughts and experiences with me. What was wonderful about our impromptu chat was that we all experienced feeling shame or being shamed for suffering with addiction – that in having this affliction our other mental health issues were delegitimised. Unanimously, we agreed that putting 'addiction' and 'mental illness' in two separate boxes wasn't helpful at all – the fact that to treat our mental health means we have to treat (and manage) our addiction to maintain good mental health shows just how grey this area is.

Basically, if Mental Illness and Addiction were on Facebook, their relationship status would definitely be 'It's complicated'.

And you know what? I'm yet to meet anyone in recovery from any addiction who, at some point in their life, hasn't had difficulties with their mental health, or experienced some kind of trauma where a bit of talking therapy or psychological intervention wouldn't have gone amiss. I'm sorry to bring *Shrek* into the mix (I've lost any hope of credibility, haven't I?) but there's a scene when the big green CGI ogre says, 'I eat because I am unhappy and I'm unhappy because I eat.' That sums up how I felt throughout my harmful drinking. There is a real need for a combined approach; in fact, a lot of psychiatrists, professors and doctors are crying out for changes in how we treat someone with existing mental health conditions and substance disorders.

When someone is diagnosed with both mental health issues and addiction it can be referred to as a 'dual diagnosis'. I had a chat with Professor Julia Sinclair, a professor of addiction psychiatry at the University of Southampton and Honorary Consultant in Alcohol Liaison in the NHS, for an episode of our BBC Radio 5 Live podcast *Hooked*. She pointed out that 'dual' suggests that there are just two issues to deal with, when in fact there are many patients who have physical health conditions, like liver disease, and also have multiple mental health disorders – anxiety, depression, PTSD, to name just a few. To this end, 'co-occurring' or 'co-existing' or 'co-morbid' seem an appropriate fit as a way to describe this situation.

Sharing her views on the challenges of getting help for both mental health and substances, she said:

Many addiction services no longer have competencies in-house to deal with co-morbid mental ill health, and mental health services frequently refuse to work with people who have a co-morbid alcohol use disorder, such that patients wanting help with the depression that they see as causing them to use alcohol are often told they can't be helped until they are alcohol-free. People in truly desperate states are bounced between addiction and mental health services, with many often falling through the gap.

Professor Julia Sinclair

For professionals to make these changes that are so desperately needed, funding is a huge factor. I'm not on the BBC with my podcast now, so I can be a bit more political ... cuts to funding have devastated this sector and I am appalled, disgusted and incandescent with rage about this. Really, it's a false economy: the 'savings' that are made in one area only lead to increased pressure on the NHS in another. If I think about my experience, I found myself in A&E multiple times, taking up general psychiatrists' and doctors' time. If there had been proper funding for me to access support or go to rehab when I needed it, then I wouldn't have been taking up resources elsewhere.

If you're a bit of a details person, like I am, you will want to know why cuts to addiction services have happened. Well ...

The Health and Social Care Act changes of 2012 resulted in addiction services [being] taken out of NHS commissioning, and subject[ed] to frequent re-tendering and budget cuts. This has disproportionately affected people with co-occurring alcohol dependence and a mental health disorder. We need mental health services to reclaim alcohol use disorders as primarily a disease of the mind, and genuinely embrace person-centred care.

Professor Julia Sinclair

The Alcohol Health Alliance UK is a coalition of more than fifty organisations working together to reduce the harm caused by alcohol. Members include medical royal colleges, charities, patient representatives and alcohol health campaigners. I have had the pleasure of working with these guys as they fight for change to a problem that is so prevalent in the UK, yet so neglected. The AHA is chaired by Professor Sir Ian Gilmore, a leading professor of hepatology and special advisor on alcohol to the Royal College of Physicians. Speaking to me about the scale of alcohol harm, he shared:

> *As a liver specialist, I witness first-hand the devastating consequences of alcohol harm every day in my work. The damage that alcohol inflicts on the health of an individual ripples out into all areas of their own lives, the people around them and their communities. Despite this, alcohol remains a celebrated part of British culture and those who either try to give up or cut down on drinking are often stigmatised by their peers. We are very happy to talk about alcohol in this country until it comes to alcohol harm and what measures are needed to end it. Sadly, for all of us that is a necessary and urgent conversation that has to be had.*
>
> *Deaths linked to liver disease have risen a staggering 400 per cent in fourteen years; alcohol harm costs our society at least £27 billion every year and 308,000 children currently live with at least one high-risk drinker over the age of eighteen. We are in the middle of a mounting health crisis which we cannot ignore.*
>
> **Professor Sir Ian Gilmore**

The latest AHA report, *'It's everywhere' – alcohol's public face and private harm*, highlights a number of areas of alcohol harm that need a serious overhaul, including funding. Within the report was the startling reality of cuts: 'There is insufficient treatment available to those who need it. Treatment provider Change, Grow, Live told us that services in England experienced real-term funding cuts of over £100 million, an average of 30% per service, since 2012.'

The next big issue I'd like to address: is alcoholism a disease? Addiction is no longer under the NHS remit. For a lot of folk, 'the NHS shouldn't be dealing with addiction as it's not a disease' is a relevant point. I know it's divisive – it's complex, and it's a conversation that can lead to hurt, anger and maybe a 'No bloody way'. Generally, those who have witnessed or been to the depths are on one side of the argument, and those who believe addiction/ substance misuse is about choice are on the other.

The fact is, I understand the main thrust on both sides because I have been on both. I'll never forget my mum's words of: 'Hold on, you were sober when you bought it, you knew what you were doing.' She's right: technically, I was chemically sober when I bought my half-litre of vodka and stuffed it down my baggy mom jeans (which, by the way, are rather snug these days) – but was I sober in the mind? Absolutely not. When I look back at my worst days, the peak of my alcohol insanity, I think: 'My god, Melissa, you poor poppet.' (It's taken quite a lot of therapy to think that of myself.) Because I know that frightened girl was me, even if now I don't really recognise her that much – such a lost and frightened soul. No 'well' person would have done the things I did, thought the way I felt, have made the choices I made … so do I think it is a disease or disorder? I do.

I wanted to chat with someone who works in the field, so who better than Michael Rawlinson, an addictions counsellor from Clouds House. He has known me from my time in rehab and we reconnected when I needed an expert for *Hooked*. He's been a fixture and a friend ever since. For the purpose of this chapter, he told me about a book called *DSM–5* (bear with me). For mere mortals like me, it is a sort of encyclopaedia for the diagnosis of mental health conditions. As the blurb says, 'determining an accurate diagnosis is the first step toward being able to appropriately treat any medical condition, and mental disorders are no exception'. Within this manual there is a definition for alcohol use disorder: 'AUD is a chronic relapsing brain disorder characterised by an impaired ability to stop or control alcohol use despite adverse social, occupational, or health consequences.'

Now, there is a list of symptoms that I was going to include, but I don't think it's responsible for me, a non-professional, to 'encourage' you to self-diagnose and potentially end up panicked. But I wanted to include this definition to help you see that excessive drinking, disordered drinking, problematical drinking, alcoholism, alcohol dependency, etc., is recognised as a disorder. It is a real thing, and you are not a bad person for suffering from it.

Further 'proof' that alcoholism is an illness comes from a funny old place – my bowels. Apart from a troublesome head, I also have a very troublesome bowel, as I have Crohn's disease. I never questioned if Crohn's was a real illness/disease: I have seen my ulcerated innards on a screen, while the blood tests, lubricated fingers up the bum, multiple operations, stoma bag and immunosuppressant injections are hard to refute. The evidence is clear and tangible that my guts are diseased, but my reliance on paint-stripper-style vodka? That *was* harder to accept as a real illness. My Crohn's is a chronic condition; I have it for life, I have to make changes to my diet, understand my triggers (those things that could set my condition off, e.g. stress), have thorough plans in place and take daily action to keep it at bay. If I were to replace the word 'Crohn's' with 'alcoholism', there isn't much difference: to me, my alcoholism and my Crohn's are both life-long chronic conditions.

These days, I tend not to go through the whole, 'I've got this shit (literally and metaphorically) for the rest of my life ... what's the fucking point?' thought process. One day at a time, folks. If I thought I would have to do anything for ever and live my days as if I had a life sentence, I'd be a miserable, self-pitying bugger. But, if I take both of them a day at a time, I have found that twenty-four hours is far more manageable than trying to live your entire life out in your head.

And then there's the next big question: 'Are you born an alcoholic?' Although I think it is an important question to raise, my simple answer is – I have no bloody clue. I don't know if I was born with it, caught it or bought it; I just know that, at some point in my life, a line was crossed: I needed a drink to get through life, to calm the nerves and quiet the head, and I became reliant on alcohol to change how I felt.

There are times when I read online articles and see discussions that make me wonder if every mental health symptom I have is just part of alcoholism, or if my alcoholism is a product of my poor mental health. Professor Julia again:

The same symptom may be either a cause or a consequence. For instance, symptoms of depression or anxiety may increase our alcohol use, which then is likely to worsen our mental state, worsening anxiety and depression symptoms, and fuelling further alcohol use, which people may regard as treating their anxiety or depression.

Professor Julia Sinclair

For my own sanity, I just accept what I am and what I suffer with and keep my focus on the solution: the things I do to stay well. (Dare I make reference to *Love Island*'s most-used quote? Sod it, why not: 'It just is what it is.')

Now, the final tricky subject to address before I get into my story: problematic language and the use of the words 'alcoholic' and 'alcoholism'. For a lot of people, whether that be academics, workers in the field or those who have a difficult relationship with drink, it is felt that both these words reinforce negative stereotypes and stigma. I get it, I really do. I only have to look at my own perceptions prior to recovery to understand it. But you will be reading that word a lot in this book, so I thought it best acknowledge it. It took me a long time to accept or consider I was an alcoholic. But through the podcast, and especially with this book, I want people to feel that being an alcoholic is nothing to be ashamed of. To be honest, it's just easier if I call myself an alcoholic – after all, if it walks like a duck, sounds like a duck ... you get the point. I really hope the word doesn't isolate you or scare you, as that's not my intention in the slightest and, please, feel free to replace the word 'alcoholic' with whatever you are most comfortable with. There is more that connects than divides us, and I really hope a label doesn't get in the way of that.

I suppose now is a good time to get off my soapbox, away from the politics and the bigger picture, and to start sharing about my pre-drinking days – well, years. Those years of unhelpful and harmful thought processes, believing that I was a piece of shit and hobbling through life forever needing a crutch to get through it.

Before I delve into the nitty and gritty ... I'm very aware that my struggle with mental health isn't of an *extreme* nature. In the grand scheme of things, my experience isn't uncommon, and my diagnoses are the timeless classics: generalised anxiety disorder (GAD), depression and a bit of PTSD for good measure – oh my GAD, what a threesome.

I suppose I want to make clear that while my own struggles are not out of the ordinary, I'm not minimising them in the slightest, either. There's nothing worse than a dick-measuring competition. We all have our 'stuff' and we all have different scales of mental health. Not all of us have 'issues', mental illness, mental health diagnoses or whatever the correct phrase is to use, but me, Melissa, I'm not unique, my experiences aren't special or different. That commonality is where I hope to offer some identification, for you to go: 'Fucking hell, yeah, I have felt like that ... I've done that ... OK, I didn't think or do that, but I have done *that* ...'

We've established I swear – I apologise if I put foul words in your mouth.

Chapter 1

Drinking won't cure your thinking

When I first got to rehab, I was under the impression that my anxiety and depression had started in my late teens or early twenties. I was wrong: they started way younger. I just didn't know it.

I had a regular everything growing up: my childhood was regular – 'dad stuff' (i.e. sometimes there, sometimes not) wasn't uncommon around our neck of the woods, but apart from that those younger years were just normal. Your run-of-the-mill, ten-a-penny childhood. I grew up in a well-presented home on the outskirts of Liverpool, in Kirkby. Just on the edge of town. It was green, it was quiet and it was a postcode lottery win for my gorgeous mum. We also fell under the catchment area for the convent high school, in a 'posh' area.

Kirkby is – how can I put this? – unique (as much as it pains me to admit it) in terms of prosperity and as for amenities, there isn't much going on. We have the accolade of ranking sixth in the no doubt much-read Parliamentary report *Deprivation in English Constituencies, 2019* – out of 533 entries I might add. Neglected as my hometown may be, it is thriving in areas that the government can't measure: heart, character, humour and, above all else, pride. Particularly pride in appearance.

My friend Sam was spot on when he summed up my hometown: 'A bubble, and the Essex of Liverpool.' I couldn't agree more. There is no expense spared for appearance and it's safe to say I can let my people down on that front: I don't dress particularly Scouse, but when the occasion is right, I'll be there, tanned up, hair pruned to perfection, with my brows on, feeling a million bucks. It's a town where everyone knows everyone; you cannot go to the 'townie' (town centre) without being stopped or having to pull a face that's a half-smile, half-'hiya' at least five times. Six degrees of separation is more like two degrees, and many conversations go a little bit like this: 'Oh, is your mum one of the Wilsons?', 'Did you used to work in X? My fella used to work there and said you were mad', 'My cousin used to go to that school, do you know [insert their cousin's name]?', 'You know Y? Well, I seen her getting lecky, and she was saying that Z was having a terrible time with her daughter.'

As you can imagine, anonymity is non-existent and nothing is sacred or off-limits. In the age of Facebook, Instagram and WhatsApp, news and 'goss' travel faster than ever – a body doesn't even turn cold before you find out who and how someone has died. To this day, I still wonder how many group chats my downfall landed in, and each time every fibre of my being winces. To be clear, that's not me thinking I am a hot commodity or even newsworthy; I just know that, in a small town like mine, someone ending up batshit and being carted off to rehab is a banqueting feast for a group chat.

When the shit really hit the fan in 2017, and my only chance at recovering was to be plucked out of Kirkby and start life over somewhere new, I had to take it. My heart still aches knowing that for me to do well – for me to be me – I had get away from my hometown, out of the bubble. But, like most Scouse people, I won't have a bad word said about the place. I can call it, but you can't. It's in our DNA to protect and defend Liverpool at all costs. What can I say – we are a fiercely loyal and proud lot.

I never really felt like I truly fitted in in Kirkby. As I got older, I just thought that was a superiority complex of wanting more, and that I had a resistance to the ready-made life that was set out for me. But as I began to connect to people in recovery, the more I heard people sharing that they too had never felt a part of anything, coupled with a feeling of, 'There's something not quite right about me, I do not belong.'

I suppose being me has never felt right or comfortable. In saying this, I'm not attention-seeking or looking for a way for people to feel sorry for me, so the tiny violin can remain in its case, thank you. I have always believed that I am weird, a burden, and not good enough. In the psychotherapy world, these 'truths' are called my 'core beliefs'. According to Michael from Clouds and reputable literature pushed my way, our core beliefs often stem from childhood and are shaped by our experiences, inferences and deductions, or come from accepting what others tell us to be true. But although no one ever told me I was not good enough, a burden or weird (well, my sister would call me tetchy, but I've forgiven her), to go all Sigmund Freud and spout the your-childhood-defines-you patter, this does ring true for me. Although I had a largely typical childhood, there was a lot of uncertainty when I was growing up: sometimes me (that's not a typo, you'll get used to the Scouse pronoun for 'my') dad was there, and sometimes he was not. He would leave, and we would be none the wiser of when or if he would return. And then, one day, he was gone for good. It was never really spoken about, there wasn't a space to process it, it was just a matter of fact. I have no resentment against me dad today: he's a loveable and funny man with a big heart, he holds court at any party, but he has his own story (and it's his, so it's not my place and not my right to share why he struggled to be a part of a family). Christ, reading that back, I'm thinking: 'Oh, how tacky – daddy issues,' but, yeah, abandonment and rejection are probably where these 'core beliefs' came from, and they have indeed played out in my adulthood: feeling desperate for people to stick around, and living in fear of being rejected.

It's funny, as a kid, you don't know any of this stuff; I didn't have language like 'belief system', or have a clue about 'processing emotions'. It was the early nineties in Kirkby, Liverpool, and if you were acting out you were simply being a pain in the arse – there was no real talk of 'feelings', and things like 'Let's talk this through' were a bit too hippy-dippy.

Does this knowledge and insight about the relationship I have with me dad mean that I blame him for my warped thinking and lush ways? Absolutely not. I remember being pissed once, screaming at my mum: 'This is all yours and me dad's fault!' I don't feel that way today. Sure, there are certainly events in my life that contributed to my mental downfall, but I can't play the blame game – it's not good for me. Hindsight can be your friend or your foe. Each time I have set off on the quest hell-bent for the reasons why, I have become frustrated, angry and further away from any kind of solution. I suppose I wanted someone or something to blame; I wanted to be able to pinpoint the exact moment and have the definitive reason of when and why I crossed the line from sociable drinking to drinking to cope. But nothing good comes from this agonising search: you cannot change the past and time travel is yet to be discovered, so all it's a complete waste of precious time and headspace. As a good friend in recovery once taught me, 'If you keep one foot in the past and one in the future, you're in a perfect position to piss all over the day.'

Apart from this warped opinion of myself, as a kid I thought I was a bit different to others, particularly in how I responded to things. I treated minor setbacks like a 999 emergency, resulting in huge meltdowns – expecting me to rationalise was like expecting me to be fluent in a language I'd never bloody learnt. And I didn't have to go very far or get very old to experience feeling odd. It didn't start on the playground, it began in the family home, comparing myself to my sister.

What are siblings for if we don't compare ourselves and question why we are, or why we are not, like them? I am one of two daughters and you couldn't get two more different girls if you tried. My sister, our Becca, isn't a bit like me. Considering there's only three years between us, you would think we would have been somewhat close as children, or even share similarities but, no, there were none. I liked learning about the Tudors, she liked penalty shootouts; she didn't give a fuck and I gave all the fucks; and, further down the line, she didn't hit the bottle and I ended up an alcoholic. I do feel for me mum (Ange): I bet when I popped out she thought Becca and I would be best friends who would share toys, clothes and values; that we would always have each other's backs. Poor Ange: a full-time mother, referee and peacemaker.

The childhood nicknames we were given perfectly illustrate our characters: we are Kitten and Big Truck. I'm Kitten. For the record, there was no intentional malice in these names, and they couldn't be more fitting or prophetic. You see, our Becca is strong willed, independent, stubborn, competitive, athletic and boisterous. She has always been able to handle her own and feels fine telling someone to 'do one'. It's also worth mentioning she has an almighty kick on her (believe me, I have felt that kick my whole life). Whereas me, Kitten, I emit a fragile frequency, a vibe that I'm somewhat vulnerable, that I need constant looking after, and am at times a royal pain in the arse. Out of interest and validation, I wanted to include my big sis's memories of a young Kitten: 'You were a brat, a crier and shit at sports.' True to form – cheers, sis!

Unlike our Becca, crying has always been my default setting; whatever the occasion or emotion, my ugly cry face and whale noises are on display for all to see. And I feel no shame about it, which to many is even odder than my actual emotional diarrhoea. Apparently, this non-stop tittie-lip and 'I want me mum' routine was the reason why babysitters were so reluctant to take the gig, and why there are very few Kodak moments of me, in comparison to my sister. I have to confess it has taken three decades and a breakdown of sorts to finally cut the cord from Ange, and I do still have my moments of 'I want me mum'. (You'll hear more of that transition later on.)

As you can imagine, these two polar-opposite approaches have their own, very different reactions to life; we were never on each other's team and as the years progressed and our personalities continued to follow the trajectories of Kitten and Big Truck, the divide between us widened more and more. Becca could never understand why I was the way I was; and rather than just accepting our differences and loving myself regardless, I automatically assumed that I was the 'bad' and the 'broken' one. For the record, she is my best mate and comrade these days.

Of course, as a kid, I didn't know myself well enough to say: 'Oh, Melissa, here we go, get a grip, calm down and look at the facts. This is all in your head,' and my anxiety started to present itself physically. Without any real thought or motive, at the age of ten, I started to pull strands of my hair out. I didn't know why I did it, I just did it. I would zone out, feeling for the right type of hair to pull out. The official word for this condition is trichotillomania, but in the same way 'anxiety' wasn't a thing back in the nineties, trichotillomania wasn't, either. I just got told to 'Stop that!' There were no conversations of, 'So, why do you pull your hair out? What do you get out of it?' I was just told to stop. By the age of eleven, I had a comb-over that could rival Donald Trump's. I still pull at my hair in times of worry or boredom – and I still get told to stop. If you look on any of the BBC Radio 5 Live *Hooked* videos, you'll be sure to see my weirdly large hands go to the back of my head.

Added to this, at around the age of fourteen, I began to scratch my arms. Again, I had no real understanding of the whys, but I would scratch and scratch until the skin went shiny, and then I would be left with a perfectly straight scab. People reacted more to the scratches: deep scratches and vertical scabs on your forearms are more shocking than a dodgy barnet. But to those who noticed the new additions to my arms, it just made for more confusion. It made absolutely no sense. Why? Because to most who knew me I was a confident kid who didn't mind the spotlight. Who knew that you could be an extrovert with anxiety and low mood? I certainly didn't.

Embodying both ends of the social spectrum is a nightmare

when you are trying to communicate how you are feeling and trying to be understood. When I used to think of someone who suffered with anxiety, I would think of someone who was painfully shy. This stereotype is just as unhelpful as the stereotype I used to have of alcoholics. I wish that we could lash phrases like 'classic' and 'textbook' right in the bin, particularly when we are talking about mental health conditions. Of course, there are groups of symptoms that are commonly associated with anxiety and depression, for example, but this one-size-fits-all approach doesn't always work. The illusion of confidence I had was again a form of self-preservation: a front; a way for people to accept me. Even to this day, I am more confident speaking on a stage in front of two hundred strangers than I am at speaking in a one-to-one with someone I barely know. When there is a sea of bodies it's impossible for me to try and read everyone; all I am thinking about is my own performance and delivering a bloody good show. One-to-one, I feel exposed, I am trying to figure out what they are thinking, I am more aware of what I am saying and begin to ramble; basically, I chat absolute bollocks and come away from the conversation mortified.

It's safe to say that I was emotional and sensitive as a kid, and that even after copious amounts of talk therapy and a prescription for happy tablets, I still am. And you know what? I'm OK with it. I'm a Tiny Tears. (Funnily enough, Tiny Tears was a nickname given to me in rehab. I think my inmates – apologies, 'fellow clients' – thought this would taper off, but they were mistaken.)

Accepting that I am a sensitive soul has taken its time, and today I am able to discuss exactly what I am feeling and talk it through without bottling it up. But up until the age of twenty-nine, I was emotionally illiterate: I knew the words 'happy', 'sad', 'fucking sad' and 'worried'. I didn't know how to talk to about my feelings, and I certainly couldn't process them, so they all ended up in a tightly wound mess living in the pit of my stomach. When I *would* try to communicate how I was feeling, the only words I could come up with were, 'I don't feel right' and 'There's something wrong with me' – these nondescript phrases would be repeated over and over again, hoping that someone would be able to tell me what it was that was wrong and, in turn, fix me.

I know now that the more I allow the pressure to build, the more chance there is of the contents of my mind exploding (a bit like a packet of crisps on an aeroplane). But leaving pain unresolved, persevering with uncomfortable feelings and allowing situations to reach crisis point was just how I operated. The concept of early intervention or 'nipping it in the bud' was lost on me, whether that was staying in a relationship too long hoping they would finish with me because the thought of ending it was just too much, waiting until I was passing blood before I went to the doctor, allowing a boss to treat me like crap until I fell to bits, or ending up completely pickled with my life burnt to the ground before I quit the booze. Not a great way to live one's life, I know. My anxiety around having to speak up and having those difficult conversations would prevent me from doing anything, so I'd remain stuck in an unhappy situation with my resentments coming out sideways. But fear of letting others down, fear of judgement, fear of the facts and fear of the outcome were a part of my anxiety, were a part of me. And still can be, on bad days. The phrase 'Melissa, can I have a quick word with you?' still turns my knees to jelly and I automatically think that I have done something majorly wrong.

I always cared far too much what people think of me. It was

all-consuming. I spent years trying to do other people's thinking for them, creating a narrative that didn't exist and always coming to the conclusion that people hated me. Here's a prime example: 'I can't come tonight, I am not feeling well.' Sounds easy enough, doesn't it? I *was* physically unwell – thanks to the Crohn's, I was shitting past myself and my large intestine sounded like a Ferrari's engine. I couldn't go out, and no one would have minded. Easy-peasy lemon squeezy to ring and make your excuses ... but no, not for me. Overthinking and overcomplicating go together like peas and carrots (insert Forrest Gump's southern drawl). This thirty-second transaction would turn into six hours of procrastinating and deliberating, drafting and editing a text message, predicting the reply, assuming the person would think that I was lying about being ill ... (and *breathe*). Finally, I would come to the awful conclusion that my friends would be finished with me for good. I would imagine the conversations they would have of me, of the friend fuming and removing me from their life; I'd think of the consequences of having no friends any more. This end-of-the-world thinking would be playing on loop. I couldn't stop the song playing; I didn't have a pause button, never mind the power button.

This entire saga would be happening in my head while I was crying, panicking and beating myself up for not feeling well enough in the first place. Then, as the event that I was no longer attending was going ahead, I would spend the time I allocated to nurse my actual illness feeling guilty and ashamed, refreshing social media every two minutes to see if they were having a better time without me.

This, my friends, is 'catastrophising', in all of its not-so-glorious glory. But this was my head, the only way I knew how to operate, and I never realised just how exhausting this all was. No wonder I wanted to escape my thoughts and take the edge off.

This panicked approach to life didn't age well. The older I was getting and the more independent adulthood required me to be, the worse my thinking went. Or should I say *over*thinking. My thinking was obsessive, I could never 'move on' from anything; every situation was pulled apart piece by piece until I had no grasp of what was true or what was not. I was neurotic. By my mid-twenties I had been given yet another nickname: Jean Slater. If you love your soaps, you will know of Jean. She's a fan-favourite *EastEnders* character who quite often looks like a deer caught in headlights. She suffers with mental illness and has a nervous disposition about her. If you're thinking to yourself, 'Bloody hell, fancy calling your mate that, that's not kind or PC,' don't worry. Piss-taking and nicknames are how Scouse people operate – it was a term of endearment, really. Although there *is* something rather sad about your anxiety being normalised, personifying my anxiety has been quite helpful in recovery. There has been many a time in recovery when I say to my friends, 'Guys, I'm having a Jean moment.' I even have a safe word, well, phrase: if I am super-sensitive, and my ability to take a joke is nowhere to be seen, I am able to say, 'Sausage surprise!' (Jean's signature dish) and the group will know that the joke or the conversation is causing me distress. Safe words aren't just for the bedroom folks.

Decision-making ain't my jam, either. I was adamant that I was unable to make any good decision. Trudging through life with this warped belief system and self-esteem lower than a snake's belly often led to a series of self-fulfilling prophecies. I would somehow find myself in a position whereby I could say to myself, 'See, I told you.' I've always hated making decisions, as you can probably guess by what you've already read about me, but the process would be completely blown out of proportion, with a whole lot of unnecessary anguish. I do have to admit, by the age of twenty, I had made a lot of bad choices, and I hurt people with my lying and avoidance. The story of my life, really: 'When you fuck up, Melissa, you fuck up big.' People who knew me at this time would tell you I was a nightmare and I'll be the first to say that I carried on something shocking. There was always a drama and I was always there, trying to think and lie my way out of it and wondering how or why I had found myself in this position. Ultimately, I lost friends by age twenty as a consequence of my actions. To them I was a lying, two-timing car crash.

I am not one for making excuses or pulling the mental health ticket, but me, then? I was gone, and was suffering with what I know now as 'unresolved trauma'. At nineteen I had an abortion. I'm not going to go into the ins and outs of the whos, whys and the wherefores. But I want to share the impact this had on me and my mental health. That experience messed me up. Whether people around me knew the impact or didn't, I don't fully know; I downplayed it, I acted like everything was fine, I carried on like nothing was the matter. I couldn't face reality so I made an alternate one.

Deep down, the decision didn't feel right but, true to form, the fear of not going ahead with the abortion was too great. In the consultation room at the hospital, I began to sob – I used to think if I cried then people would know what I was thinking and know there was something wrong, and help me – and perhaps take the responsibility of making the choice away from me? The nurse said, 'If you don't stop crying, he won't do it.' So I did what I was told. (I've always responded to authority: doctors, teachers, nurses, bosses

– I would never have dreamed of challenging someone in that type of position. What can I say, I am a wimp and a kiss arse.)

I woke up in that room and I don't think I was ever the same after that.

I remember screaming, 'What have you done?' but by that point it was all too late. I left that hospital numb, and for years I would avoid having to go anywhere near it. That day haunted me, asleep and awake; each time a flashback took over my brain, I would slap my head as if to knock it out of my skull. I didn't even tell me mum about it until eighteen months later and yet, truthfully, if I think about everything I have ever been through, that was a time when I probably needed my mum the most. I was a young girl with poor mental health in a situation she wasn't able to manage. I didn't get immediate help, I don't recall even being asked if I needed to talk to someone afterwards. I didn't think I had any right to feel sad so I just put up with it and, in a perverse way, I welcomed all the misery that came thereafter. I thought I deserved it.

I thought the bad things – bad bowels, gynaecological issues and unhappiness – were stuff I had brought on myself because of the abortion. I even thought I was being punished by god – which was really bloody odd, because I wasn't particularly religious; but a convent high school education (complete with nuns) and a constant Catholic drip feed will do that to you. The darkness stayed with me. I was no longer just acutely anxious: I now had a shadow that was always with me.

I never really connected the dots; I never once thought that this darkest of moments was playing out in other areas of my life. I knew of other women who had been through the same and felt very little about it, so I thought I had no entitlement to feel any type of sadness.

Furthermore, I saw the abortion as the evidence as to why I should not be allowed to make any decisions.

If there are any women reading this who, like me, have struggled with an abortion, you are not alone, your feelings are valid, and you're all in my heart. Please don't suffer in silence.

Sorry, that got a bit dark, didn't it? I was umming and ahhing whether it was important or not. You came here to read about drinking, not to find out about a nineteen-year-old having an abortion. I just want to say that I'm good today. I've processed it and I have come to accept that the timing wasn't right and there was another path for me. The one I find myself on now. I had a good chat with me mum about whether I should include all this and, ever the protector, she wanted me to think long and hard about sharing this part of my story. She and I don't often talk about it – it's one of those topics that you have a code word for or just allude to, and you never say it out loud. But someone does need to talk about it: there are too many women in a similar position for me to not talk about it. My closest friends in recovery know how significant this experience was to my mental health and for me not to share it would mean I am omitting a significant part of my 'journey' (cringe – I hate that expression).

The thing with any type of untreated pain and suppressed emotions is that quite often these feelings need numbing: we may not consciously know that we are anesthetising ourselves, but booze, drugs, food, sex, gambling – all these change how we feel. They are a way to escape and avoid dealing with pain for a brief moment in time. For some, including myself, this sense of relief and freedom from my own thinking was worth holding on to. There's no real handbook on how to cope with life's difficulties; there is no right and wrong way to cope – there *are* healthy and unhealthy ways to cope, but it's just about that – coping: getting through and surviving. There are those amazing creatures who, when facing adversity or when they are mentally in the gutter, throw themselves into something positive. There's the type who cope through physical exercise and take up yoga and running, employ healthy-eating lifestyles and have a life overhaul. There are those who develop a new hobby or skill; there are even those who immediately think of ways to help people in a similar position to themselves and raise awareness and even funds. Did you know there are even people who go the GP and ask for help? Blimey. I was not those people.

Although I won't be running a marathon or cutting out the chocolate anytime soon, I am now better at choosing the healthier ways to cope. But me pre-recovery? I needed an instant fix. The unhealthy ways to cope often only give short-term relief with negative consequences. The healthy ones are generally the complete opposite: they may not provide instant gratification, but they will have a positive, lasting impact. But I was impatient, and playing the long game was never an option for me, in any area of my life. I wanted it all now.

Self-medicating using alcohol is like pouring petrol on a burning house hoping it will put the fire out. Did I know that nothing good could come from looking for the answers in the bottom of a bottle? Absolutely. That's what was so baffling. I knew alcohol would exacerbate my anxiety the next day; even before I started to 'secret drink' and drank 'alcoholically', I always suffered the next day with 'beer fear'. This feeling after a big night out would have me crying, in a foetal position, begging for answers: 'Did I do anything wrong? Did I upset anyone? Are you sure I didn't do anything? But how do you know that no one is upset with me?' You may not have rocked, sobbed or put the shower onto the hottest temperature to burn the night off your skin, but you have definitely felt that dread. And then I would be in a god-awful cycle. If I went out on a Saturday, I would eventually mentally and physically recover by Wednesday, I'd have a productive Thursday, the Friday feeling would get me and, boom, we were back to Saturday to start it all over again. Remind me why we did/do this to ourselves again? Oh, that's right – it's 'fun'. (Insert staring eyes emoji.) It blows my mind that in the 'glory days' of my drinking – the times when alcohol was still only reserved for nights out – severe 'hangxiety', the lowest of ebbs, was a price I was willing to pay to send myself to another realm for a few hours. For all my slightly higher-than-average intelligence, I still thought drinking was the solution.

Because drinking to cope isn't just reserved for the major life events or when the shit really hits the fan, is it? It's a part of society and a social norm to have a drink for the most regular of life's hiccups. Broken up with your fella of two months? Get the wine in. Tough day at the office? Pour us a drink, please, love. The kids doing your head in? Make it a double. For the majority of people, that is fine – I will never condemn or point the sober finger. You do you, hon, and if you ever need to chat, my DMs are open. But it's important to know that for some, including myself, this game-changing elixir becomes the only way to find relief, to the point where it becomes such a well-trodden path in our brains that in any time of trouble reaching for a drink becomes automatic. Alcohol did for me what I couldn't do for myself: it gave me a quiet mind, confidence, happiness and freedom. But it also took away all of the things it had once given me, and then some. Sure, alcohol is fast-acting, cheap, accessible and normalised, but it is bloody dangerous. Alcohol is a drug (fact). Your trusty sidekick quickly or slowly becomes your captor, and the fun and balanced relationship you once had with each other descends into utter obsession. It's toxic in every sense of the word.

The short-term fix that alcohol provides starts to become the problem as tolerance develops and we need to drink more to have the same effect. Once that happens alcohol starts to cause or add to the problems we were trying to solve (feeling anxious, low mood, poor sleep, etc.).

Professor Julia Sinclair

And, just like the professor says, my anxiety and depression worsened at the same rate my drinking did. As my drinking progressed and my life was falling between my trembling fingers, my mind was out of control. I wanted out, I had thoughts of and half-arsed attempts at ending my life; I just wanted it all too stop, as the consequences of my drinking were too much to bear. I wasn't a teacher, I had no one in my life. I lost my freedom and I couldn't see a way out. I don't know why I held on – I didn't have hope – but what I did have was my mum. I couldn't harm her any more.

What all this comes down to is that treating and managing your mental health is difficult, and when there is any substance abuse in the mix, it becomes much, much harder. I had to address the drinking first, which felt near impossible as it was so enmeshed with my mental health. I know I said earlier that the two can't be separated, but you have to start somewhere. Perhaps if I had known about the anxiety, etc., that it wasn't right, and was treatable with (legal) medication, I would have started on that route first, and my drinking would have reduced as my mental health improved. It's a chicken-and-egg situation. As Michael says:

> *A lot of people who have mental health issues use substances to manage those issues. Over a period of time, what they don't intend to do but what happens is that they develop a dependency on that substance. So you have the mental health presenting issue and you have the substance misuse and it's important to treat that substance misuse so that mental health services can then be accessed. There are excellent services and facilities to support trauma and mental health conditions, post-practice (after treatment). We're cautious at Clouds House, we try not to open people too much. There are other residential treatment centres that really crack people open like a walnut, but our clients are only with us for a maximum of forty-two days, so in our clinical view we have to be cautious and appropriate on how we are managing emotional well-being.*
>
> **Michael Rawlinson**

Whether you're a raging alchy like me or aware that you are drinking that bit too much, when we have a sabbatical from the booze we might start to notice life feels just that bit more manageable. Thinking may become clearer and those situations – the things we like to put off – feel right-sized. Now, I am not going to sit here and say that as soon as you stop drinking any mental health issues will magically disappear. That's utter horseshit (in my opinion).

Stopping the drink, for me, was just the start of the 'journey'. My drinking was a symptom of my thinking and therefore just quitting drink wasn't enough to get any peace of mind. I still had the same head, the same thoughts, when I put down the bottle, but I then had the brain function to finally address the painful memories that haunted me. I was finally able learn about myself and how my mind operated, and I could at last identify those triggers that would send me down a dark path, and unlearn twenty-nine years of harmful thinking patterns.

Takeaways

- **My drinking was a symptom**
- **To manage my alcoholism is to manage my mental health**
- **Supressing emotions only causes harm**
- **Alcohol, drugs, sex, gambling all change how we feel – a way to escape or manage our feelings**
- **Self-medicating using alcohol is like pouring petrol on a burning house hoping it will put the fire out**
- **The short-term fix that alcohol provides starts to become the problem as tolerance develops and we need to drink more to have the same effect**
- **To get support with your mental health, you're advised to stop the drinking first.**

Chapter 2

Drop the act, it's fooling no one

Who likes to admit that they are having any type of difficulty? I've always loved turning a blind eye, having my head buried in the sand and avoiding reality. ('I think that's called denial, love.') As long as I looked the part, I was the part, and if you'd asked me if there was a problem, I would have said no. If you'd asked me if I had a problem with my drinking I would have bitten your head clean off, regardless of whether you were coming from a loving place. I would have the audacity to profess my innocence loudly and with ferocious intent, an empty bottle in my bag, a she's-had-a-few look on my face and stinking like a brewery. My aptitude for denial has always been a bloody nuisance. But I know I am not alone.

I also know of the dangers of pretending everything is hunky-dory when the reality is far from hunky or dory. 'I'm fine' – surely this is one of the most-told lies? Think about it: how many times has a friend told you they are fine and you came away from the conversation thinking: 'They aren't fine at all, I'd better do something about this'? Why is it that we won't declare that there is something the matter? Is it because we cannot be bothered to make a big deal out of it? Maybe we are avoiding how we are really feeling, or maybe we just don't want to talk about it. But for some reason, to keep up the façade for as long as humanly possible is the norm and, I'm sorry to say, usually welcome. It's easier for everyone if everything is 'fine'.

Keeping up appearances and perfecting your brave face is exhausting and actually requires more effort than admitting there is a problem and showing your hand. Not only do we have to convince people face to face, we have to do it virtually now, too. But social media is a wonderful tool to keep the 'dream' alive. It allows us to project what we want projecting and edit out the unsavoury parts; it gives us the power to curate our lives to suit our brand. We use these platforms to show that we are 'living our best life' and that all is well. (Me mum is adamant that social media has been the unmaking of modern society, and for many years Big Truck and I have told her she's boring and to piss off, but I think she might have a point.)

Apart from denial (which I will be pulling apart a bit later), to be someone and something that we're not comes from that desire to be liked and accepted – those pesky core beliefs again. A lot of my life has been spent conforming to specific roles, but when the curtain fell and I could clock off, I would feel broken and uncertain. I was never really one person all of the time: I didn't know you were supposed to be. I know that may sound daft, but I genuinely thought that, as people, we are expected to act in the context of our setting; to adhere to the social protocols that are set out, and that we are supposed to be who people want us to be.

I've often changed myself and adopted a persona; like a chameleon, I would try my best (and fail) to blend and morph myself to suit whatever situation and social group I found myself in, because in my head just being me was not enough and therefore not welcome. My shape-shifting powers were an automatic response, a survival instinct. There wasn't much thinking involved. I wouldn't say my actions were particularly calculated – I certainly didn't go all *Killing Eve* and have a wardrobe full of costumes and a back story to match – but trying to 'be like everyone else' was just like breathing for me. You'd never catch me disagreeing with you, I would always be sorry and assume all blame, your shit joke was hilarious, and your behaviour would *never* offend me.

Today I know and accept that l am an inherent 'people-pleaser'. During my first week in rehab a counsellor shone a light on this instinctive trait and diagnosed me. What a lovely thing to hear and for someone to acknowledge; that for all my faults and mishaps, really I just liked to make everyone happy and be liked. I felt seen and I felt heard, and I was that flattered I replied, 'Ahhh, thank you!' and gave a bashful smirk as if to say, 'Aw, shucks.' Little did I know that being a personality contortionist and trying to keep the world and its wife happy was just as destructive to my life as the Russian pickling juice. And it never once occurred to me that this behaviour wasn't OK and that it causes harm and upset to those you are desperate to please and keep onside. I suppose there is only so much pretending one person can do before the cracks begin to show and people are completely burnt out by your bullshit.

I had a PR way of life: I would keep certain parts of my life hidden to different groups. I had no problem worming my way into a new group, but maintaining and nurturing friendships was a different story entirely. If you are a people-pleasing shape-shifter, you will know that mixing pockets of friends, work, family and a boyfriend is a recipe for disaster. What mannerisms would I use this time? What have I told or hidden from who? I kept my life in separate bubbles: I thought it would make life easier. Turns out, anything I thought would be 'easier' was always the bloody opposite.

So, what were these roles I played? Well, you have the bog standards of 'the daughter', 'the joker' and the 'drama queen', but I'd say the two most significant roles were that of 'party girl' and 'primary school teacher'. Can you get two more different roles?

Heading to sixth form is wild. You go from a uniform and fearing detention to your own clothes and freedom. You can get yourself a job, earn your own money; you are expected to make choices that will set you up for a career; you're of the age of legal consent; and it is completely acceptable to go on nights out. All in the space of six weeks. I was not prepared for any of it; well, not the real-life stuff, anyway.

Back in 2006, I was the right side of seventeen. I thought I was the dog's bollocks and cat's pyjamas, the big *kahuna* of what was cool and what was not. Where had this newfound confidence come from? Alcohol, drugs and going out on the town. I'd arrived, I'd found my calling and who I thought I was meant to be. I was reborn; I was Party Girl. (What a wanker.) I do wish there was a better way of putting it, as this title sounds a bit too *Hello* magazine meets *Daily Mail* 'pardy girl', like I was some kind of high-society debutante who was invited to all the best parties and loved champagne. Actually, I was that much of a nightmare that I just about received invites. I was more high-risk than high-society, as there was no real guarantee that I wouldn't do something to make the party all about me, or get so wasted that I would pass out. Ashamedly, there was a better chance of me offending your mum or doing something or someone (and regretting it for the following ten years) than there ever was of me respecting the fact it was your birthday. I was there for a good time, not a long time. However, if you had me on a good day and I didn't partake in pre-drinks, I would like to think I was an asset to any night out. I loved to laugh, to be carefree, to be strange, to be free. Of course I was still a nuisance, but less toxic in my manner due to less toxins in my liver. I was, as the kids say these days, 'extra'. I loved the laughs, the spectacle; I was there for the party. So, yeah, I did live for the weekend and you would always find me out with a bra full of class As, and a belly full of JD. That's the type of 'party girl' I mean.

I had age on my side, but I abused my 'early twenties privilege' by consuming way too much. On the surface that was fine, a completely acceptable justification for my behaviour, but I had an inkling. I knew I had my 'shadow', I knew I had my Jeanisms, and I knew nights out were fast becoming respites from this internal affliction. I thrived on people thinking I was 'wild' or 'nuts' – it makes me cringe even to say that, but it is true. It was validation, it didn't matter that after these big nights out I was a wreck and ball of fear; I was providing a service and I was receiving attention. That was enough.

Do I have regrets for some of the states that I found myself in? Absolutely. But, at the same time, I have to allow that some of the nights out, parties, festivals, have the greatest of memories. When getting sober, there's a temptation to regret every substance you've ever sipped, sniffed, inhaled and swallowed; to hate yourself for ever drinking or getting 'off your chops'. But that's not realistic and it wouldn't be my truth. There's really no use me lying about it: I had a ball – but, ultimately, that ball came at an extremely high price.

The more I performed – literally *acted* my roles – the more I would be trying to forget the pain this caused. As time went on, the emotions started to bubble to the surface on my beloved nights out. I would be crying in the toilet, chatting shit that was too deep for a club venue, and quite often I'd be melting the ear off someone in the smoking area, pouring my heart out to anyone who'd listen. Those poor unfortunate sods. And don't get me started on the drunk texts. I always wanted an after-party and my nerves would be shot to pieces if the sun began to come up – or worse, the host would say they wanted to call it a night. I wanted to stay in the (not so safe) safety of the party bubble. I didn't want to return to real life; I wanted to stay in the play-pretend.

I have a friend called Sarah; we've been friends since we were about twelve thanks to morris dancing. (It's a Kirkby rite of passage to join a morris dancing troupe – it's a weird hybrid of Irish dancing and, well, morris dancing. There're no sticks and dancing around a maypole is involved – there are bells on your feet, though. It's basically council ballet.) At a tender age we connected over our oddities and our bizarrely wonderful sense of humour – like myself, Sarah didn't fit the conventional Kirkby mould and I loved her for it. She's the type of girl who, when every other girl dresses sexy at Halloween – a chance to get the 'girls out' and wear a tutu – she'll be there dressed as a carrot.

We carried on being weird and we took childhood friendship into our twenties. Nights out with Sarah and her gang were guaranteed fun, but even she knew I took things too far. She's currently living her best life in Vietnam, so finding a time to put her on the spot and ask her if she thought I was a) mental and b) an alchy was a bit of a challenge. With a pretty-looking cocktail in her hand and that sea-salt beach-hair that can never be achieved in England, we video-called and dug deep. And when the call had finished, she put her extra thoughts down via a message from her phone: sometimes there are things that are too challenging to say to someone's face, even virtually. I do love a deep and honest conversation these days: they keep me 'well', and who even knew that friendship was all about honesty and trust? There are things she has shared that make me want to peel my skin off and wring my heart out, but the truth hurts and it's important for me that I know the extent of the pain and worry I caused.

So off we went on a trip down Memory Lane. She reeled off about five examples of when my drinking was taken too far: waking up at 7 a.m. and downing vodka at Glastonbury was the first. Unafraid to speak up and concerned, she told some of the group that this was not OK, but it fell on deaf ears. I never realised that her worries and observations were pooh-poohed; she was advised to stop being a killjoy. I was hiding in plain sight. Another example from Sarah: I totally forgot about the time we went to get our teeth whitened and I brought bottles of wine with me. Why I thought wine would be a good thing to drink pre- and post-teeth whitening is beyond me. But to me, these were the fun and happy times (awkward). What I never realised was the guilt she felt – alcoholism is such a selfish condition that you don't even think of other people's feelings. Her exact words? 'Mate, it was guilt in the sense that you did show signs of needing help before the rock bottom, but how are you meant to approach a situation when you are the one advocating the party?'

Sarah isn't alone in this guilt, it's a legitimate conundrum for many friends.

Then our trip down Memory Lane took a turn down a darker, more unpleasant alley.

She reminded me of the time when I turned up to the call centre we worked in completely inebriated. It was the day after Boxing Day 2012, and I was due in for my shift. Boxing night is a big deal in Liverpool and I had a ticket for an event. Something quite dark happened on that night, the lines of consent as blurred as my vision. I came to in a place I didn't know, not remembering how I got there, and with a person I didn't know. I went from the hotel into work.

I'm not afraid to admit it – my understanding of consent was limited back then. I thought that because I was drunk and because I had agreed to go back I 'had to'. Like I was obliged. Not every time, I'll give myself that – but there have been some very uncomfortable experiences that were batted off as early twenties silliness when, really, it was not OK. But this day after the Boxing Day massacre, I kept the heavy parts out of the story and just pretended life was one big party. I fronted it out, I was acting 'Billy Big Balls' as we say in Liverpool, thinking it was fine to turn up drunk to work, a bottle of JD in my overnight bag. I should have known then that there was something seriously wrong, that my priorities were all wrong. I genuinely thought that not going into work would be worse ...?

Rightfully so, my spectacle at the call centre went rife among the stalls. I was mortified – why wouldn't I be? I blew a raspberry in an older woman's face, I told people to fuck off, and someone had to take me home. The next day, not only did I wake up with bruises where there shouldn't have been any, I woke up without knowing anything. I had blacked out.

Blackout is terrifying. I think this might have been my first ever experience of it. I spoke to a medical professional who specialises in alcohol harm in older people on what blackout is.

An alcohol-related blackout happens during an episode of heavy drinking, during which the transfer of memory from short- to long-term storage becomes disrupted. This can either be complete (en bloc) or fragmentary (partial). It is not the same as intoxication, which does not, in itself affect memory storage unless accompanied by a blackout. Blackouts are also a strong indicator of alcohol dependence.

A blackout can be quite frightening following a night out, especially if a drinker has no recollection at all of events during the blackout itself, which is confined to the duration of time that there is a high blood alcohol concentration. It also leaves the drinker more vulnerable to exploitation, as there will be no subjective memory of events to substantiate the authenticity of events that happen during a blackout.

Dr Tony Rao

Although Dr Tony raises the point that alcohol blackout suggests dependency, many 'muggles' also experience these:

Although alcoholics do usually suffer from frequent alcohol-induced blackouts, a person does not have to suffer from alcoholism to suffer a blackout. Blackouts are a direct result of how much alcohol a person drinks at once or in a single sitting and not of how much they drink over a longer time period.

Michael Rawlinson

Science lesson over, back to Sarah. I didn't see her face on the video call when she was relaying her memories of this, but I felt her upset. To be honest, my initial reaction to her telling of this story was, 'Nah, that ain't going in the book.' But I realised my knee-jerk defiance was another defence tactic to avoid uncomfortable memories and shame. Therefore, that woeful moment of embarrassment has to be aired and thus finds itself here.

On a roll now, Sarah and I pulled up a pew at the memorial of mental health. Here was where we recognised our differences; this was where our similarities and love of the party ended. At first glance we are similar, with big personalities and unafraid to take the piss out of ourselves and do daft things. But under the surface our intentions for a good time were so very different, I was a bag of nerves, Sarah was not. Sarah had known me long enough to know that I was a good actress and could see that my persona of being carefree and acid-tongued was all an act. In her truth-bomb mobile notes, she relayed a story of being at an after-party. True to form, I had started to show off and I took the piss out of her – I made fun of her arse in her red disco pants and belittled her in front of a group of partygoers. I'm glad she brought this up ten years later, first of all because I had no idea I did it and second it has given me an opportunity to make amends for specifics, rather than a universal, 'I'm sorry for everything.' And she went on to confirm that I was different people: 'There was "crowd" you and then there was "one-to-one" you.' Basically, one-to-one Melissa was her mate, crowd Melissa was everyone's mate.

I never understood why people liked or, dare I say, loved me. My self-hatred got in the way of receiving love. Sarah isn't the only person who didn't allow the gossip, my reputation, to get in the way. All of the people I have in my life today from my pre-recovery life are those who didn't give up on the real me and who allow me to be me. They are the people who I have always felt the most authentic self with.

I'm still quite surprised Sarah put up with me at all; but that could be my low self-worth rearing its hideous head.

As my early twenties got underway, I didn't feel fulfilled. Who does? I desperately wanted to put the shit-show behind me; I'd had more jobs than hot dinners, several hair colours and styles, my friendships were unstable and the men in my life were one after the other. I hated being alone because I hated myself. I felt empty. I knew I had more to give to life and I wasn't reaching my potential.

As much as this may shock you, I was bright and intelligent. Grades were never an issue in school, or as a university student (I studied Drama and Theatre Studies and you won't be shocked to know that I stayed at home), and I was well behaved – again the fear of letting my mum or teachers down prevented me from relishing any recalcitrant ways. So, leaving university and not using my degree made me feel uncomfortable. In my infinite wisdom, I went on the ultimate rebrand: I became a primary school teacher.

I had always felt a pull to work with children. I wanted to help children who felt fear in school and who had that same 'nut in the gut' that I had as a kid. From a skills-set point of view, I was academic and a good performer. I knew I was able to deliver, it felt like the perfect fit and I gave myself to it completely. I was able to prioritise teaching and finally say the words, 'I can't go out, I have books to mark.' I was growing up. FOMO (fear of missing out) wasn't bothering me like it used to. With glimmers of commitment and shouldering responsibility, I thought this new chapter, this new career, had 'saved' me. And for a while it did. For me, I was always looking for a sense of purpose – for that one role that would make life make sense. The happiness I felt on the course and in the classroom and the connection with the kids was like no other feeling I had had before. I felt like I was doing good in this world for once. The feedback from tutors, from the colleagues and teachers was unbelievable (although I still lacked any self-confidence). My teaching philosophy was: 'It's OK not to know, but it's not OK not to try.' Rich coming from me, but seeing children stressed about work never sat well with me. Building confidence and giving children the space to feel proud of themselves felt more important. My heart was big and this didn't feel like a job, it was a calling.

But my happiness and grasp on life was short-lived. The pressure I put on myself to be a cross between Mary Poppins and Miss Honey from *Matilda* was unhealthy. But the pride in my mum's eyes when all my hard work paid off and I got the job of my dreams was magical. And she gave me a Parker pen with 'Miss Rice' engraved on the back.

Unfortunately, it wasn't just high expectations that were causing me distress; at the beginning of my new career, my Crohn's was off the scale. No treatment would cut the mustard and I would not ask for time off – that felt like failing; the people-pleaser in me would never allow healing time. I was in and out of hospital; experimenting with different immunosuppressants; I was on liquid diets – the whole shitty lot. I would not and could not share that I was both miserable and terrified. I played it down to friends and colleagues. I was embarrassed and, to be perfectly honest, I didn't want to hear: 'That sounds awful, I have irritable bowel syndrome, I know how hard it is.' No, you don't. I didn't want to hear about your boyfriend's cousin's dog's brother's owner's miracle cure for it. I didn't want to be known as the girl with Crohn's. I wanted to detach from my body and live my life as if there was nothing defective about my innards. I asked me mum about her memories of this ill-health era. She wrote:

> *Melissa tried her best to hide her illness to the outside world and has shared little with very few – she always said she felt embarrassed and degraded and that she lost her dignity. She was always anxious and she worried constantly about everything from: can anyone smell me? Have I soiled myself? Can I make it to the end of the road? Where's the toilet? What's happening to me? When is this going to stop ...*

This detachment from and avoidance of my physical illness was a big issue. In 2015 I had an infection which escalated, my lymph nodes in my groin turned necrotic and sepsis kicked in. I'd had a bout of sepsis before, but this time it felt different, felt more sinister. I was heavily reliant on paracetamol to get my temperature down, but the effects of the simple tablet we all take for granted were wearing off. After an MRI I was dropped off by a porter in my side room. Ange was there. She had got the visiting times mixed up and whether this was divine intervention or not, it was a good job me mum was in that room. I started to fit like never before. I remember everything going quiet and still around me, but doctors and nurses frantically doing their thing and my mum hysterically crying. My body was convulsing but my mind was at peace. The doctor was trying to keep me talking and noticed my *The Thick of It* box set. So there I was with what felt like the Grim Reaper's hand on my shoulder, trying to quote Malcolm Tucker and Terri Coverley. I was rushed into surgery to have the dead mass in my groin removed by Mr Arthur. Mr Arthur is in my top five favourite humans of all time. He is my colorectal (bowel and bum) surgeon and goes above and beyond for his Crohn's patients. I trust him completely and I have never feared any op I have had because of my faith in him. He knows me inside out (quite literally).

This was the scariest moment from my bowel saga to date, but all that went through my mind during this time was: 'I need to get back to work.' And I was back in work three weeks later, pretending everything was fine, that it was no big deal.

It was not fine. I was in complete denial and removed from the situation. Now I look back and think to myself, 'What in god's name were you doing? You were running on empty, your head was a mess, your body was in bits and all you cared about was keeping up appearances.' Is it a surprise I that drank?

I can't remember the first time I lied about my drinking and kept it a secret. My decline into the abyss was a progressive one. I didn't wake up one day and be all, 'Eureka, that's it! Today is the day I start to self-medicate with vodka, but only strictly on the down-low!' (I never drank vodka, I was always a double Jack Daniels and Diet Coke with no ice and a shot of Sambuca girl. That order still rolls off the tongue far too easily if you ask me. So why did I drink vodka? Well, somewhere in the depths of my brain was this 'fact' – vodka doesn't smell. Before you get any bright ideas, this is fake news, vodka fucking stinks, nevertheless I held on tight to this useless misinformation and ran with it, all the way to the offie.) It was a subtle and secretive affair. You know what? An 'affair' is a pretty accurate way of describing it: the lies, the cover-ups, the selfishness, the gaslighting, the pain and misery and, above all else, the destruction of lives. Deception and addiction go hand in hand, and I often wonder whether this deception and dishonesty is why addiction is often met with such contempt. It is also the only disease I can think of that convinces you that you haven't got a problem; it's a disease of denial. Here's a sloppy acronym for you: Don't Even (K)Now I Am Lying.

Denial is a characteristic distortion in thinking experienced by people with alcoholism. For decades people have been baffled over why alcoholics continue to drink when the link between alcohol and the losses they suffer is so clear. Denial is an integral part of the disease of alcoholism and a major obstacle to recovery. Although the term 'denial' is not specifically used in the wording of the diagnostic criteria, it underlies the primary symptom described as drinking despite adverse consequences.

Denial can be life threatening. It can literally kill people; it is – for most members of the addicted population – the big struggle. Psychologically, it is a huge block; a barrier – usually it's there to mask elements of fear, a lack of control, and usually to manage the big one, shame. When people are under the influence they behave in a way they do not intend; it's far better to have that shame protected by this real complex strategy – denial. It can be quiet or loud; denial is the series of lies told to self to protect us from the truth. 'I'm not that bad, I can stop after Christmas, I can just have one, I'm not a real alcoholic.' This little voice, I know to call it the 'poison parrot'.

Michael Rawlinson

My denial around my drinking manifested in all kinds of weird. I became adept at concealing my habit. There were a number of reasons why I think I went straight into secrecy: I wanted to protect my career, I wanted to avoid dealing with my mental health, I was ashamed, I didn't want to be judged for struggling and – I didn't want to have to stop. Keeping this my dirty little secret felt natural – I've always been a secret squirrel. I just knew that no one would understand it. There was certainly no way my mum would understand it. I was still very attached to the apron strings and my dependence on my mum for decision-making and crisis management was very much alive and kicking. And, as saints tend to go, she's never really been a drinker, so for me to come home from work and say: 'I'm going to pour myself a drink, it's been a tough day,' was out of the question. We aren't an 'alcohol in the house' family; I grew up with five aunties who are like extensions of Ange and none of them were really drinkers – we are more of a tea and cake family. Today, I love that there isn't a culture of drink in the family, but back then it was a bloody nightmare. So, as drinking wasn't normalised in the place where I lived, honest conversations were a no-go, and I can see why I went straight to the secret swigs.

My early purchases were pretty vague, which only goes to show how cunning and baffling alcoholism it. What I do know is that it started off with a quarter of vodka here and there. I would buy it on the way home, along with my stench-busting paraphernalia: the classic combo of chewing gum and cheese and onion crisps. As soon as the seal cracked on that lid, I could feel my shoulders drop, appreciating it like one of those 'Ahhhh, Bisto …' moments.

And then I would neck the whole lot back.

My partying ways had prepared me well: I could neck any spirit without a grimace or a flinch. In fact, I used to pretend that the shot of whatever it was served on the bar was disgusting and far too much for my girly body to bear. Lies. I put on the amateur dramatics just to be like everyone else – classic Melissa.

The effects of my cheeky quarter bottle would soon kick in. My worries would dissolve and for an hour, tops, I felt stunning. I would be warm, fuzzy and snuggled into the evening ahead – or so I thought. I always knew that my vibe would be killed by either me mum or my boyfriend of the time smelling it on my breath, so to keep them off my back, I would make sure that the house was well ventilated. I'd have the windows open, the tea (dinner, for you southern folk) in the oven and the most potent of perfume on.

The more I drank to cope – by now outside the boundaries of nights out – the more I felt compelled to keep it a secret. I still thought that it was just me mum and my boyfriend at the time who noticed a problem. It was as if my mind could handle a couple of people questioning a problem, but there was no way that it could handle others questioning it. One of my main drivers for always keeping my shit to myself was to avoid people talking about me, which is laughable because I was always doing ridiculously alarming things that warranted people talking about me. I was still healing from my name being dragged through the mud in my early twenties – the result of 'Party Girl' – so the thought of everyone gossiping once more was unimaginable. But guess what? People will talk. When you are turning up drunk, acting unhinged and slurring your words in people's houses at 11 a.m. when you're supposed to be there for a cuppa, of course people are going to talk. I remember once I was on the train going to Liverpool City Centre; it's an eighteen-minute journey but you are guaranteed to see at least five people you know and two you probably want to avoid. Sat there with my headphones on, as if to say to the world 'do not disturb', I was tapped by someone I hadn't seen for a while, those kind of people who you don't really know how you know them, you just do. The first thing that came of her mouth, 'I heard you turned up pissed at X's house, her mum told me in the Home and Bargain.' I wanted the train to open an emergency exit beneath my seat. This skin-crawling conversation happened while I was at the third stop on the line, Rice Lane. To this day, whenever I am at the station that I share a name with I shudder. But people were worried and people weren't daft; it was concerning behaviour and people just don't know what to do for the best. I was shifty, twitchy, cagey, jumpy, sweaty, sloppy and sneaky – all of the seven dwarfs of alcoholism – and I *still* thought that I had everyone fooled.

I was in dangerous territory. What started out as a bit of vodka here and there after a stressful day soon turned into reaching for the bottle for the majority of life's emotional pulls and events, whether they were stressful or not. And as the empties began to mount, my behaviours became bonkers. We alcoholics, addicts, are a resourceful bunch and the ways of obtaining and concealing your substance of choice are almost genius. For example, I would rotate the off-licences just so my order would not be known. I would buy those gift-bottle bags and thank-you cards to convince the cashier that this bottle was not for me. I would pretend to be on my phone while being served so I didn't have to look them in the eye. I would buy an entire 'big shop' so that I looked as if I was making a special tea for the hubby I didn't have, and this litre bottle of vodka was an after-dinner treat. Do you see how absurd this all this? But I still couldn't accept I had a problem.

Bottles would be found by me mum in the most random of places around the house and she used to be so cross, confused and understandably heartbroken; it was then she realised that my drinking was a bigger problem than my Crohn's. Under the mattress was for rookies, and I knew I had to get creative to outsmart my astute mum. If I found a good hiding place, I would take a picture of the place I was about to conceal a bottle in, so that after I had stuffed it in I could go back to my original pic and make sure that everything looked just so – the places near the gardening tools were always a good one, as were the bags of childhood relics of years gone by. Something rather poignant about hiding a vodka bottle in a big bag of happy memories. Further down the line, I buried a bottle in the back garden. I. Buried. A. Bottle. What the actual … Have you ever heard the like? It looked as if we had buried a dog in the back garden the way I did it. I remember moving soil with my bare hands to hide a bottle and not even thinking that this was out of the ordinary – it was something I had to do. I think my personal best has to be my decanting idea: I would divide my drink into several water bottles and have them located in different bushes around the local park. I had a bit of string on a branch to signal where a bottle was. What the *actual* hell? These bottles could have been covered in rat piss and there I was, swigging away.

Apart from the desperation of keeping things hidden and maintaining a regular supply of alcohol, the lies that would come out of my mouth were frighteningly effortless: 'Why are you kicking off? That bottle was from ages ago!', 'No, I bloody well haven't had a drink!' After a while of my refusal to tell the truth about my drinking, the lies turned more manipulative. Ashamedly I would resort to gaslighting my nearest and dearest: 'I can't believe you think I've been drinking – you always think the worst of me' or 'You're paranoid!' I would stoop so low to make my mum and my sister question themselves, and there were even times when they apologised for accusing me. Truly awful.

Lying about drink isn't just for alcoholics. I remember stumbling across a YouGov survey to assess how much Britons lie about drinking and, more importantly, who we lie to. It may come as no surprise, but 59 per cent of respondents admitted to telling a few porkies about their drink to a healthcare professional, while 43 per cent have lied to their parents about their drinking at least once. The 18–24-year-old bracket contains the biggest number of liars to their parents, with an unsurprising 60 per cent. But the most intriguing fact arising from the report? Women are twice as likely as men to lie about their drinking to their family and friends. It makes me wonder why that is. Maybe, as women, it is deemed more shameful to have an issue with alcohol? Regardless of advances in women's rights, we are still viewed by a lot of society as child bearers, mothers and the less reckless of the two sexes. But even three years into sobriety, it's still good to know that I was not the only boozy liar. Everyone's at it – alcohol and lies go together like ice and a slice.

My tall tales and yarn spinning weren't just alcohol related, though. I even lied about things I had no reason to lie about. I lied about what I had for my tea, what I was watching on the telly, how many books I had to mark, what time I went to sleep, how much my dress was. Ridiculous. I created a mega web of spin, but there was no silk involved in this web: my thread was made of utter bullshit. A therapist told me my lies were a way to 'compensate the shame' I was feeling. Sure, that may be true, but let's call a spade a spade: I was just a barefaced liar.

I also started to steal alcohol when I was in peoples' houses. As much as it pains me to say it out loud, never mind writing it in a book, I did it. Drinks cabinets, fleeced; the selection of booze bought for parties rinsed by yours truly. And, I kid you not, but at this stage I did not think I was an alcoholic. It didn't even enter my pickled mind. To make matters worse and more insane, I would find myself being genuinely *hurt* by people asking me if I had been drinking. I believed my own narrative: people were accusing me of drinking and I was innocent. This was a whole new level of head-fuckery. I had gone from keeping up an illusion of being fine, to being outright delusional.

You would think that wanting and needing a drink would mean that nights out and boozy social gatherings would become easier. Not in my case. Nights out became harder and required more effort. Why? Because I would be trying my bloody hardest to show restraint and not wallop drinks. Obviously, I always had my 'handbag vodka' – I thought I was ahead of the game – as this practice was both efficient and economically savvy. Why pay £4 for a single shot when I could have a quarter bottle for a similar price in my bag? Fools. There was nothing social about my social drinking, there was no respect for the 'bar experience'; it was just a room for me to get sloshed in. And, as time went on, my behaviour on these nights out became more unhinged. Pissing myself, tick. Swapping clothes with a stranger in a toilet cubicle, tick. Waking up under the chassis of my mum's Fiat Punto after a night out, tick. Calling the police because someone took my shoe, tick.

When I find myself in a pub today (yes, a recovering alcoholic can be in a pub) and I see a drink left or people slowly sipping or even saying, 'Better not, I've had two, got work in the morning,' I am floored. My denial about my own problem had me convinced that everyone drank like me; that no one could just have one. Socially, I could never have one. What was the point in that? The fact that I would rather have no alcohol at all than one or two used to be one of the reasons to prove to you all I didn't have a problem when really, I should have been more occupied with the fact that I couldn't stop at two drinks. Stopping at one or two was awful, it almost felt painful; I'd always be the person to say, 'Oh, stay out, have another one' – taking people hostage to carry on the buzz. But if my manipulative ways weren't up to scratch and it was a firm and resounding 'No', I would feel panicked and think of ways in my head to carry on. So I put a stop to that scenario. If it wasn't guaranteed carnage, I wouldn't bloody bother. I genuinely couldn't have cared less about cocktails and girly nights – a shit-load of juice, a long wait at the bar and not wanting to break loose in case you looked bad on pics? No thanks.

With nights out becoming more infrequent due to people going out less, I didn't mind too much – I had life sussed with the secret drinking. There were several times when people in my life tried to have a word and I wouldn't listen; my friend Fran (code name – if you're reading this, 'girl', you know who you are) for one. She would often try to bring it up but I always batted it away, coming up with a plethora of justifications as to why I was drunk or why I was more drunk than everyone else. There was a time when it was me and Fran against the world – she got me and I got her. I'll never forget when we were at an after-party and she rubbed my back as I had my head down the toilet. I lifted it up and said, 'Everyone in Kirkby hates me,' and she said, 'Well, everyone in this bathroom loves you.' And that was when I knew she was the one for me. But I put her in horrendous predicaments as my mental health and alcoholism worsened and I don't blame anyone for not wanting that in their life. And I still refused to say that I had a problem with drink. I had a problem with parts of my life, yes, but drink was not the problem.

Around the beginning of 2016, I was eight years into my drinking. I had distanced myself from some pockets of friends; from those who would confront my behaviour, including Sarah. As she would say, I gave her 'the chop'. Cutting yourself off isn't uncommon: addiction is an isolating condition. I've run away from so many people, good people (granted, not everyone, as some people are meant to be gone and, likewise, people are probably glad I'm out their life, too). But there were good humans who I fucked over, people like Sarah and others like Joanne, Cat, Jonathan, Sam and Fran, who would have helped if I hadn't been in such denial – the majority of these people, along with my recovery mates, are now part of my support network.

My decision to distance myself from certain people was similar to my people-pleasing, secret drinking and hair pulling. It wasn't a conscious choice. Now that I have processed this period of my life, I realise that this was a way to protect myself. I didn't want them to see me any differently. I didn't feel worthy of them and I certainly didn't want to worry them. My self-obsessive selfishness and non-existent self-worth would prevent me from considering their feelings: I never once thought that going on the missing list would cause pain or worry to these people (today I know it did). I saw myself as disposable and someone they would be better off without.

Self-fulfilling prophecies and repeated consequences are a part of my story. I suppose that's because I was repeating the same behaviour over and over again and expecting a different outcome. I hadn't stopped the people-pleasing, the denial, the lying; I had unresolved and unprocessed pain, so of course history was going to repeat.

In the summer of 2016, I finally blew it. I had already turned up pissed ten times too many to parties, and after one particular day of secret drinking, 'hiding it' from my mates thinking they didn't know, I was found out. I was a holy show. I was making no sense and I was offending people; ultimately, I caused an almighty scene and ruined my friend Fran's celebration. My behaviour wasn't harmless, it wasn't amusing and it certainly wasn't acceptable. I wish I could give you details, but I do not remember much of it at all, how could I? I was out of it. It was the straw that broke the camel's back: my friends had reached their limit and I don't blame them.

What I do know is that I left that party obliterated, mortified and hysterical. I was found hours later by me mum in a nearby field, cold, frightened and in a terrible state. Waking up the next day was dark: I was consumed by fear and shame and that was that. I was 'out' and this time I accepted I was out. I *was* a liability and I understood why they could no longer have me in their life. After that night, I had no fight in me to try and win them back; I was resigned to the fact that I wasn't a person anyone would want to be associated with – as far as I was concerned, I didn't deserve friends or support. Today I know I was not a bad person with a bad heart; I was a complicated, unreliable and admittedly a nuisance of a person, but I wasn't evil or cold.

This severing felt like the end of the world and my mental health plummeted. I believed that I was the most abhorrent human that had ever walked the planet.

Why don't we talk about the loss of friends more? We all know about the heartbreak from romantic relationships that break up: the majority of songs, films, books and memes are all centred around a partner breaking your heart. But the loss of friendship to me is a loss like no other. Your allies, confidants and main bitches, poof – gone. Your left arm is amputated, your heart crushed and your head, well, your head is mushed.

It took three years to build up the courage to reconnect with Fran. It was my three-year sober-versary, and although I had achieved a lot personally and professionally, I still felt a fraud and a coward. I'd held on to this remorse and pain for so long, but there was a person in my life who I loved and who I still hadn't tried to make contact with. I can't describe the release that came from that experience.

I want to make a final point about friendship loss: I see myself as no victim when it comes to being alone and losing people. I crossed lines and therefore ties had to be cut. Loss in addiction is inevitable. I have never held any anger towards anyone involved; the only anger I had was towards myself. I think there can be a belief by people that the messes I created didn't affect me. So, if you are reading this, all those many associated persons, please know that they killed me. Each heart broken, told lie, hurt feeling, messed-up night out or time

I let you down chipped away at my heart. You may not have felt as if I cared, as I was good at that. But know, I did.

After this experience in the summer of 2016, it was the beginning of a new chapter, but not in a good way. This was the start of my 'confinement'; I was signed off work by this point on mental health grounds. There was an incident with a belt that will forever remain on my doctor's notes. I didn't want to be seen any more; I didn't want to show my face in Kirkby. The paranoia was overwhelming, so I fell off the face of the earth, my head as my only companion. Few Instagram posts, no Facebook status, no liking of pictures, no one to really talk to outside the family home. In theory you would think that would be easier, as I had no audience to perform to, and for a while it was. Every so often, when someone popped up, I wouldn't tell the truth. I would say I was fine. Same old lying ways; same old shit with a different shovel.

The secret drinking evolved into full-on drinking sprees. Bursts of days where I would only be conscious to drink. I wanted nothing from my day. I just didn't want to feel anything. I didn't care about the hiding, the lying; I was a brazen drunk in the house. And it was around this time that my mum asked me to the garage. We have fold-up tables in our garage, you know the type that you dust off at Christmas. I walked into the garage and there it was, a display of bottles all lined up on the table I had sat and laughed and eaten at with my family. There were miniatures, quarter bottles, half-bottles, litre bottles. So many bottles, so many tears and so much damage.

That was it. Every justification I had held on to to prove I didn't have a problem no longer had meaning.

I was a drunk.

My mum and sister had called me this many a time in heated rows, but I had never believed it. But that summer, I saw my problem. I had the fear of god put in me, and so many questions. How had this happened? Why didn't you try and tell me? What about my job? What do I do now? Does this mean I am an alcoholic?

What will everyone think of me?

I wish I could say to you, 'And that was it – I stopped drinking and I never looked back.' That's not my story. All that happened is that I dropped the act. I couldn't pretend any more. I'd spent five years trying to prove to the world that I wasn't an alcoholic; now, my mind was cleared from having to lie and show others that I didn't have a problem. All that I was left with was the facts, the reality. I had a problem with drink and if I didn't get a grip of it, I was about to lose whatever I had left. My family and my career. It was time I tried to take back control … Oh, dear.

Takeaways

- **Keeping up appearances feels like the right thing to do**
- **Putting on an act is exhausting – playing a role takes it out of you**
- **Social media allows us to deceive the masses**
- **People pick up on your drinking even when you think it doesn't show**
- **Denial is dangerous and can fuel 'secret drinking'**
- **Cutting out people who would confront you is not uncommon**
- **Alcoholism is progressive and powerful.**

Chapter 3

Trying to stop will reveal a lot

As the cliché goes: the first step to dealing with any problem is admitting there's a problem, right? I did that. So what next?

I knew I needed to stop the harmful drinking. I didn't say I wanted to *stop* drinking – are you mad? I wanted to go back to the glory days: the binge drinking on weekends when life was a party. I wanted to be one of those girls with a cocktail who I slagged off in the last chapter. I wanted to a prim and proper drinker; the type you see on the TV adverts; those groups of girls with the perfect teeth, laughing, joking and raising a glass, with some kind of Mediterranean salad in front of them.

And, on that subject, what the hell is wrong with these alcohol companies, by the way? I've never known a substance that causes so much death, destruction and misery be able to market itself in such a wholesome and positive way. Could you imagine if cocaine was advertised to kids? Cocaine-flavoured desserts, billboards depicting cocaine as the best way to have fun? Outrageous. It's a dangerous diet we are fed. I'm no prohibitionist, but I do look at the changing face of campaigns for cigarette and gambling advertising and question why alcohol advertising isn't changing too. There is some hope, the AHA (Alcohol Health Alliance) are working hard to address this:

> *We are calling on the UK Government to introduce evidence-based policies to address the harm alcohol causes and improve health outcomes. We know that measures such as minimum unit pricing of alcohol (which already exists in Scotland and Wales) and restrictions on alcohol marketing work. We need the government to introduce these measures to create a healthier future for us all.*
>
> **Professor Sir Ian Gilmore**

So, yeah, I did not want to give up alcohol, I wanted to be like the adverts. For me, a life without booze wasn't a life worth having. I had all of these theories and notions in my head, the most significant and ridiculous ones being that without drink I wouldn't have a personality and that my life would be over. Bearing in mind that my secret drinking turned me into a dithering, non-communicative, emotional wreck, still my head told me being sober would be worse.

I know now I'm an alcoholic, which makes sense as to why I wanted to keep drinking, but wanting to keep alcohol in my life was more than wanting to stay drunk. I wanted to keep drink in my life because I didn't want to be judged for not drinking.

We are used to a bit of subconscious sober-shaming in the UK. How many times has someone on a night out said they don't drink or 'worse', don't *want* to drink, and their choice is made into a 'thing'? I'll hold my hands up and confess – I have called people bores and encouraged people to drink: 'Go on, you can just have one' or 'God, you've changed, you used to be fun' have fallen out of my ignorant mouth many a time. Appalling behaviour, really. I even went as far as to say that people who didn't drink were weird. So, what is it about the booze? Why don't we feel comfortable around people staying sober? If someone told me they weren't going to take cocaine, I wouldn't bat an eyelid or think any less of them. If someone told me that they didn't want to eat fish because they reacted badly to it, I wouldn't embarrass them and apply the pressure so that they eat it. I certainly wouldn't judge them for not putting into their bodies the thing that causes them haddock – sorry, havoc. But sobriety breeds a distinct distain.

Wonderfully, there is this incredible 'sober curious' movement that has now started: people are simply choosing to be sober for no other reason other than they are healthier and happier without it. Sobriety is not life or death for them like it is for me; it is a lifestyle choice, and I salute you all. But even with this trend plastered all over Instagram and gaining traction, there are still hurdles to overcome. The normalisation of sobriety still hasn't fully taken place. I hope one day it will be the norm for people to be completely unfazed by not drinking. I hope it happens before I snuff it.

As my need to take back control of my drinking came before sobriety was cool – dare I say, 'woke' – going teetotal was out of the question. So I thought I would put everything into *controlling* it. What a complete disaster.

People say if you have to Google: 'Am I an alcoholic?' then you are an alcoholic. I don't know how true that is, but it certainly was the case for me. The one good thing about the internet – it never judges you. And you can always count on the world wide web to prove or disprove whatever conspiracy or belief you have. Even when the online quizzes were all conclusive that I had a drink problem (one quiz told me that I was a sociopath, for god's sake), I discounted the abstinence-based solutions. Instead, I asked the omnipotent oracle for ways to avoid having to give up the booze. My Google searches were as follows:

- **How do you control your drinking?**
- **How do you stop drinking alcoholically?**
- **What alcoholic drink is the least harmful?**
- **How to keep alcohol in your life?**
- **Do you have to give up drink?**
- **How to be a functioning alcoholic?**
- **I don't want to quit drinking, I want to reduce, what to do?**

I was trying to gain control over something I knew I had no control over. I still thought I knew best and that these top tips I found on some random website were putting me on the right path. I didn't need professional help; I was an educated professional myself. Surely cutting down on the booze is just like dieting, right? Wrong. Considering I was so dependent on drink, my mum, boyfriends and validation, I was oddly dead set on doing things my way and was being quite self-reliant about it. I know what you're thinking: 'What a contradiction – what is she on about?' but my drinking-stinking-thinking days were full of contradictions and paradoxical ideals; there was a complete disconnect between my actions and my thoughts. I wanted control; I had no control. I wanted to be independent; I was dependent. I wanted to be loved; I pushed people away. I wanted to be understood; I didn't open up. I wanted to be trusted; I was acting untrustworthily. I wanted to be heard; I didn't use my voice. I wanted stability; everything was unstable. I wanted to be happy; I made my life a misery. But still adamant that my way was the best way, I gave 'controlled drinking' a bloody good go.

Controlled drinking is, according to the American Psychological Association, a controversial harm-reduction approach for those with relatively mild alcohol problems and low alcohol dependence. Research has not supported controlled drinking as an efficacious primary goal of intervention for moderate to severe alcohol dependence.

Michael Rawlinson

Now, I'm not here to piss on anyone's chips and turn my nose up at controlled drinking or reducing drinking. The statistics are there: for some people moderating and tracking alcohol consumption works to reduce their drinking and alcohol harm, and to those I sincerely say hats off to you. I'm no abstinent AA evangelical; you could tell me that you stand on your head in the corner for two hours a night because it helps you to live a happier life and I would support you. (Not literally, though — I haven't got the upper body strength for that.) Whatever method people employ to get well, happy or sober is down to the individual. Tolerance is key and having been judged many a time in my short life, who am I to comment on anyone's route to wellness and freedom?

Finding out what works for you, however, isn't like trying on a pair of jeans and seeing if the cut is right on your arse. When it comes to matters relating to your booze consumption, the chances are you have to fuck up and throw up a fair few times before you find out what works for you, what looks good on you. Suppose it's a bit like Goldilocks and the Three Hairs (of the dog). Suffice to say, Melissa Rice and controlled drinking was a bloody nightmare, let me tell you. I am a binge drinker through and through; in fact, I am a serial binger: TV shows, food, exercise, coffee are all exhausted until I go, 'That's enough! I need a breather.' Switching from a mindset that had a total disregard for units, to counting *and* pacing my units, was too much like hard work. It seemed counterintuitive. I drank to be carefree, to escape the noise in my head and to worry less about the past and the future, not to sit with a pen and paper, monitoring, tracking and panicking. I must admit, when I was *compos mentis* enough to complete a drinking diary, the results were astounding. I was gobsmacked. My go-to half-bottle was a 35cl, and that one bottle that I would sink in a few swift swigs was 13.1 units. Say I did that four times a week … that would be 52.4 units a week. Did you know it is recommended that we drink 14 units of alcohol a week? You read right: 14. And four half-bottles a week was probably during the times when things weren't too bad; later, down the line, I moved up to a 75cl bottle, which is a whole different ball game, leading to chemical dependency.

In tandem with the counting, I read about setting some goals and rules to get a handle my problematic consumption. These rules, I felt, were a great way to change not only how I drank but why I drank. They were as follows:

- **Only drinking on weekends**
- **No more vodka, switch to beer**
- **No drinking at home in secret**
- **No drinking when I'm sad**
- **No more doubles and no more shots if I am out**
- **Drink slower**
- **Drink water in between drinks**
- **No drinking on dates**
- **No drinking before 6 p.m.**

Jesus Christ, this was all rather exhausting and, truthfully, I was miserable. I thought more about drinking when I was trying to moderate it than I ever had before. I wished days of my life away to get to that next drink, and for the weekend, when I would permit myself a blowout. I wasn't fully present in anything that I was doing – all I could think about was bloody drink and worrying myself daft that people knew that I was thinking about drink. My head was full of, 'A drink would sort that out,' or 'Only a few more hours to go.' I had been to the GP by this point over my anxiety; he put me on an antidepressant and I responded so badly to it I thought they weren't for me. Drink was a quicker way (or so I thought). And so I found myself chained to the stuff even when I wasn't even drinking the stuff; all of that precious headspace and time spent obsessing, wasted on a bottle of plonk. Is it any wonder that my anxiety and mood were worsening by the week? But I still firmly believed that this was what I had to do if I wanted to have it all – drink in my life, a career to return to and my mother's nerves in order. I was prepared to be miserable.

I am fully aware, at this stage in my drinking career, that I,

Melissa, was not one of the reasons I wanted to get my drinking under control. I didn't want to stop for *me* (that would have meant that I cared about me). Nope, I wanted to get a handle on it for the sake of others and to keep hold of a job. Please note, you have to stop for you and make the change *for you.*

My attempts at controlling alcohol were obviously ill-fated. Each and every rule was broken at some point. I would either come up with an exception to the rule, or I would move the goalposts slightly. Rather than seeing these oopsies as evidence that I needed to seek professional help, I saw my 'Sod it, why not?' guzzles as examples of how much of a useless idiot (twat) I was. The feelings of failure were crippling. But it's important to acknowledge that I did still try. You know that annoying saying you hear after coming last in a sports day race: 'It's the taking part that counts'? Well, that. As condescending and pitying as this phrase is, when it comes to drinking or changing any harmful habit, we really should acknowledge that the person is at least trying. It may be hard to celebrate someone for trying when they are pissed and causing so much pain and upset for themselves and unto others, but to even attempt a change in drinking behaviour is a huge step. So, if you are ever in a position whereby you are trying to change your relationship with drink and you feel like you have fallen at the first hurdle, be kind to yourself. This shit is hard, and you deserve compassion and support, and that has to come from *you* first. I was never kind to myself in my early days, and I certainly never gave myself any credit for at least *trying* to gain back some kind of control.

Breaking my rules felt like a series of epic failures. Each time I fudged it up, it would take me to an incredibly negative place that chipped away at my heart and soul. As me mum said:

Melissa would battle with drinking and win, gain strength.
However, this was short-lived – she was going round in circles.

I would call myself every vile name under the sun when I would slip back into drinking; I felt worthless, stupid, frustrated and weak-willed. There're a lot of people who still use the old 'They have no willpower' remark when talking about people who are struggling with addiction. But how could willpower ever prevent me from doing something over which I had no control? Willpower alone couldn't have saved me from the depths of despair I found myself in. My need for drink was not a moral affliction or a reflection of my character: I was suffering from a recognised condition.

While we are on the subject of 'failure', before recovery I never appreciated how important getting life wrong is. I am who I am today because I have learnt from past mistakes and misjudgements. When I was in the madness, I also had a bad habit of setting myself up to fail. My targets were overambitious, to say the least, and my expectations ...? Well, they were always in the sky. I know when my mates read this next bit, they will piss themselves laughing, but I do struggle with perfectionism. They'll laugh and say, 'Is she messing? She never got anything right, something always went wrong.' And you know what, they would be completely just in their opinions. Back in the day, I had the remarkable gift of the reverse Midas touch – everything I touched would turn to shit; a shambolic disaster rather than just a blip in the road. There were so many examples, like trying to organise a night out and we'd arrive at the bar and the table would be booked for the wrong day. Or when I had given it my all for my dissertation and on the last hurdle lost five thousand words of the assignment and had to stay up all night on god knows what. My mate Fran always used to say the phrase, '*Of course* this has happened to you.' The molehills of life would be the Three Peak Challenge, and I certainly didn't have the gear or knowledge of a mountaineer. But perfectionism comes in two forms: the adaptive (healthy) and the maladaptive (unhealthy). Guess which one I identify as?

The adaptive perfectionism folk are the type who achieve their goals and have that whole conscientious, go-getter, high-standards vibe about them. Yeah, I am definitely not that kind, although I seem to surround myself with them. I am the maladaptive perfectionism type. If you're in my unfortunate gang, you'll be haunted by your past mistakes, fearful of new mistakes and afraid of not living up to expectations. Let me tell you, the amount of pressure I've always put on myself to get everything right, to be who you wanted and needed me to be, was as unbearable as it was ridiculous. Failure was never personal: I never think to myself, 'You've let yourself down.' No, my first thought is, 'You have let everybody down.' My jugular. This unhealthy perfectionism in relation to my drinking was off the chart, and incredibly damaging to whatever self-esteem I had left.

Maladaptive perfectionists are also more likely to seek positive feedback from the environment and attempt to gain approval from their peers. If they see imperfection in their lives they are apt to become discouraged and seek an alternative way to gain acceptance, including depression, suicidal ideation, anxiety, stress, eating disorders, emotional deregulation, recurrent physical pain and other medical problems, insecure adult attachment, marital and premarital difficulties, and low academic performance. Both maladaptive and adaptive forms of perfectionism can moderate an individual's response to disruptive events. However, for maladaptive perfectionists events that can cause loss of status, worth and failure can result in behavioural avoidance and withdrawal.

Michael Rawlinson

Although my dalliances with mindful, controlled and measured drinking may appear a total flop, it was a process I had to go through. I had to find out the painful way that drink was my kryptonite. These losses against the drink pushed me closer to accepting that I needed to go completely sober and, later on, get expert help.

Today it is clear to me (and probably to you) that I had no defence against alcohol. As soon as a drink went into my body, that was it: I'd unleash the beast within, and I was away.

Inevitably, my drinking worsened yet further and I was becoming more and more mentally unwell. I couldn't have it in my life any more. Every binge was becoming more chaotic, more dangerous; I was sick of people on my back, I was sick of the life I was living. I had to quit.

Once more, I returned to the internet for the answers – Google felt far easier than confiding in someone and, let's face it, I didn't have many people around me I could turn to. The shame was too much to reach out and ask for help from outsiders. My mum wouldn't even tell my family members what was going on, so it became our immediate family secret. At this point in time, I still thought that I wasn't an alcoholic and, therefore, that I didn't need Alcoholic's Anonymous. I certainly didn't need a drug and alcohol service, or even the GP. I clearly needed a hobby and a healthy substitute in my life. That's right, I thought a fucking hobby would save me. (Funnily enough, new hobbies *are* recommended when you are in recovery, to discover your creative side and all of that palaver.) But to think that a hobby would stop me from drinking was just as naïve as thinking I would adhere to my own rules around drinking. My hobbies:

- **Yoga course – lasted two sessions.**
- **German lessons – lasted four sessions, and for the last one I had to be picked up by Mum, absolutely stinking drunk.**
- **Meditation apps – lasted two minutes as I couldn't handle the stillness and the images in my head.**
- **Knitting – don't ever try knitting when you have the shakes.**
- **The gym – didn't hate it actually, but I have distinct memories of hiding two small bottles of rosé in a sanitary bin before I went into the circuit training class.**

Each new hobby and interest were things I had always wanted to get into. They may not sound that cool or interesting to you lot, but they were to me. I must say, each phase was met with enthusiasm and determination – I genuinely thought having a new focus that was outside work, a focus that wasn't harmful to my head or liver, would be good distraction from the drinking thoughts. If only there *was* a way to knit one, purl one out of alcoholism.

And then something sinister started to happen with these new hobbies and interests – they became alibis. I started to use these new 'outside the home' hobbies to get the units into my system. What else was I to do? My mum had the eyes of a hawk and the nose of a police-trained Alsatian. With few friends on the scene and no real social life, I had to get the drink in somehow.

Things became more hostile in the family home. I won't dwell too much on that here, but in the early stages of me trying to get sober my mum was rightfully sick and tired of the three-weekly blow-ups.

- **Week 1 – I would be determined to do well, chat the big 'un about how things will be different this time, I'd have my shit together, I would be attentive at home and I wouldn't be a crying mess of an evening or utterly paranoid.**
- **Week 2 – the 'I got this' novelty would be wearing off.**
- **Week 3 – the fear and panic would set in, my head would wobble and, boom … away she goes.**

This cycle went on for a while. My mum saw it as her responsibility to clear up the mess of the aftermath and get me back on a sane path after my sprees. It was wholly unfair to her, and draining. Each episode was getting worse and it was becoming harder to stay motivated. I needed help. I needed professional help.

Even though I was signed off sick, the fear of my employer finding out I was getting outside help was massive. I dared not tell them – I couldn't do that, they were never to know. As a society, there are certain professions that we commonly assign 'role model' status to: nurses, doctors, social workers, teachers, lawyers, etc. There's a credibility and an understanding that these people have their shit together, they are respectable, and we trust these people with our health, life and offspring. There is hardly room for humanness. Think about it, would you want a surgeon who suffered with anxiety? Would you want your child to be taught by someone who drank to cope?

If you have heard the podcast *Hooked*, you will be familiar with my co-host, Jade. By trade she is a mental health nurse and, you guessed it, an addict in recovery. We met in October 2017 on my first day of rehab. She was the first person I had met who had the same catastrophic thinking as me and we bonded over the 'disgraced nurse/teacher' feeling we both shared. Personality-wise, we are oil and water and in theory we shouldn't mix or get on, but much to the counsellors' surprise, our oil and water differences turned into something quite beautiful – a friendship lava lamp. (Jade, I can feel you squirming at my analogy and my mushiness; just allow me this one moment. Please.) Back to why I have brought in Jade: our professions. I'll never forget we were interviewed on live radio once, and the presenter asked us: 'What do you have to say to those people who trusted you with their children or their health?' Jesus Christ, what a kick in our imaginary balls, what a way to take a rusty knife to wounds that were barely healed! My response: 'I'm a human being who was suffering and needed help.' We have to remember, folks: we are not our jobs or our roles. We are human, and no one is infallible.

Both of us clung on as long as possible to our jobs; of course we did, they were the last good thing we both had in our lives and without them what would we do? Who would we be? Allowing your job, or any role, to define who are as a person is risky business. We both learnt (the hard way) that trying to keep up the pretence causes more personal and professional damage than good.

In the podcast, I asked Jade: 'What was it about your job that prevented you from asking for help?' Apart from stating the obvious – 'I didn't want to lose my job' – Jade pointed out a very good point – that her job as a nurse fed into her denial. As long as she was performing in her job, she did not have a problem.

Employment – and the fear of losing your job – is a massive barrier to seeking help. Letting any employer know you are struggling with your mental health can be daunting in itself; I was signed off on long-term sick leave with anxiety and depression after my summer of hell in 2016. Which is technically true, but it wasn't the whole truth. I was still living a lie and, as I have been taught in recovery: 'Secrets keep you sick.' It will come as no surprise that during the time I spent off to get well, I became more mentally ill because I was obsessing about being off and worrying way too much over what my employer thought of me. I was already the Crohn's girl who would sprint down the corridor to get to the bathroom in case I had an accident; now I was the mental health girl. Imagine being the alchy girl. Letting your employer know that you are drinking to cope is a different beast entirely, something that takes courage and one of the bravest acts I can think of. (I mean that.)

Since that particular podcast aired, I have received so many messages from people who are scared to let their employer know the truth, to drop the 'everything is fine routine', because they feel their job will be at risk. Each time this very real and justified fear-filled message appeared in my inbox, my heart would sink: I had been there.

Now, I have to make clear, not everyone shares this worry. I know many fortunate folk who have been able to be open with their employer about their drug or alcohol issues, and have gone on to get the in-work support they need. But back in 2016, I didn't have the confidence to share the full story of what was going on. I was riddled with shame and I was too desperate to hold on to my career. To no longer be a teacher or be in the classroom would have been too great of a loss for me. (I sometimes wonder how different life might have been if I had opened up to my employer about drinking to cope, but if the trust wasn't there and I didn't feel safe to, then I won't punish myself for that.)

Instead, my mum made an appointment with the GP. He was a lovely man who took his time and had one of those glowing auras – a way about him that made me feel secure. Feeling safe enough to open up is crucial. Going through my medical history, he was able to see that physically I had been through a lot, what with my guts and my arse, and he could also see that throughout my twenties I had made the odd visit regarding my mental health: this wasn't my first time at the rodeo for declaring to my GP that I wasn't 'reet' in the head. But it was the first time I had talked about alcohol. I'd received some counselling sessions around the age of twenty-three, crying my way through those sessions. Didn't say that I loved a drink, though. Didn't tell them that I had intrusive thoughts of seeing my arm wrapped in a cheese wire with blood pouring out in times of worry. I had just sobbed like a baby for ten sessions and that was that.

This time, though, things were different. I had my mum sharing what was going on – she was the only person who knew how bad things really were of an evening, lest we forget I was pissed for the most part. My poor mum's thoughts and memories painted the harrowing picture for the doctor: her having to pick me up off the floor, having to put me in the shower, checking that I was still breathing when I was sleeping. Listening to her describe me on my bad days was so very difficult – was this really me? What is wrong with me? I just couldn't believe that this was me, I was that person. I remember the doctor took my hand and gave it a squeeze; a squeeze as if to say, 'I understand, and I am not judging you.' I appreciated that, I needed that – we all need that. Then, as I waited for him to provide some miracle cure, he referred me to a local drug and alcohol service.

Every gorgeous thought I had about him went out the window. I was fuming. A drug and alcohol service? Really? I had been hoping he was going to tell me that this was a mental episode, but it was not. He did, however, put me on another prescription for antidepressants, and I was glad to take them. But I may as well have been prescribed Tic Tacs – this medication only works if you don't drink …

The drug and alcohol service was in the middle of the townie, near the Maccies and facing an icon of Kirkby's civic pride: the market. (If you ever want a decent sausage and find yourself in Liverpool, do yourself a favour and buy a pound of Kirkby sausage.) Granted, I'm no town planner, but I do wonder what the powers-that-be were thinking in putting a drug and alcohol service slap-bang in the middle of the townie. I know there should be nothing to be ashamed of, but at that point in my life, there was plenty to be ashamed of. I have done the walk of shame before (we've all been there, haven't we, when we've drunk too much and ended up going back to someone's place and partaking in sloppy and sometimes weird inter-human relations, then waking in the wee hours, picking up our shoes, knickers and pride, and embarking on that walk of shame home?), but walking into that drug and alcohol service to seek help was the worse walk of them all.

There I was, at this drug and alcohol service, full face of make-up, hair done and a smasual (smart-casual) ensemble – I had the full armour on. (Besides, me turning up in my mental health uniform of slept-in pyjamas with a bun on the top of my head looking dug up wasn't acceptable – presentation at all costs again.) Inside, I was a mess. I began to cry to me mum in the waiting area, looking and acting like a child who was waiting to go into the dentist. I didn't want to be there; this wasn't where I belonged, where either of us belonged. You have to bear in mind that we both had archaic understandings of who or what an alcoholic was. I was riddled with a chronic case of the 'don't you know who I am(s)', a dreadful condition that inflates the ego, attacks your pride and has you convinced you are better than most. In an instant, I would be able to reel off a plethora of reasons as to why I, the 'respectable' Melissa Rice, couldn't possibly be an alcoholic:

> *I was female, I wasn't a super-rich celebrity, I was educated, I had a loving family and regular childhood, I was in my twenties, my mum wasn't a big drinker, I suffered with anxiety and depression, I was a teacher, I wasn't homeless, I did not drink cider in the park, I didn't drink every day – 'excuse me, I am a binger' – I hadn't been to prison, I was not homeless, did I mention I was educated? I wasn't yellow, oh and I had my own teeth.*

Notice how the list progressively becomes more offensive and desperate. I'm ashamed to say, that list has not been exaggerated for dramatic purposes, I really was that ignorant and arrogant towards alcoholism. I now know that addiction, mental health and 'falling on hard times' couldn't care less about who or what you are – we are all fair game.

The worst part about the whole experience of this drug and alcohol service was that my biggest fear of being spotted came true: I knew the girl behind the desk. Of course that bloody happened. My head came clean off. I was imagining her breaking her employer's code of conduct to tell people that I was in there. I remember trying to hold my shit together and hoping that she thought I was there to supervise someone else (even though she clearly had my referral notes on her desk).

Apart from my paranoia of people knowing I was there for help, I felt frightened. I was frightened by the signage, by the stain on the couch, by the argument that occurred between two clients in the waiting room and, most of all, I was frightened by the reality of it all. This is where my drink had brought me. How the fuck had it all come to this?

Going into a drug and alcohol service can be daunting for anyone, particularly if your shame and pride levels are on a par with your drinking levels. If you are nervous, embarrassed and all of those other feelings that don't serve us well when we are in need, I get it. If it makes you feel any better, avoiding drug and alcohol services isn't uncommon. One charity in particular is doing great work to ensure that they are accessible in every sense of the word. We Are With You was formerly known as Addaction;

speaking on this decision to rebrand, Chief Executive Laura Bunt says:

> Through changing our name to We Are With You and creating a new visual identity and website, we hope to be more accessible to people who use or might use our services. Our research shows that language around addiction can in itself be a huge barrier to people seeking help. As We Are With You, we will use everyday language and focus on the help we offer, not the problem.

We Are With You have also made great strides in their virtual offer as they know just how unsettling and challenging walking into a service can be. In recent times, the way in which we connect and communicate has changed. Zoom, Google Meet, Teams, all of these applications that we never really bothered with are now our life-lines, and in the addiction and recovery community they are proving to be hugely successful.

> Online meetings have had extraordinary outcomes; for many people the thought of walking into a meeting or a drug and alcohol environment is overwhelming. The social anxiety, not knowing what is going to happen; a blend of intense fears. These virtual meetings allow people to enter this world from the safety of their own home. There are more and more support groups for addiction, probably more than there have ever been in existence, and although services have been cut dramatically, there is support out there. It's just about taking that first step and asking for help in the right place; a lot of people ask for help in the wrong places,

which leads to rejection. I heard someone say once, 'There's no point going to the hardware store for a pint of milk,' and this analogy is perfect for addiction. You have to go to the right place and have a bit of responsibility.

Michael Rawlinson

Virtual meetings were not a thing back in 2016/17 – I wish they were. The staff in this service I attended treated me with such kindness. Recovery workers are remarkable beings who quite often have 'been there' themselves, or been affected by addiction in some way. When you think about what the role of a recovery worker requires, and everything they see and hear, it takes a special person, a compassionate person, to be in a field that is steeped in trauma. There's very little money involved in recovery work and if I had my way, they would be paid handsomely. They support some of the most vulnerable and broken members of society and I'm yet to meet a recovery worker doesn't want anything more than for you to never have to see them again. They want you well and they want you to be free.

Despite this, my first experience of a service was too much of a shock to the system and clearly I wasn't desperate enough to take the help I needed. Regardless of the kindness on offer, I was so shell-shocked by the experience and the realisation of my alcoholism that it actually worked as a deterrent. I never wanted to have to go in there again. I feel so bad to state that baldly here, but I genuinely never wanted to step foot in that seventies concrete building again. My ego had gone through nine rounds with a heavyweight champion and I wasn't prepared to go in the ring again.

I was still dead set on wanting to show to my mum and prove to myself I could do this alone.

I white-knuckled it. Each day, I was holding on for dear life and living with obsessive thoughts, when I should have been accessing support from those services to pick up tools for how to cope. I became a miserable, dry drunk – an alcoholic who no longer drinks but otherwise maintains the same behaviour patterns as an alcoholic. I was still mental. I was still broken. I was still being deceitful. I was still angry. I had no kind of treatment or solution; I was just the same, only without the drink.

I remember I got a good stint of sober days under my belt, and I thought I was cured. I knew nothing of the illness I was suffering from, I didn't know about things like 'triggers' or 'relapse'. So it's no bloody surprise that the mental obsession became too much again, and I needed to act on it. And each time I drank again, it set me straight back to somewhere less than square one. There were times when I relapsed without even knowing it was going to happen. You could have put me on a lie detector test and asked me if I had intentions of drinking and I would have said no. I'd have passed with flying colours and been found not guilty. But alcoholism, or any kind of problematic use of anything, is a sneaky fucker: without your mental weapons you don't really stand a chance. It will sneak its way back in quicker than you can say, 'Litre of vodka, please, love.'

Hopelessness really began to set in; the days were long, meaningless, miserable. I was depressed, and life felt the heaviest it had ever been. When you're depressed you lack motivation, so how could I have the requisite fire in my belly and test my resolve when I just wanted to give up? I wouldn't leave my room and I wouldn't really speak to anyone in the house. Apart from vodka, my only other escape was the TV. I would zone out watching it, spend hours staring at it, watching series after series, mindlessly. I didn't have to speak if I was watching the telly, I didn't have to notice the state of my life if I was watching make-believe. Actually, I still can't sleep if the telly isn't on – my lecky bill is through the roof, but trying to drift off in silence makes my mind wander and race. By concentrating on what others are saying – usually in some British monarchy documentary or Malcolm Tucker in *The Thick of It* – I don't need to hear myself, and I can drift off to the land of nod without the usual, 'Urgh, why did you say *that* today?' and 'What the hell are you gonna do about your life?' I'm sure you get the picture.

In the space of that year, I went from being cocky, thinking I knew best and that my way was the right way, to ending up on my knees, begging for help, drinking holy water from Lourdes in an attempt to purge me of this illness. If you're rather confused, you'll find most 'Catholic' houses in Kirkby will have a bottle of holy water in a phial shaped like the Virgin Mary somewhere, whether that be on display or in a cupboard. Someone *always* knows someone who has been to Lourdes and they always bring back the holy water. If you're still confused, Lourdes is the place where many sick people go on a pilgrimage; the spring is said to have healing powers as it's the place where the Virgin Mary appeared to a young girl call Bernadette. So yeah, this was not my finest moment – unscrewing Our Lady's blue crown to get to the consecrated H2O and then filling her back up with tap water so my swig would go unnoticed, but there we have it.

This year of trying to gain back control taught me that you can't do this on your own and that I had no control. I was sitting, stewing in my own memories, reliving my past, but this time I didn't see a future. I saw no way out. I needed a friend, I needed someone other than my persecuted mother to talk to. My mum was too involved in the situation, and we were both as demented as each other, just in different ways. So I reached out to a friend who I hadn't spoken to for quite a long time. Joanne.

Joanne was close with Sarah: she is a strong, private and a very fair person. She knows right from wrong and I have always respected her and her approach to life. She couldn't give two shits about gossip or hearsay, and when I say everyone needs a Joanne in their life, I mean it. Your business will never be shared, she is fiercely loyal, but also able to call bullshit if she sees fit. We have enjoyed many a gig (our favourite being The Pixies) and many a night putting the world to rights.

Existing in my room, I remember sending her a message on Facebook, asking her if we could meet. I didn't say the words 'I need help', but I think she knew something was up.

We met and we spoke and as much as I appreciated her listening to me, I couldn't bear the thought of her knowing the whole truth all in one go. Instead, she listened to a slow and steady drip feed: for the next twelve months, Joanne, the girl I met at twenty-one at parties, became my only friend. The more we would meet up and talk, the more the heavier stuff was revealed. But I always managed to hold parts back; you know, those locked-up boxes stored in your brain. But she knew, and she knew that I was under some heavy-duty family surveillance too.

It's always good to include someone else's observations on what was going on at the time, so just like I asked Sarah, I wanted to include Joanne's voice.

Before I knew what you were struggling with, I remember getting a random text from you asking if I wanted to go for some food with you one day. I was made up to hear from you, as we hadn't spoken much around that time. We hadn't fallen out, we just hadn't seen each other in a while. I can't specifically remember what happened then but we started going for food every few weeks or so after this. Always PG fun, haha.

One time we had a table booked at a restaurant on a random weekday for lunch. I met you outside and your Becca and Noah [my nephew] were with you and I remember thinking it was a bit strange because it was like they were dropping you off, which must've been the case, but I wasn't really aware of everything that had been going on at this point so I was just a bit confused. I didn't think much of it, but it popped back into my head once I did get to know what was going on because they were probably just being extra-cautious that you were going to be somewhere safe and we weren't going to a pub or something.

I knew you had problems with drinking, but I never pushed that conversation on you. I knew you were sensitive around it; anyone would be if they're dealing with something like that. I didn't ever want to be a person who would challenge your drinking because I knew your mum and Becca were doing that. I felt that if I started to pick you up on it you would hide it more, and I just wanted to be someone you could talk to about anything and not have to edit out any parts. I would rather know about it than it be a secret. I started to come and see you through the week on my lunches while you were at home; this must have been around the time your mum wanted you to stay home.

One time I was trying to get in touch to come down. It was a Monday and you weren't responding so I just texted you and told you I was on the way. When I got there no one was home but you pulled up in a taxi and we went into yours and sat in the conservatory. You seemed a bit strange; I wouldn't say you seemed drunk to me, you just seemed a bit odd. You weren't making eye contact and kept looking at the floor. I was just making normal conversation and you seemed to relax a bit.

Your mum came home not long after we got in and slammed the door, and I remember her shouting, 'This house stinks of drink!' She didn't know I was there and when she came in the kitchen she saw us and, normally, I would expect your mum to try and avoid confronting you until I had gone because she is very private, but she just said the same thing, that you smelt of booze, and asked where you had been. She said she knew you had been drinking and asked me if I could smell it. I honestly have the worst sense of smell in the world and I wasn't sure, so I just said as much.

When things got really bad, I came to see you during a hospital admittance and I think this was the first time I properly told you how scared I was of what was going to happen if you carried on. I am NOT a crier and I remember crying so it must have been a heavy conversation. I remember you saying that you wanted me to tell you how I was feeling because you needed to hear it.

Diluting my pain and keeping things back from Joanne wasn't

because I didn't trust her, or that I thought she would judge me. It was my insecurities and my own way of avoiding the truth – I didn't want this girl to run or feel too worried by me, and I didn't want to impose on her life. I remember thinking: 'I should have done this a long time ago.' Her friendship took me out of my head, it almost gave me a purpose.

She asked me to be her bridesmaid when I was at my lowest and just before I went into treatment, on the unsaid condition that I got my act together. And, you know what? I did it. I didn't have many goals entering or leaving rehab other than the obvious, but putting on a frock and seeing her get married gave me something worthwhile to hold on to. I never really knew how much she was worried; again, I think it another avoidance tactic of the mind. She not only supported me but she checked in with my sister and my mum. I don't think she will ever realise what a cup of tea or a trip to see the squirrels did for me. I get told off by most people for telling them how thankful I am for what they did for me, but these typical gestures that regular friends did (and do) felt like grand acts of kindness.

Bloody hell, I'm blubbering again here.

Apart from Joanne, I wasn't ready to reconnect with anyone else just then: I cared too much and didn't want to be a drain on any more people. Social media would show me that the other friends I had distanced myself from were in their prime of life and I didn't want to show up uninvited with more drama. I wasn't ready to answer too many questions with too many people. So, I remained on the missing list. But the relief from even sharing a third of my problems with someone I could trust goes to show that when we get our worries out of our head and into the light, we lighten the load.

Problem drinking is a heavy cross to bear and I thought it was my cross to carry.

Although I had a friend and antidepressants and I was a regular at the GP, I still couldn't stay sober for long. One glimmer of hope was that opening up became easier as my drinking worsened and my mind deteriorated. Little did I know that life was going to get much, much worse.

Takeaways

- **You have to find what works for you**
- **Be proud of yourself for even trying**
- **Don't be alone with your problem**
- **Open up to people you feel safe with**
- **Put yourself before your job**
- **If you need help, get the bloody help.**

Chapter 4

Rock bottom is a gift

How many times do you see an inspirational Instagram quote, sent by a well-meaning friend, saying, 'You can't have rainbows without rain', or 'Better days are coming', or 'What doesn't kill you makes you stronger', and you think to yourself: 'Oh, piss off, have a day off, will you'? But as much as I find forced positivity as uncomfortable and unbearable as forced fun at Christmas, those 'things can only get better' quotes do have truth behind them (sorry, don't hate me). When we're really up to our eyes in 'it', and we find ourselves in so much pain and fear and we are convinced that there is no way out, the idea of holding on to hope, having faith or believing there is a solution, can feel impossible and pointless. I never once thought that anything good could come from being at your lowest point. But as a wise old owl taught me, if you're at the bottom, surely the only way is up. (Damn it, that's two pop-song references I've put in the one paragraph.)

The phrase 'rock bottom' is bandied about quite freely these days, particularly on the old mental health and well-being circuit. But in the addiction and recovery world, 'rock bottom' is a real place; a hellish destination people have to reach in order to get to the point of waving the white flag while screaming, 'I am done, I can't do this any more.' I know not all people find the phrase useful, so I chatted with Michael: 'Rock bottom is a useful phrase; for some it is not, because it suggests you have to lose so much, but as a practitioner it is a phrase that most people understand. Rock bottom means you can't get any lower and in a way the rock bottom can be the greatest moment because it is the turning point.'

For me, that very moment of surrender in alcoholism is called 'the gift of desperation' (Alcoholics Anonymous). The gift of desperation means that a pickled person, like myself, is finally willing to do whatever it is that is necessary to make the change. This 'gift' allows us to finally admit defeat and accept that alcohol/drugs have beaten us. According to Michael, 'For addiction treatment to be successful, people have to want to change and the rock bottom or the moment of change can drive that want.'

Does admitting defeat or powerlessness make people weak? I don't think so. I didn't have to keep trying, I no longer had to compete with an enemy who only wanted me dead. When I finally realised the booze had beaten me, I felt free.

Seems odd, really, that to gain freedom from addiction, you have to experience loss. But not everyone has to reach the lowest of the lows before they remove alcohol from their life. You do not have to lose your house, family, job or sanity to find sobriety – this is not a prerequisite. I know folk whose drinking looked quite pleasant to a binger like me, but to them, it was causing too much disruption and damage to their life, so they quit while they were ahead. Michael added to this: There are people who have 'high rock bottoms' or 'low rock bottoms' – it doesn't really matter; the moment they decide to change is personal to an individual.

For instance, I have a friend called T – we both self-identify as alcoholics and both abstain from the stuff, but our stories are very different. For him, he was able to see early on that whenever he had a few drinks or a big bender on a weekend, his relationship with his wife and his ability to perform in his job were both affected. He didn't like the person he was with a drink in him and these feelings were enough for him to say no more. T could see where this unhealthy relationship with drinking was going and he made the decision to end the relationship before he lost the parts of his life that he cherished. I suppose your pain threshold is yours to gauge. Clearly, mine was pretty high.

Your rock bottom is personal to you. No two rock bottoms are the same. Towards the end of my drinking, I was scared of my own reflection and I became utterly paranoid. I was hearing voices and was having the most intrusive of thoughts; I would imagine inflicting all kinds of harm on myself and, ultimately, those childhood behavioural soothers returned. My arms were clawed more times than a cat's scratching post and my hand seemed welded to the top of my scalp, so that I resembled a chimpanzee vacantly picking pests out of its fur (I'm sure you get the gist).

You may read about my darkest days and be tempted to say to yourself: 'Phew, I'm not as bad as her' or 'Maybe I don't need to look at my drinking after all, as my life isn't that bad.' And that may be true: your final days, months or years probably won't comprise hospitals, bruised vaginas, lost careers, being locked up in the family home or jumping out of windows. It really doesn't matter how much we do or don't drink, what we lose or keep; what matters is how our vice/habit affects us, how it impacts our life and how much we can tolerate.

There's been many a time when I have questioned if I was a 'proper alcoholic'. I thought my story wasn't tragic enough to belong to an alcoholic, my lack of liver damage wasn't alcoholic, and the way in which I drank and what I drank wasn't 'classic' alcoholic. What a load of shit. Alcoholism does not stay in one place. It doesn't plateau, and it keeps deepening, affecting the person physically, mentally, morally and spiritually.

Sharing my unsavoury last hurrah with you isn't intended to scare you into quitting booze, nor is it here to suggest that a reliance on a tipple to cope will lead to this. The rest of this chapter won't contain every war story and drinking disaster that occurred in that twelve-month period for a number of reasons: I haven't got the time, I don't know how much use they are after you've heard the first few, and for certain people involved it would be unfair to blow any anonymity. I'm not in this for shock value; there're enough movies and books out there for you to know how dark addiction gets.

Aside from the repetitiousness of obliteration, my rock bottom is not just about the danger, or the states I got myself in; it involved the emotion, and pain, around the events. As I keep saying, drinking was a symptom; a part of a much bigger problem. This period of my life may be marked by the depths of despair, but it was also filled with people who held me when I needed holding and supported me when I couldn't support myself. When I was in the darkness, I may not have truly acknowledged the love that was shown to me but today, and in this chapter, I also want to celebrate the folk whose support, big or small, contributed to getting me to the point of getting the help I needed. I thought I was alone, but I never really was.

So, here we go ... rock bottom.

I walked away from teaching in the end. I couldn't do it. I wasn't ready to go back after the time off, and I didn't feel safe. I'd been away for so long and I wasn't getting any better. There were glimmers of hope at one point, but they weren't enough for me to be fit for work. I surrendered to the fact that I needed to leave that world, that environment, and get Melissa back. Not the teacher. Just Melissa.

As endings go, this was the most harrowing for me. The lynchpin that I had to keep everything in place was removed and I absolutely chucked it (went cuckoo). I can honestly say that I have never hated myself more than I did during that period. There was nothing for me to hold on to any more.

I fell hard and fast into a deep depression, coupled with a frenzied state of mind. My life as I knew it was in tatters. All remnants of my teaching life had to be removed from the house: cards that I received from the kids, any class photographs that I might have been in, green biro marking pens that I had marked the books with, keyrings and mugs that the kids bought, and my graduation picture.

As far as I was concerned, I had nothing left and nothing to give or lose from that point onwards. When I look back at this now, I can think, 'It was only a job.' I can sometimes get angry at myself for putting that job and all what and who came with it on a pedestal, but I can't change that. When it comes to rock bottoms and reflecting on the hardest moments of our life, we can't beat ourselves up for not knowing what we know today. I never thought I would recover or move on from that ending. But leaving that world was the first big act of kindness I gave myself in recovery. By walking away, sure it messed me up – I went on a series of ridiculous sprees afterwards – but my job was the loss I needed to say, 'No more.' And because I had no pressure, no more secrets to keep, no more worries about who thought what, when I finally got to rehab I could concentrate on getting well without any distractions.

I realise how much of a luxury and privilege this is. Not everyone gets to walk away from employment if they have bills to pay and mouths to feed.

I'm glad that's out of the way.

My binges at this point were longer and filled with more booze. Halves didn't touch the sides, they weren't blocking out the pain or the noise in my head any more. I had moved up to 75cl bottles of vodka. The intrusive thoughts were getting worse and I just had this feeling that I would be better off dead. It was a feeling; a knowing. There didn't seem to be a point in trying to get well because there didn't seem to be a point in living. The drink stopped working for me, it used to make the pain go away, now it brought the pain to the surface and each drunken rant to my mum she would hear the words 'I'd be better off dead'. I was twenty-nine and couldn't stop drinking, I considered myself as damaged goods – too broken to offer this world anything other than misery.

One particular spree resulted in my first chemical detox; there's no use me trying to remember what happened because I can't. I tried to get my mum to think back to the first detox to remember what had happened, but there were so many frequent sprees that neither of us can figure it out. What I do know is that we went to A&E because I was presenting with symptoms of alcohol withdrawal – my body was shaking and my temperature went through the roof. For those of you fortunate enough to not know what an alcohol detox involves, it might be worthwhile giving an idea here:

When a body becomes dependent on alcohol, if you were to stop drinking alcohol straight away … you could die. A heroin detox you cannot die from, but yep, alcohol you can die from the withdrawal. You have to 'wean' off alcohol gradually before you can begin the process. The alcohol withdrawal symptoms – the delirium tremens – are horrendous, the stuff of nightmares: sweating, shaking, insomnia, seizures, being violently ill, feeling like you have spiders under the skin, jolting knees, a racing brain. Basically, you are the living dead. To help aid you through those withdrawals you are prescribed Librium or, if you are 'lucky', Valium. The prescribed medication is a sedative/anti-seizure medication that takes the edge off, to give the body and mind time to restore. With this in mind, I can't stress enough the importance of seeking help from your GP if you are drinking increased quantities and want to quit. A supervised medical detox may be required.

Mum monitored my condition, forced water down me to flush out my system and administered the meds. The detox was so traumatic that I thought it would put me off ever looking at a drink again. You would think it would, but it didn't. This detox would be my first of four.

It was also the trigger for my being seen by the crisis team. I had also started to harm myself and found myself making some fleeting, half-arsed attempts on my life. Unfortunately, it was at this point that the system started to unravel for me (and the chicken-and-egg discussion of a 'dual diagnosis' rears its head again): for the longest time I was bounced between services. The alcohol team would say this was a matter for the mental health team. Likewise, the mental health team would say this was an alcohol problem. While you're the ball in this dangerous game of tennis, you become beaten and bruised until you're no longer a ball that's fit for any game. And my experience is the experience of so many – you are told to get your drinking under control before you can access the help for your mental health, but you find yourself drinking because of your mental health.

With no real communication between services, I was falling between the cracks, stuck on a not-so-merry merry-go-round.

When my mum explained the desperate situation to the crisis nurse – that there were no beds for me in hospital to get the help I needed – she was told: 'If you put her out on the street, she'll be picked up and will get into services quicker.' This advice was coming from a brutally honest and caring place – this nurse knew the state of funding for mental health and addiction and knew there was little she could do. But how this (dare I say) sobering advice was received and acted on was with shock and fear.

I was locked in.

I was locked in the family home several times, in fact.

I can't explain to you how awful this was – for everyone. Controversial? Yes. Successful? Depends what you deem success; it kept me alive but as you'll soon read it took its toll. The *anger* I felt when I would wake up from a drunken stupor covered in piss, unable to piece together what had happened and why I had ended up drinking again, only to find out that I was on lockdown again: phone, card, keys all confiscated – they were accessories to the crime and would allow me to access money, and money meant booze. Windows and doors would all be locked. Knives, medicine, tablets and anything that had the potential to cause harm were kept locked in the garage. I would be screaming and screaming. The screams were not like your regular screams, they were unnaturally animalistic.

The first few days of a lockdown were always the worst. Whether it was the rage, the adrenalin or the vodka, I don't know, but I somehow found the strength to tip over two full-size wardrobes, walls were punched, glasses, photo frames and mirrors all smashed. I often describe my 'active alcoholism' as if I were possessed. Let's look at *The Exorcist*, a 1973 horror classic, banned in many countries and renounced by the Vatican. Poor Regan is a girl is taken over by a darkness, the devil himself. This corruption of her mind, body and soul distorts every part of her character until she is unrecognisable, no longer resembling a young girl, let alone someone's daughter. She was a damned lost cause, powerless over what was happening, her family in despair and frightened by what they were witnessing. Rather familiar, if I do say so myself. Although I didn't levitate, spin my head 360 degrees and, thankfully, didn't tell a priest that his mother sucks cocks in hell, I was, in the context of my former self, demonic. And while this possession comparison isn't to shirk any responsibility or accountability, this is me saying that I was so mentally ill and ravaged by the obsession and compulsion to drink that it warped me as a person.

My poor mum at this stage was living in hell. Her daughter was in the grips of addiction, and she hadn't a clue what to do. Addiction is often referred to as a family disease, either because there is more than one member of the family suffering with addiction, or because it is a disease that has a devastating impact on the entire family.

The more me mum and sister tried to rescue me and put out the fire that was my addiction, the more they were burnt by the flames. The lengths that my family went to in order to keep me safe were extreme, lengths born from love and despair.

It wouldn't feel right or sit comfortably for me to write this book without acknowledging the feelings and experiences of my family members. So I want to include me mum's voice – but a bit more about Ange before I bring her in. She will do anything for anyone and wants little to no fuss being made about it – I know, how weird, right? She is a reserved character but do not let this fool you, as she can end you in one short sentence if you dare try to take the piss or cross her path. In fact, there has been many a family gathering when my mum was called upon to sort the kids out if they were being cheeky; we call this 'getting Anged'. Every hospital appointment, or lengthy Crohn's battle, Ange will be there, with a bag of M&S goodies, new PJs and toiletries. I have never known a woman to have so many life hacks and to be so handy: bridal dress-making, DIY, cooking Christmas dinner for thirty-two, going back to school to get a degree and getting a super high-flying job – no sweat. She only ever wanted the best for Becca and me, and didn't want to see us fail and fall. (But the thing about protecting and preventing – sometimes, falling is the only way to learn how to fly …) And so, to Ange:

> At the time, seeking help for Melissa was so hard; it took a lot to convince her to admit she needed help and when we asked for it – it wasn't there. We were caught up in a viscious circle, professionals weren't prepared to support Melissa's mental health as they felt her drinking was the problem – they didn't

know Melissa and didn't recognise that as her parent I too was desperate for their support, and capable of speaking for Melissa when she didn't have the energy to fight for herself. The system let her down – change is desperately needed, people shouldn't be left to struggle as we were.

To be told that having her sectioned by the police could be the quickest way to get support, or to lock her out of our home, where she was safe, left me feeling horrified and terrified for her future. We didn't know what else to do but keep her in the house. We were alone. I would never wish this experience on any family but throughout it all, I never gave up hope that my beautiful Melissa would return back to me – I missed her.

Reflecting back on the darkest days of 2017 generates feelings of anger and disbelief. We went through so much to try and mend Melissa, every day brought different challenges. Melissa was at her lowest point both physically and mentally, it was heartbreaking to see your amazing daughter in so much pain and there was nothing you could do to fix it – there didn't seem to be an end to her suffering. I felt a failure, felt like I let her down and worried immensely what would happen to her if we (Becca and I) were not around. We were living in fear of what would come next – it was horrendous, we were all shattered physically and emotionally.

What I put my family through when I was at the peak of addiction was torturous. I was at times violent towards my family. Those privy to Melissa prior to 2017 would know this was not who I was, but such was the power of the obsession and need to drink that I lashed out. I have the most vivid memories of screaming on loop: 'You can't do this', 'Let me out', 'You cannot keep me a prisoner'. I would scream until I had exhausted myself, like a baby going through the Ferber method. I would be pacing and running around the house, looking for a way out or a way to make everything go away. Never in my life did I think I would end up pushing and shoving my mum. Ever. But I did, and more than once. There is no justification or excuse for it. In those moments, me mum and Becca didn't know the torment that was going on in my head or my body; how could they? They are not addicts and, unfortunately, only someone who has found themselves desperate to escape their situation in order to get their fix would understand the lengths and lows you stoop to.

I truly hated being locked in – it would go on for weeks at a time. I could not be trusted outside but this detachment from society did not act well on my mental state. The longer I was kept in the house the more I regressed; it was as if I was a teenage girl all over again. Often in the addiction field, they say you find yourself stunted – frozen at the age when you first started to blot out any pain. I was a teen in the body of a near thirty-year-old woman, grounded for my behaviour. My regression also had me reaching out to people from my teenage years, causing them worry and concern. I was reaching out to people who were harmful to me, reaching out to old friends I hadn't seen for twelve years. The ghosts of my past were flying out of their boxes and living and breathing in my present day. It was fucking bizarre and I had well and truly lost my marbles. I genuinely thought it was 2007.

Like most teenagers who get locked in, I would find a way out. I was like the great Harry Houdini himself. As sharp objects were hidden, I went on the hunt for something that could unpick the window locks – there was no point me trying to unpick the front door as it was a heavy-duty lock. One time, deep in the kitchen cupboards – you know those one or two cupboards where you put the miscellaneous, non-essential shite – I found a steak griddle kit. Within the kit were some metal tags with pointed ends that you stuck into the steak to see if it was cooked. What a touch: it was thin and sharp enough to fit into the teeny window lock. As this meat-testing contraption went in and I felt the mechanism inside lock the turn, the feeling it gave me was as close to the relief that I would get from vodka. Out of the window I climbed, in broad daylight, and made my way to the bank with my passport, withdrew cash and got vodka.

In American coming-of-age films, those teenagers who climb out of their window to go to their fella's house or those parties with the red cups and kegs make it look a piece of piss. I remember Rizzo from *Grease* slithered down a drainpipe like it was no big deal. Well, I was no Rizzo. Don't even try it, folks. Climbing out of any window and jumping from a garage roof is hard. One time I bust my ribs on a wheely bin – I never tried escaping through the landing window after that, although I must say I did make it to the offie. It was less hop, skip and a jump and more limp, hobble and a shuffle.

Once I got back to the house from my illegal jaunt, I would consume the contents of what I had bought, be knocked out for the day – and that's when murder would kick off all over again, when my mum would come home after work. After one particular episode, my daily routine began to include a room search.

Getting sober and back on the straight and narrow during my lockdowns wasn't about me getting well, it was a way for me to get early parole.

As I sit writing this, I'm asking myself, 'Why the hell did I go back home?' The truth of the matter is simple: I had nowhere else to go, and I was one selfish bitch. Really, I wanted to have my cake and to eat it too. I wanted the safety and support from my mum, but I wanted to drink as well. If I were to run away – which, by the way, I had tried before – I was always found, or I would last hours and then fear and panic would set in because – let's have it right – I didn't have the independence to start life over. Plus I was already known to the police and to the hospitals as a 'vulnerable person'. Nightmare.

Over the years since, many counsellors, fellow recovering alcoholics and even friends have tried to poke the bear, to try and get some kind of angry reaction towards the measures put in place by my family. But how could I hold any anger for a desperate mother and a heartbroken sister? They knew how vulnerable I was, what I was doing to myself under the influence of drink. And when not under the influence of drink, they heard what I was saying; they could see that I was nothing more than a frightened child, covered in scratches, unable to eat, sleep, wash or hold a conversation even when 'sober'. I know now that they were as powerless and as helpless over me as I was over alcohol and my dwindling mental health. For them to never give up is probably the most selfless act of love I have ever encountered. They didn't give up. Not once.

I know that if I had been out of the family home and living independently, without those unprecedented measures, I would be dead. If you have never been in that situation before, how are you to know what to do or how to react when you are watching your child slowly killing themselves? We know as a family that this wasn't the best way to handle the situation, but it happened and as always, you live and you learn. I have explicitly told my sister and my mum, if I were to drink again, that they are to detach from me, for their own benefit.

I pray to god that day never comes.

The experiences of the family and friends of alcoholics are often lost. All emphasis is on the drinker getting sober, the drinker getting their life back. Knowing that my drinking robbed my mum of her peace of mind kills me. Knowing that my sister at one point thought I was dead and had to ring an ambulance because I was no longer breathing kills me. Knowing my dad was that disappointed and fed up that he no longer wanted anything to do with me killed me. But knowing I impacted the childhood of my nephew – well, that crucifies me.

I was a former teacher who genuinely loved kids. My beautiful nephew was an innocent boy with the purest of hearts seeing things he should not have seen. No boy of five should see his mother rugby-tackling her alcoholic sister to the ground to get the drink out of her hand. It's easy to say or think of children: 'They were only five or six, they won't remember.' Well, I have vivid memories from that age, really vivid memories. Trying to protect children from the truth is natural, but when it came to my alcoholism and my Noahsaurus, when the time was right, I explained to him in a gentle way what was going on. I didn't want him to feel uncertain; I know what that uncertainty does to a child. He came to visit me while I was in rehab, looking out at the fields filled with cows, and I said: 'Noah, remember when I was very silly and naughty in Nanny's house?' He nodded with vigour. 'Well, I wasn't very well. I have come here to get better and see the doctors.' He looked, tilted his little head, patted me and said, 'Very good,' and that was the start of a new relationship with him.

I've gone. Tiny Tears again. You know what's causing tears to stream down my face? That I couldn't stop for my mum, for anyone in my family who I loved so much. If love could have stopped me drinking I'd have been sober six years sooner. Thank god my mum had the support of her closest friend, Maria, and her husband, Peter (who are like family to Becca and me). It's hard to imagine our life without them: every stage of my life they have been there. I am grateful that they stood up to me and were the cavalry my mum needed. You see, not only did I isolate – my mum did too. Can you see the connections between the person suffering with addiction and the ones who are supporting or caretaking?

My aunties and uncles also started to know more of what was going on, as did my closest cousins – we are a large but close-knit family (like most of Liverpool). But none of them could help me: for every supportive chat and crisis meeting, nothing could get through to me. I used to just repeat and ramble and cry the same old 'You don't know what it's like.' Raising my voice to my aunties and uncles was something I would never have done before. Ever. Both Becca and I respect the hierarchy within the family – the aunties and uncles are the 'elders' and we uphold that respect.

It pains me to say that even my granddad was involved. God bless him, he is a church-going man – we aren't a massively religious family and we aren't all practising Catholics, but when it comes to the big sacraments – christenings, communions, weddings, funerals and memorial masses – we are there, in our Sunday best. It's a very Liverpool thing. I remember him saying to me, 'You won't find what you're looking for in a bottle, girl.' He was right.

I ran away from home once and turned up at his door; again, it was unfair of me to do that, for him to see me and even have someone that unwell and unpredictable in his house. He put me in the spare room, but my stay didn't last long as my mum collected me to bring me home. I deeply regret him seeing me the way I was, and that I was exploiting his house so that I had a way to drink and to get away from the lockdown. He has kept me in his prayers since. You'll laugh at this bit – a couple of years into sobriety, I was in me granddad's house, and he asked me to 'Get a tea towel from the landing, queen.' Off I trotted up the stairs. I hadn't seen that spare room since I was incapacitated and I don't know why, but I wanted to see it. Maybe I wanted to remember how far I had come, or maybe I wanted a reason to beat myself up (standard). I went in and there it was: my school picture from year four – next to a candle of St Jude. I remember thinking to myself, 'Who is this Jude and what is he the patron saint of? Why am I next to him?' Because I was a sober gal now and allowed my phone (phones were always troublesome, they gave me access to internet banking, taxis and escape routes), I quickly researched. St Jude is only the patron saint of 'desperate cases and lost causes'! (I'd like to swear at this point, but I won't – I am resisting profanities in a paragraph that has both my granddad and a saint in.) I couldn't *BEEP* believe it. I felt terrible. So I pulled him up on it: 'Granddad, what am I doing next to Jude?' And his reply, in the most resplendent Scouse accent you ever did hear: 'I had to do *some*thing, girl … it worked, didn't it?'

Who was I to question it? Throughout that *annus horribilis*, the climax of my addiction, there were so many moments when I could have and should have died: I ran off to a hotel and locked myself in with litres of vodka, waking up in pools of vomit. I was found by the police passed out in the middle of the city centre. I was found collapsed in a train station in Preston covered in mystery blood. Someone or something was looking out for me. Maybe it *was* St Jude;

or maybe it was my nan and Aunty Sandra, both of who had passed away ... I don't know, but for reasons unbeknownst to me, I escaped death and consider myself one of the lucky ones. I could have died from choking or alcohol poisoning or made a successful attempt at taking my own life. But that didn't happen. Me dad always says I was the cat with nine lives, and although I joke and remind them that my name is Kitten, it's not that bloody funny.

The lockdowns and all that chaos were not sustainable. I was the shadow of the girl I once was. I was dead behind the eyes and no amount of make-up could sort it. It was time I tried to access help once more from a specialist drug and alcohol service.

After yet another visit to the crisis team (like many, my rock bottom was repetitive), a nurse began to talk about a service called The Brink in Liverpool city centre. She explained that it was a recovery café that held groups and offered counselling if you needed it. Hearing that this wasn't a sterile or clinical setting seemed appealing; I trusted the nurse and I had to try it. We went to an assessment and I felt safe; I didn't feel scared in the slightest. What I did think was that it was strange that this hub of recovery was right in the middle of the trendy bars, etc. (why am I obsessed with town planning?). It wasn't just a recovery café, it was a venue that had open-mic nights, played the footy on the big screen, etc. It was simply a bar without the booze that ran a few groups in the back room.

During my assessment there, I could see people laughing and socialising. The music playlist was cool and right up my street: The Pixies came on and I thought that it was a sign from above; this was where I was supposed to be. I never once thought that the people sitting drinking their lattes and eating their paninis were alcoholics or addicts. I just thought they were regular people. I reckon this was the first time I had ever seen real 'recovery'. I did not know that one day I could be like them – enjoying life. I just wanted to stop drinking and stop crying: that was my only goal.

I signed up to the twelve-week abstinence-based programme and, you know what – I responded really well to it (thank god, a bit of happy news). I remember walking into the first group meeting, which was set back from the rest of the café – I felt like a child on the first day of nursery when they keep looking out of the window waiting for their mum to collect them. Ange waited in the café area with a coffee and cake combo (classic). The room itself was Scandi-chic, the lighting was pretty subtle – which I appreciated – and they had these trendy orange chairs in a circle. The group was already seated when I entered, head down. I had come prepared: I had my tissue at the ready, scrunched up in a ball. I knew I couldn't pick at my arms or pull strands of my hair in this group, so I took out all of my anxiety on this ball of tissue.

I opened up to the people in the group; in fact, I sang like a canary. It was the first time I could tell people what was going on, and I couldn't stop. I don't think anyone else could get a word in edgeways, to be honest. I shocked myself at how willing and able I was to open up. I felt exposed afterwards, but I also felt relieved. So I returned.

It was a daily group meeting and I met some of the loveliest people on the programme. For the first couple of weeks I was chaperoned to my meetings – to get to The Brink from my house solo I had to travel to Kirkby train station. That eight-minute walk had two pubs and two offies in its path, and I wouldn't be able to count the opportunities to access booze when I made the walk from Liverpool Central to The Brink. At the start of each group we had a check-in: we spoke about how we were feeling and what was going on for us, then we would have a topic to cover. The groups were facilitated by Paula and Eve, two incredible women who had been there, done that and bought the T-shirt. They didn't put up with bullshit and they saw right through any excuses – but they weren't militant in the slightest; they were simply unapologetically honest. My confidence began to grow with each session. I had a structure to my day and this group held me accountable.

I didn't drink for the thirteen weeks I attended the programme, and for some weeks after.

When I completed the programme, I thought I was cured. I really did. There was talk of me going on to another day programme after that – a more intensive, rehab-style scenario. But I didn't feel the need to. I felt a whole lot better, and I had earned my privileges back. I knew best (uh-oh). I had my keys, my card, my freedom and I remember thinking that life was good once more. My antidepressants had been given the chance to kick in and I was one step closer to getting my life back.

I disconnected from anything recovery: I didn't need it, I had it sussed. Then, *boom*. Out of the blue came an almighty relapse. The thing about addiction, it is a relapsing condition, that's the nature of the beast unfortunately. The other unfortunate thing about relapse is that it usually happens way before a drink or a drug is consumed. Through my disconnection from anything recovery, I was back to doing things my way. I went to the off-licence to pick up the old Marlboro Golds; I had no intention of buying a bottle and the order just rolled out of the mouth and the vodka rolled down the back of my throat. The shame after the relapse was like no other shame I had felt before. I had blown it. Upon reflection, I had been trying to run before I could walk. It was devastating and I was crushed. And, just when I thought that life couldn't get any worse, I needed another operation.

Again, I thought this was what I deserved; this was karma and I just got on with it. I was used to surgery by now – genuinely, I haven't got a clue how many times I have been under general anaesthetic, but it's a fair few.

My colorectal (bowel and bum) surgeon, Mr Arthur, he is truly, without a doubt, a hero. As you know already, he has saved my life more than once, and he gave me a brand-new life when I got the stoma bag in 2018. We had always had a good relationship but this time when he saw me, he looked confused and quite shocked. He was used to me all prim and proper, but that had all stopped; I didn't even shave my legs and other places that needed shaving – which was unheard of. I just didn't have it in me. I didn't care any more, because I couldn't care. I had no energy for pretence or protocols.

I was slumped in the hospital bed, staring into space with glassy eyes, and I remember him asking me: 'Where have you gone?' I just cried. I didn't have the answer I desperately wanted to give him: I didn't know where I had gone, I just knew that I *was* gone. He looked at my arms and he picked one up gently and then looked at me. They were covered in scratches, those vertical ones I perfected at the age of fourteen. He spoke about the procedure with me, and I just nodded; I had no questions to ask, no concerns, no worries – I was just there in body. I just thought, 'Do what you want.'

He pulled my mum to the side and quizzed her further. For some bizarre reason I didn't think he knew about my drinking; maybe that was because I couldn't cope with the thought of him knowing. I respected and valued him so much, I didn't want him to be disappointed in me. But he knew. He asked her if I was still drinking. Limited in what his powers were, he was able to get my antidepression prescription reviewed and I must say, the increase of dosage made a difference to my head. He didn't have to do that. He was there to treat my Crohn's not my head, but he did, and I am so grateful to him.

Recovering from that surgery meant another lockdown; it meant nurses coming out daily to dress the wound when all I wanted to do was be alone and to fade away. But I wasn't so past it that I wasn't polishing off the morphine that was supposed to be taken for pain relief. I didn't have alcohol, so I did what I had to do to get out of my head.

Convalescing from this operation, I reached the end of my tether. During an eight-week period from June to August 2017, I was the hottest of messes due to a series of head-on collisions. I was breaking free all the bloody time and I was trying to escape the life I was in, as well as the house I was trapped in (never once thinking that wherever I went I would still have the same problems). I was once more pickling myself. And the cravings − holy cow. Imagine living life 'needing' something to get through each day or emotion, and you no longer have your crutch in your life. The reasons as to why you need that something haven't changed or gone anywhere, but your solution isn't an option any more. It's torturous. Craving a drink is both physical and mental. When I used to crave a drink, it would feel like I had itchy bones and, I hope you forgive this next overshare, I would sit and squirm on a chair, the craving making me want to cross my legs really hard. The mental obsession would take over and further exacerbate the physical discomfort: your mind telling you that all of this would go away if you had a drink; that you would feel better, you would be able to go about your day easier, if you just had that drink. I don't know if you have ever had cravings like that, but for me, when they happened, nothing else mattered: I couldn't focus, and certainly was not present in anything I was doing. I was just fixated on drinking and also on not drinking.

My mum contacted The Brink again. But there was no way I could go back there – I felt much too ashamed. The thought of having to go back with my tail between my legs being all 'Hi, guys, it's me again!' was out of the question. I honestly thought that as I had relapsed, they would not have me back, that if I drank again, I would have let them down. What a numpty!

But I did return and they were concerned. I was a different girl to the one they had first met. I was a good few kilograms lighter, and more of a creature than a human. They showed me kindness, compassion and support – not just to me, but to my mum too. Paula and Eve understood why the lockdowns were happening but could see they were taking their toll on both of us. They asked if I had considered residential rehab.

We had tried that route before but had been told that I would not be eligible for any public funding. On paper, I had a home, I had a job, I didn't have children, I wasn't under Social Services.

All I could hear from this series of 'no's was that I wasn't an alcoholic and my drinking wasn't bad.

We didn't have the money for rehab – that was for the

super-rich. We were working class; we didn't just have a spare £15k lying around, and there was no way I would allow my mum to take out a loan or remortgage her house. If I hadn't been rinsing payday loans maybe I could have got a loan for treatment myself; so, all in all, rehab felt out of the question.

That was when we were introduced to Clouds House. Both The Brink and Clouds House are a part of the charity Action on Addiction. At this time, Clouds House was offering bursary beds – charity places at their rehab. I applied for admission there.

I still have the application form. When I read it back, I felt sad but I also laughed to myself – the way I had written it, I clearly wanted them to know that I was an educated human being and I didn't want them to know how bad I was. I was careful to keep the true nature of the crazy hidden – I didn't mention much about the self-harm or the suicidal thoughts. I did let them into the social anxiety I experienced:

> It is fair to say that I have lost all confidence when being outside the house alone, and therefore have resorted to isolation. I severely struggle to walk through the city centre and local town centre due to my social anxiety, feelings of regret/shame and slight paranoia. I have suffered multiple panic attacks on the way to Brink of Change group due to past events, dangerous situations I have been in, flashbacks and the several off-licences/bars/ public houses I have to walk past. Public transport now causes major distress and now my family are unable to chaperone me to and from meetings/appointments, as they kindly did previous. This mentioned struggle and inability to feel safe/confident/ comfortable in and around Liverpool has led to relapses.

At the end of the application I wrote:

> *I am determined for a life of abstinence and honesty and to address my obsessive/addictive traits. Essentially, I want to be able to feel at peace with myself, learn to love myself and be a happy and confident person who can finally begin their life. I understand that residential rehab is neither a cure nor fix, however I believe the structured programme provided by Clouds House will equip me with the knowledge, understanding and tools in order to achieve my goals.*

Bloody hell, I meant every word of that an' all, even if I did write it in a weird, corporate style.

After I submitted my application, I felt a slight boost. I had put a lot of effort into the application. My brain function was quite limited due to the detoxing, the drinking and the general unwell state of mind, but when I apply my obsessive thinking to something, I will give it my all.

The wait to hear if I had been accepted was a killer for an impatient addict like me. I held on as long as I could without a drink but, in the middle of August 2017, I blew it. It was the final swig, my swan song with the booze, the divorce, the termination – the moment when I dropped the bottle the same way that Obama dropped the mic.

It's 24 August 2017 – Leo season, and the summer is in full swing. It's just before a bank holiday, one short week before the kids go back to school and the anniversary of my last drink. There is a lot to be grateful for on this date, but for me it is not a time to celebrate.

It's not a day that I like to remember, let alone lift a Diet Coke to. That entire day and period leading up to it is branded on my brain and my psyche. As is the aftermath. The 'ordeal' is a permanent, tattoo-like reminder of how and where my drinking took me (a more painfully embarrassing tattoo than the two German words I woke up with after a blackout three months prior).

My last drinking binge was a gruesome crescendo of pain and fear. The period itself is pretty hazy, but I have vivid, standout memories of it. One being that I climbed out of the narrow living-room window for the final time while being filmed by my sister. My sister thought filming my behaviour would be a deterrent, a way to show me just how 'mental' I was, but shock tactics and visual representations were never going to defeat the obsession I had. Before the excruciatingly painful shimmy out of the window, I screamed the house down, begging her to let me out. But she wouldn't (and rightly so). By this point my sister was practising tough love − she thought my mum was pandering to the situation, babying me (which is kind of true), and Big Truck had taken it upon herself to knock some sense into me. But you have to remember, she was angry about what I was doing to our mum and couldn't see why I was repeating the same shite over and over again. My sister knows how to push every button I have and she would push them all at once. I am getting angry now, just at the thought of her sitting laughing at me while I was crying. (Little did she know on that day, I had her bank card.)

Setting off that day, I remember knowing it had all gone too far, got too dark, and I had seen my addiction head-on; that I was no longer able to deny or justify it. Not only had I lost a lot, the things that I managed to hold on to − my family − were broken.

From that point on, as I shuffled down the street in my green coat, things got weird. I'm talking weird phone calls to people, shitting myself, buses, strangers coming up to me, being found by the police and waking up in hospital not being able to see. I was actually blind drunk. I thought it was just a saying, to be honest, but I couldn't bloody see for hours. I remember feeling my mum's face to see if it was her … I'll be right back, I'm just going to bite a pillow and maybe throw up.

I'm back.

There I was, fucked again in hospital after being found by an ambulance, even further from the girl I once was. And again, I was in need of another home alcohol detox with my mum at her own near breaking point. She was, as always, determined to get me back.

This time though, I wasn't eligible for Librium right away. Why? Because the levels of alcohol in my system were too high. It was white-knuckle time again.

This leads me to my final drink. It was roughly 7 a.m. and I was due in hospital for 9 a.m. to be breathalysed and assessed. As my mum poured it and fed me it, I was crying. I was crying because I didn't want it, but I knew I needed it. I had been 'administered' small amounts of vodka throughout the night by my persecuted mum – enough to prevent a seizure and the DTs, but it was never enough to satisfy the beast within. For each three-hourly 'dose', my mum poured a single shot of vodka into an Ikea glass tumbler, which she diluted with Diet Coke, much to my disapproval (I drank neat: I wanted it to hurt, to punish me). The night before had been mentally and physically excruciating. Being an alcoholic who knows there is vodka under lock and key, and not having access to it, will take you to some dark and desperate places, believe me. Each minute feels like an hour and throughout each hour your head is the boxing ring hosting a fight between what's logical and what is not. In the red corner: 'You can stop next week, the drinking is not the problem, it's your mental health, being alcoholic isn't all bad!' And in the blue corner: 'I can do this, it will be over soon, think of Mum.'

How my mum was able to pour the poison and supervise my drinking, I will never know. To this day, I still can't drink out of those tumblers or watch *Shameless*; how ironic that the only box set I had available to get me through that night was that of an alcoholic in a green coat.

On that first day of the beginning of my alcohol detox, I knew something had changed in me, something had shifted. It was a profound feeling, as if the vodka-tinted glasses had been removed and I could see myself, my drinking, the pain and suffering I caused, in all of its glory. I remember hugging my mum and just sobbing into her and I couldn't let go and she didn't let me go. We aren't a hugging family, really, but she held me in her arms so tight that I couldn't fall apart. She told me it was going to be all right and I believed her. It was going to be all right. This time around, I wanted help. I couldn't save myself, my family couldn't save me, jobs couldn't save me, and drink certainly couldn't save me. It was time to fight back. That shift, that epiphany, was my moment of surrender. I had put down my sword.

I was still white-knuckling it – I had no spiritual, emotional or psychological support to fill the hole, the same hole that I had filled with drink – but, during that time, from my last binge to entering rehab six weeks later, minor changes began to take place – mini miracles, in fact. I got up and out of the bed each day, I got washed and dressed, I would make people a cup of tea, I would eat with my family, I was holding conversations, and the biggest change ... my mum left the key to the house, *but I didn't want it*. Joanne visited me quite a bit and took me out on a few 'day-release' visits; I was too frightened to be in the community on my own. I didn't want to relapse and I knew the risk was too great. So I imposed my own lockdown, can you believe it? All that screaming like a banshee, carrying on shocking and worrying the neighbours – here I was now, locking myself in. I just had to get to Clouds.

This year of our lives is one that we never want to relive, but together, as a family, we are able to use those darkest times to appreciate what we have now; to see how far we have all come. We are stronger for it. There are positives to take from burning your life to the ground and it's important to me that I actively search for the positives, otherwise I will slip into victimhood and self-pity, and both of these character traits are as damaging to my life as vodka. When I find myself moaning or wasting too much energy on 'Look how much weight I have put on', 'I don't know if I should take this job', 'That fit bloke ghosted me', 'Some twat just rear-ended my car', I have to remember that the regular-thirty-something problems I have today are the problems I would have wished for when I was at my worst.

As I sit here, remembering the shit-show that was my life in 2017, I feel awash with sadness while peaking a solid ten out of ten on the shame scale. And while this may sound peculiar to most, I am rather relieved by my physical reaction. My recoiled state of being keeps the fear alive, in a comforting sort of way. It's reassuring to know and feel that the mere thought of history repeating itself petrifies me and that my mind hasn't romanticised my drinking too much. My past is my greatest asset: without the hopelessness and horror I wouldn't have received the 'gift of desperation', the 'rock bottom' I have talked to you about. This may sound utterly bonkers, but I really am grateful for my rock bottom. This doesn't mean I'm happy or proud of the things that went down or the pain I caused, but without that lowest point, I would still be in a constant tug of war with booze, I'd be in denial about my deeper feelings, and I would be prolonging the pain and misery for everyone. Although this dark period is one I would wish mostly to forget, I can't, because if I were to block out those painful moments, then 'Just a little drink. One will be fine' would be the famous last words I'd tell myself.

Takeaways

- **Your rock bottom is personal to you**
- **No rock bottoms are the same**
- **Admitting defeat is not a weakness**
- **You don't need to lose everything**
- **How much you drink is irrelevant**
- **Alcohol withdrawal is lethal**
- **People care**
- **Recovery isn't linear.**

---

* It is worth referencing that as of June 2020 The Brink, the place to which I attribute who I am today, has closed. Due to the impact of Covid-19, The Brink was unable to reopen. Although Action on Addiction still offer services for the people of Liverpool, The Brink was unable to return. This is a great loss to the city of Liverpool and to the recovery community; it will forever be in my heart and this is an unfortunate reminder of the battle faced by many drug and alcohol services across the UK.

Chapter 5

Trust the process and hold on tight

I won't lie – when I got to rehab, I felt somewhat robbed as there were a lot of people turning up drunk and smelling absolutely lovely (stinking of booze). For some strange reason, I thought you couldn't go to rehab if you were drunk – thanks for that, Mum. (I can't believe I fell for it.)

Starting anything new brings up all kinds of emotions: jobs, partners, houses, exercise – you name it, the initial phase for me is always the worst, when I'm at my most mental. I am a creature of habit, whether that be a good habit or a bad habit. Hate is a strong word, but I can say comfortably that I used to hate change – today, I just dislike it very much and prepare myself in advance, usually with a shit-load of 'It's going to be all right' affirmations, and slathering myself in something lavender-based. The thing is, as much as I would be happy keep the status quo, I know that the discomfort that I feel when I am forging a new path or trying something new is healthy. It's something I have to power through and, guess what, that's life. Sobriety, or in my case, coming to recovery, felt the same. But this time, I had to ride the wave and have faith that that recovery would work for me.

I had to 'trust the process'.

Me mum, Becca and I drove from Liverpool to Wiltshire in October 2017. Throughout those seven hours, the mood in the car would go from encouraging and positive to doom, gloom and misery. The air was thick with nervous energy. You know when someone is going through a hard time and you don't know what say; the silence is deafening, and you're trying to keep it light and breezy because you don't know if you are OK to mention the problem, so you find yourself chatting the most nonsensical, irrelevant bollocks to fill the space? Well, that's what this journey was. There was a giant elephant in the white Vauxhall Corsa and all three of us ignored it as much as we possibly could. But, every so often, that elephant would wave its trunk and loudly trumpet all around the car. The nearer we were getting to the place, the more rapid my mood swings were; I was having contractions of anxiety. Aside from the frequent outbursts of panting and trembling, odd and unwelcomed thoughts would enter my head as we were going down the country roads: 'I wonder what would happen if I just opened this door' or 'Imagine if we just crashed, that'd be easier.' Thankfully I did not act on these thoughts or even share them out loud, but the fact that my mind gave me graphic images of road traffic accidents says a lot (I watched far too much *Casualty* as a nipper). My intrusive thoughts are always at their worst in times of distress. Uninvited little shits.

As well as envisaging being carted off in an ambulance with a neck brace on, there was a part of me that was intrigued. I had never been to Wiltshire before – I'm one of those annoying, egocentric Scouse people who has only been to London, Glastonbury Festival and nowhere else south of Birmingham. But in the days leading up to my admission date, Wiltshire had been popping up everywhere, and it was doing my nut: the ham in the fridge – Wiltshire; the butter for the ham sandwich – Wiltshire; my favourite couple from the sugary-cup-of-tea-of-a-TV-programme that is *Gogglebox* – you guessed it, they were from Wiltshire. Let's not get it twisted, there are worse places to visit or have on your mind, and it is a stunning part of the UK, but I didn't want to leave Kirkby or my mum. I thought I would have been happy to stay in the house in a town I didn't feel comfortable enough to show my face in. I would have gladly watched the world go by, living without drink and with a family that was exhausted and worried. Comfort zones don't always have be comfortable. What I mean by that is, my comfort zone at this point was being cut off from society, remaining childlike in the household, feeling deflated, staring at the TV, smoking twenty a day in the garden, hoping that my neighbours who were used to hearing all kinds of screaming would not talk to me. I was conditioned to it. The prospect of going to a strange place, with potentially strange people and learning strange things, was daunting to say the least.

With the seven-hour journey coming to the end, and minutes away from my perceived incarceration, can you believe that one of my biggest fears around going was about the food? 'What if it's all fish and veg? I can't eat salmon fillets, the flakes knock me sick. What am I going to eat? I can't eat the veg – my Crohn's! I'll shit myself! I'll have a flare! I'm not fucking going.' (In my defence, I have never eaten fish: my granddad told me, 'You don't know what's in the sea, girl, it's full of dead bodies,' so I don't eat it.) In reality, 70 per cent of my breakdown wasn't fish- or food-related: I was using this 'problem' to find faults and reasons why I shouldn't be going.

Clearly, I couldn't come up with many valid ones.

When I arrived at Clouds, it hit all my historical erogenous zones. It was the most beautiful building. I am a sucker for a period drama, country estates – basically, anything from a time when a woman had to wear a corset. But I couldn't get the twinge to last – no number of high ceilings or *Downton Abbey*-style settings could have made me want to go in. I didn't want to leave the car; I was hysterical. Remember that elephant in the three-door Corsa? Well, you couldn't ignore it any more, let me tell you. I jumped on that elephant's back and rode it all the way into the foyer with me mum and Becca in tow, watching in horror – but also taking part in the spectacle.

For all my family's genetic predisposition of holding it together in front of professionals, I can confirm that we Lost Our Shit. You would think we were never going to see each other again by the way we were acting. I just assumed everyone reacted like this. (Turns out not many did.) But to us, it was real, this was huge. Kitten was going to a new home. It was a new start for us all, the first time in a long time when they weren't going to be the caregivers, and this was the longest time I would ever be away from them. I can safely say I made a holy show of myself when it was time for me to see them go out of the door. When my mum and sister left the foyer and headed back to their car, like a child I ran to the window and shouted for my mum. I even did the classic, 'Don't leave me here.' Oh, dear. I'd like to think that I wouldn't be that dramatic and devastated if I had to do it again ... well, for a fucking start, I don't want to go back to rehab again. But Clouds wasn't a goodbye to my family; in the back of my mind, I knew it was a needed separation, and the end of a dark and needy era.

I had flown the nest at last, but landed in what us residents liked to call the cuckoo's nest.

On the subject of the perception of residential treatment, Michael (from Clouds) believes that more should be done to make residential treatment seem less daunting:

Never underestimate people's anxiety and fears around residential treatment. For a lot of people they imagine white coats, people being handcuffed to beds and all other very unhealthy and outdated clinical imagery. That's not what treatment is like; well, not at Clouds anyway. The more that can be done to change the fantasy and perception around residential rehab the better; it shouldn't be feared.

Michael Rawlinson

When my crying stopped, I was shown to my room. For obvious reasons, bags were searched, and a nurse commented on how lovely my pyjamas were. Well, that was it: 'Me mum bought me them!' and I was off again. I couldn't handle that for all the pain and anguish I caused, this woman was buying me essentials and had meticulously packed my case.

At the end of my bed there was a pin board for any pictures I had. I had a couple of photographs that I put up, a drawing of a dinosaur that my nephew had thrown together in approximately thirty seconds, and a card with a colourful illustration of the Liver Buildings from Joanne.

When we were done in the bedroom, I was assigned a 'buddy' to show me around. She was a lovely woman with a personality you would describe as *eccentric*. I do love the word 'eccentric': for one class of people, 'eccentric' allows you to get away with all sorts (in the lower classes, the relevant adjectives are not as kind). She showed me around the building and introduced me to people, and I was made to feel nothing but welcome – although who knew what they were thinking about this twenty-nine-year-old childlike Scouse girl.

When I was initially transferred to the care of my buddy, I asked the member of staff if I could keep my coat on when I went to meet the rest of the community. She didn't think anything of it: little did she know that I had no intention of taking it off. It was my trusty green waxed rain coat. I still have it in the wardrobe – it has seen me at my worst and at my mediocre (I've not reached my best – yet). I've always had a weird relationship with coats. Since I was little, I have always felt safe and snug if I just kept my coat on. I am basically that little boy from the nineties movie *East is East*. Maybe it's because I like to think that if I have my coat on I can escape, or maybe I keep it on so no one sees me. Whatever the reasoning behind it, I kept that battered green coat on in Clouds until it was noticed by a fellow resident, which means one thing – you have to talk about it …

Rehabs run as a community. No community means no treatment. Within the first hour of being a part of the community I was asked, 'Are you a bedwetter or a junkie?' My Hyacinth Bucket-mode booted up: 'Excuse me?' I asked, with raised brows and look of gentle distain. What a load of baloney – I knew exactly what was being asked of me, but I was mortified by how plainly and simply it was put. Once more the question was asked, and with the stained mattress and sound of squeaking rubber sheets in my head, tail between my legs I just replied: 'Bedwetter.' It was official, I was not in Kansas any more, and this was the start of me owning my shit (sorry, piss). Questioning and 'challenging' someone on their behaviour (including wearing your coat) is a part of the treatment. The act of calling someone out on their behaviour is to hold them to account, to force the person to realise their traits and behaviours, as generally these entrenched behaviours come from unhealthy thought processes and are a part of our addiction. At first, I couldn't challenge people for toffee. Jade, my podcast sidekick – she bloody loved to challenge people, and I used to watch in awe at her confronting someone on their unhelpful and harmful behaviour. But as much as I liked to watch her in action, it was always hard to be on the receiving end of it.

After a couple of weeks you were allowed visitors on a Sunday (I did say that my family farewell was a complete over-reaction). Sunday was family day. Each visit, I would be done up to the nines and dressed like I would be for church. One Sunday, Jade and I were having a smoke in our beloved smoking shelter – aka the bus stop – and I spotted a tiny hole in my tights. You would think that I had relapsed. I remember being confused as to why Jade could not see the severity of this situation. 'My tights have a ladder, and they arrive in fifteen minutes!' After that visit, in the next women's group, I was pulled up on it: 'You are a different person on a Sunday; why do you dress up?' Yikes! I was caught, I had nowhere to escape and no way to justify it; it was the truth and therefore I had to work on it. In rehab, every person in the community is a mirror to yourself, and although at times I didn't like to look at the reflection staring back at me, it was the only way to accept who I was, what I did and how to change my ways.

Being in rehab felt like a relief. According to sources, one of the first things I said was, 'I am just so happy to be around people.' (Everyone was also completely confused by my length of sobriety running up to rehab, and my nonchalant attitude towards being locked in.) It was the first time I had been around people who had been through the torment I had been through, proper. I think the relief came from the fact that I didn't have to pretend I wasn't an alcoholic; I didn't have to save face. There was no one to impress. I was what I was, and there was no judgement to face. That's not to say that I didn't feel an intense level of shame, but it was the first time in a long time that I didn't feel alone. The more people would share their shenanigans and their deepest, darkest moments, the more at ease I felt in sharing mine. There were times when I would think, 'Bloody hell, I can't believe they have just shared that,' and this would stay with me and give me permission to open up about all sorts of horrors. Rehabs cultivate honesty, and with honesty comes trust, and trust means everything.

I met all walks of life there, and I mean it. Our community was a melting pot of folk from a variety of socio-economic backgrounds. I only wish I could go further into the characters I met, but I am sure you understand it would be unkind and unfair to break any anonymity: rehab is a sacred place. I am perfectly OK with blowing my own cover, though, as that was a decision I made for myself. The folk in my life today from my stint in rehab have given me the go-ahead for all this, but there were people there who are now out of reach: I don't know where they are, or even whether they are still with us.

This brings me to another important point to raise about rehab: it is not a guaranteed fix. Annoyingly, like most things in life, you get out what you put into it. The counsellors made that clear throughout our stay: 'Not all of you will make it.' At first I thought to myself, 'What a bloody cheek, I've come here to find a cure and to never drink again and you're telling me there's a chance I might not.' This thought was followed by, 'Well, that's bad marketing,' when actually it was just the truth without any embellishments.

Being stuck in a house with people from so many walks of life smashed my old ideals. The community I was in showed me for the first time that addiction *really* doesn't discriminate. Titles, wealth, degrees, homes you own or the childhood you had – it made no bloody difference. Rehab was indeed a leveller. Naturally, there were some folk, including myself, who did feel that there was a certain hierarchy, or that their 'problem' wasn't as bad as others due to things like: 'I'm not a heroin addict.' But the truth is, you can't polish a turd. Addiction is a turd. You can roll it in glitter made of justifications, and rationalise it until it begs for mercy, but it's still a turd. Humility is a part of the recovery process. The way I see it, I had my thinking smashed to pieces. I had to be brought down off my high horse and by a peg or two in order for me to get well. Let me tell you, rehab will serve you the biggest slice of humble pie you'll ever eat.

When it comes to the day to day of rehab, it's no health spa. Routines are vital in rehab, in fact in recovery. In the drinking days, I was always bending rules, pushing my luck and doing things my way. But where did that lead me, lead any of us?

We have those deliberate boundaries in order for people to bounce against them and feel safe in the knowing that they are there; our boundaries are consistent. If we're wishy-washy about these boundaries it can cause anxiety. Let's say you're a parent and you say to a child, 'You're very naughty, that it not acceptable … Here is a sweety.' This causes uncertainty and conflict. It is the same in adults. If you are clear with boundaries this can be avoided.

Michael Rawlinson

Today, structure is glorious. I thrive on it. As the old saying goes, 'The devil makes work for idle thumbs.' Too much time on my hands always led to a mess; breaks from work or even recovering from surgery always resulted in destructive behaviours, bouts of depression and a wheely bin of empty bottles. Give me a timetable and I'll be fine; take it away and I'm useless. I learnt this about myself in Clouds, so now I live each day with a loose structure. (I say 'loose' because if I was militant about my routine that would leave no flexibility for life's curveballs, which would only lead me to some kind of meltdown.) In rehab, however, there is no excuse for not adhering to the structure or the rules. By turning up to group late, not doing the chores (oh, yes, there are chores) or, even worse, conspiring to take drugs, you are harming the whole community. You aren't thinking of the consequences and therefore you are being self-centred. You were never told off by the counsellors – they were way cleverer than that – no, you were always addressed by your peers, which was worse. Like when your mum says, 'I'm not angry, I am just disappointed.' Thinking of others and practising accountability in such a concentrated way worked wonders – I didn't realise how much of a selfish bugger I was.

I was shocked and borderline sickened that there was no telly, no phones, allocated times for music and no sweets allowed. I soon realised that these everyday treats – that in the western world we take for granted – are distractions, escapes. Believe me, if they had said I could have watched telly, listened to music and eaten cola bottles and Angel Slices all day, there is no way that I would have made the progress I did.

I have to confess, I did not stick to the 'no sugar' rule; few did. Each Saturday we would all pile on a minibus and head to the local town, Shaftesbury. We would all be in groups of three – without supervision. This level of trust was new and very uncomfortable at first. I thought the counsellors were absolutely bonkers letting a bunch of freshly detoxed people into the big wild world, but I see now that trust and 'doing the right thing' are a part of the treatment. We were accountable for ourselves and for the group we were in. Some would go the barbers, others would go the Superdrug for nice toiletries. Me? I would go to the charity shop and look for bargains. I still have a gorgeous tartan blazer from there (check it out for yourself, it's on my Instagram – £3.80).

Before the groups went to the shop of their choice, we all went to the Tesco. It was like the final round of *Supermarket Sweep* on that sweet aisle. I often wondered what the townspeople thought of us. It was clear where we were from, the oddest group of people all piling off a minibus acting like kids on a school trip. Sometimes there were a few looks here and there and a feeling of 'this is a local shop, for local people', but who cares, this was our freedom and we were people who made a choice to get well. Not wanting to bid farewell to sugar, we would stuff our trousers, sleeves, bras with whatever we could – Angel Slices don't quite taste the same when they've been squashed down your knickers. For some there was no guilt or remorse about the smuggling, but I was a mess. Upon our return we would be bag searched and questioned. My guilt would last all of fifteen minutes.

Having the relationship with Michael I have today, I thought I ought to apologise for my rule-breaking, and you know what he said? 'We knew, we all knew – that push back is what we expected. But ask yourself? Could it have been worse?' It was astonishing really that no one bought drink, that no group allowed other members to slip – we were there for each other in what could be seen as a high-risk setting.

Michael taught me that the treatment for addiction is human connection, and these rules, regardless of how draconian and overzealous I deemed them to be, forced me into connecting with others. For many of us there, we had spent much of our time isolated physically and/or mentally, therefore missing out on valuable human interaction. Or, for some of us, we were either pissed and off our nut for the majority of the time and therefore unable to have coherent and 'normal' communication. At the time of going to rehab, I didn't know how to communicate without tears, I wasn't able to look people in the eye. But, little by little, and as the weeks progressed, I began to find my voice.

I had spent a lot of my years not standing up for myself, avoiding confrontation and ignoring my gut instincts. A member of my group didn't take to me at all. It was good learning for him and for me.

Every day, I would say or do something that would ignite something in him. He would erupt, then hours later hand me a book that he thought I would like. The hot and cold routine was too much for me, I don't respond well to the wolf in sheep's clothing routine. Whether that be a boss, a stranger, or a friend – it sends me west. This man's behaviour was weighing me down. I remember thinking, 'I didn't come here to put up with this.' Being in Clouds was my lottery win so I had to make a choice, cower and cry or have it out with him. In Clouds there was a group called 'Community Health'. It was for some the highlight of the week, and for those who hated confrontation (me) the worst group of the week. In a huge circle, every member of the community would have the chance to 'discuss' any issues that were impacting the health of the community.

It. Was. Wild. Mine and this guy's issue was brought up; there was no booze and no Mum to lean on, so I had to put my big girl pants on and say, 'Aye, I have had it up to here with you, what's your fucking problem?' (or similar). I don't think anyone, including myself, expected it. I'd say this was probably the most honest and direct I had been in a long time, and it felt kinda good. I didn't whimper or do my Baby Jane routine, I just let the person have it – I told him how I was feeling, what I had tried to do to resolve it and exactly why I couldn't tolerate his ways. I know I shouldn't gloat, but I wiped the floor with him. But as good as I felt after that, I did have to take responsibility for my side of things. I had said a few choice words, but I couldn't believe that I was given a warning. This warning sums up how Clouds runs:

Melissa, the treatment team are concerned that you made provocative remarks to one of your peers and that led to discord in your group. Throw-away remarks can be easily made and, as you know, can leave others feeling hurt and angry. Being in treatment and recovery is about changing behaviours and learning to be responsible for our actions and well-being. By not adhering to this you may have left you and others in a state of anxiety and turmoil.

Please ask your group to help you process this written condition so that you have all the benefit of seeing how these seemingly irrelevant actions can affect how you feel about yourself and your effect on others.

(Signed by Michael I might add.)

That telling off really hurt me and taught me a valuable lesson in effective communication. I learnt that feeling angry and telling someone why you are angry isn't a bad thing; in fact, it is a very healthy process. I had gone through life thinking that getting angry was negative, that it was a 'bad emotion', but it isn't. I also thought that people don't like it when you pull them up, that I would be rejected if I said to someone that they upset me. Sure, if anger tips into aggression and each day you are acting out on that anger, that's not healthy. But to deny your feelings when someone has pissed you off only leads to built-up tension and, in my case, passive-aggressive tendencies.

I am not afraid to admit it: I can be one passive-aggressive madam. If someone had done my head in or ground my gears, rather than tell them, I would just do something sneaky to sabotage or wind that person up, asserting my anger in that indirect way. Let's say I was asked to go somewhere with the perpetrator – I would choose to be noncommittal and arsey, leaving them hanging for a bit. Or maybe I would show up late, or I would sit there at the event with a face like a smacked arse. What a dick. Again, I thought this was totally normal and perfectly acceptable, and I didn't know there was a name for it.

I was learning all these new things about myself in such a short amount of time. I'd like to say it felt good, but really what I learnt was I wasn't actually a victim, that I wasn't special or different, and that I had a whole heap of dishonest and manipulative ways about me. *I* was the problem.

As much as there were hours and hours of talking therapy, there were also a lot of written assignments to be completed. Each night there were daily journals to complete, which were then handed in to the counselling team. I can't help but think that they must have had a right laugh at some of the stuff that goes into these journals. I'd never really had to write out my thoughts before; I had never been given assignments based on myself. And it was a lot harder than it sounds – these weren't light assignments. They were based around deep-rooted issues.

My first assignment was on intimacy. Immediately, I was defensive and embarrassed. I came out of that session with my booklet in hand and turned it over so no one saw the title. I genuinely thought that intimacy was about sex, and I was so embarrassed: 'Lovely Jo [my counsellor] thinks I'm a trollop.' I had no understanding that intimacy was way more than sex. I had a problem with relationships of any kind. Other assignments were on shame, perfectionism and control, and grief. They all cut deep and burst open the locked-up boxes that I had buried deep for so many years. My recovery truly began when I was in rehab, sitting in lectures and groups, and learning about the illness I was suffering with, and the pain that was holding me back.

That to me is what rehab is about: a safe space to open up and take the first steps in trying to make sense of your life.

There were good times to be had in rehab and that enjoyment is just as important as dealing with the horrors of your addiction. Recovery isn't a miserable existence, so rehab shouldn't be, either. We had a mate called Si, the ultimate cockney and one hell of a wind-up merchant with a ruthlessly sick sense of humour. If a new client came in and they were in bad shape, perhaps on the brink of a full-blown cluck (opiate withdrawal), well, Simon and his sidekick T would take it upon themselves to impersonate the prison guards from the film *The Green Mile*. With an exaggerated southern drawl, you would hear them shout: 'We've got a live one, boys, walking the mile, they're just walking the mile … you're gonna fry like a turkey …' That humour, however inappropriate, made a dark situation somewhat tolerable – even for those who were shuffling to what felt like their death. I remember those early experiences of enjoying myself and feeling an incredible amount of guilt – surely I had no right to be enjoying myself, as I've hurt the people I love? But you can't think that way. We were sick people. Hurt people – well, they hurt people. If we right the wrongs and put in the effort to work on ourselves, then why shouldn't we be happy?

These moments of enjoyment and hilarity showed me that you don't need a drink or a drug to belly-laugh, to feel free, and that was an important lesson to learn. There is a certain absurdity in rehab – where else would you find yourself watching *One Flew Over the Cuckoo's Nest* with a bunch of people who, like you, found themselves in an institute to address mental health and addiction? Where else would you find yourself in a basement chapel with a tambourine singing along to pop songs like 'Because I Got High', versions of Robert Palmer's 'Addicted to Love' changed to 'Addicted to Drugs' and other pop classics with members of the local church community?

Music was a huge part of rehab and it is a huge part of my recovery. You see, in addiction music felt painful – every song on my Spotify was attached to someone or something, which all led me back to self-pitying torment. We were allowed a Discman – yup, a portable CD player. Who has CDs? I didn't bother with one at first; I couldn't be fucked to feel sad over songs. But I was struggling to fall asleep. Bearing in mind that at night my room mates turned into wrestling crocodiles – they had restless legs from opiate withdrawal – one morning, I went to the tuck shop and bought a Discman and me mum sent me some CDs that I hadn't seen or held since I was a kid. That was the beginning of enjoying music again. My most played CD was *Absolute David Bowie*. I remember being about nine and hearing 'Life on Mars?' – I played it on repeat until I was told off. I listened to that album in the middle of Wiltshire and I felt like I was that young girl again, hearing it for the first time. A lot had happened in those twenty years, but for the 3.29 minutes of that particular song, nothing had changed: I was just a girl who loved Bowie.

Little by little, other things also start to return – my sharp tongue, appreciating nature, creative writing and eating ... Much to my surprise, during my vacation in Costa del Clouds, the more I was learning about my addiction and off-loading years of pain to counsellors, the heavier I was getting. *Sure* I had weight to gain – we all did – but the way in which I ate, as it was for a lot of us – it was like we had never seen food before.

In fact, it was a joy to see some of my closest comrades gain weight. In the medical room, there was a wall of photographs from our admissions (I still have mine – it's on my Instagram), and those mugshots brought us all so much joy. Every visit to pick up our medication (in those classic paper cups), we would laugh at each other's admission photos and the state in which we had walked in. Si, well, we used to say he was the invisible man – his picture simply looked like a photograph of a pair of floating glasses: there was no man, no Si to be found. So when he piled the weight on, it was something to be proud of, to be happy about.

But for me the eating didn't stop. I was eating away my feelings. This wasn't about being hungry, this was a way for me to change how I felt. I took all-inclusive eating to a whole new level. I'd thought I would come out of Clouds with abs and be able to run 10k in under an hour. The only thing I was running was a bath.

I'd say for the first twelve months of sobriety, I smoked like a trooper and ate like a horse. I could inhale a pack of chocolate muffins, no probs, and toot all day on a cig or a vape (smoking got really expensive and I didn't have a pot to piss in). One tale from around this time springs to mind, when I went on a visit home to Liverpool after I had left rehab. I am a carb queen anyway, and my mum knew my penchant for supermarket bakery muffins. With the cupboard stuffed with all the finest beige food money could buy, I couldn't handle just having one muffin – and I went about my muffin consumption with the same secrecy I once did with my bottle of vod. I didn't want to be judged, chastised or challenged that I was going in for yet another cake, so when that needing-to-eat feeling came once again, I went downstairs, I put the taps on in the kitchen – you know, so it sounded as if I wanted a drink of water – and concealed the sound of the single-use plastic muffin package by stuffing it down my pyjama pants and trotting back up the stairs. Then followed: 'What's that in your trousers?' Fuck. I foolishly didn't realise the panic my behaviour would cause. The poor woman was so used to it being a bottle of vodka or something harmful. She got a real scare. I slowly pulled out my slightly squashed muffin and heard the words: 'You don't need to lie.' It was a real moment of, 'Wow, you really are an addict.'

I'd like to say that those moments don't happen today, but they do. There are times when I go the shop to buy a bottle of … Pepsi Max, and I catch myself downing that pop like I would a pint of vodka circa 2017, and think, 'You ain't well.' I'm aware of those behaviours today and know I have to share them before I start to keep secrets. If you're thinking, 'Bloody hell, Melissa, it's only a few muffins and a few litres of sugar-free pop', it's much more than that. I'm trying to fix a feeling with something external.

I consider myself lucky: since entering rehab, I have had no desire to pick up a drink. That's not me bragging, by the way – for all I know, I could have a craving tomorrow. But while I may not obsess over a bottle of vodka any more, I have had moments of thinking, 'I would love a gary [Gary Ablett, tablet] at a festival.' But I know recreational drugs would lead to alcohol which means relapse, and I certainly don't want that. I may not have any control over the thoughts that enter my head, and the associations that lead to wondering about chemical escape, but I am not my thoughts, and as Michael says, 'Thoughts aren't facts.' I don't need to act on them. If you ever see me randomly blowing a birthday candle out in public and there is no candle in front of me, let alone a cake there, I am blowing away the harmful thought. Seriously, I don't know why I began doing it or if anyone told me to do it. Sometimes

I just find it easier to physically blow that thought away. My AA sponsor Jo does something similar – she stamps on her negative thoughts.

Someone told me once to doodle when I got a craving and I wanted to punch them square in the chops. 'You want me to colour in and draw pictures when every single part of my mind, body and soul wants to pour a drink? Dickhead!' But I see now that those sorts of suggestions, however patronising we perceive them to be, are just people trying to be helpful; I really do understand the importance of distraction. And when it comes to cravings there are a few tactics that I learnt in Clouds:

- **Trust that it will pass. Thoughts will come and thoughts will go; when I am experiencing intense feelings, I have faith and trust that this will pass. It may feel like it won't but it will. I take some breaths and even say out loud, 'This will pass.'**
- **Play the tape forward. If a drink is presented to us and we are tempted, what would our lives look like in twenty-four hours after that drink? The chances are – pretty bloody awful.**
- **Break it down into blocks of minutes. If the thought of being sober for a whole day is too much and we are thinking about a drink – practise 'for the next hour, I won't drink'. You might even need to go further and say, 'for the next 15 minutes, I won't pick up a drink'.**

The most powerful thing I can do if a thought creeps in or I find myself staring at a drink too much is … share it. Get it out of my head, say it out loud and take the power out of it. Tell someone, tell anyone. Cravings may feel like they will never leave or will never pass, but they do. Knowing your triggers also helps to avoid cravings. What are the feelings, situations or environments that make me want to drink? For someone who was as pickled as I was, towards the end everything was a bloody trigger. But they can be broken down into different categories – emotional, environmental and mental.

Below are a few common 'relapse triggers' for you to see where I am going with this.

- **Stress. Feeling under intense pressure is bound to make us want to drink/use.**
- **Sights, sounds and smells. Smelling that stale pub smell, seeing your old stomping ground or maybe hearing a song that reminds you of a difficult time.**
- **Emotions. There's no avoiding emotions, but if you relied on a substance to cope with them in the first place, feeling emotions may be so unbearable that a drink may seem like a good idea.**
- **Sex and relationships. A lot of my relapses have been induced by a new suitor. Being worried about acceptance and the challenges of romance caused my liver a great deal of harm.**

- **Euphoric recall.** Reminiscing about that one time at age X when I had the time of my life and all was well …
- **Drinking dreams.** Those goddamn drinking dreams. Drinking being that engrained in your psyche that when you sleep you are consumed by the stuff.
- **Positive things happening.** Oh, would you look at that, I have a new job, my life is great, I am buying a new place, may as well celebrate, I've clearly got my shit together now, so why the hell not …
- **Being around boozy and druggy people and places a bit too much.** Oh, look, I'm in a bar, no one's watching, I feel OK – I'll have a double, please, bartender.

But the biggest triggers in my life today – and one phrase that I use all the time to tackle them – is HALT (hungry, angry, lonely or tired). If I am any of these, I shouldn't be making any rash decisions or take my reactions too seriously. Have you ever been so hungry that you snap? So tired that you end up feeling sorry for yourself and feel worthless? So lonely that you reach out to someone toxic? So angry that you do something that you would never usually do? Yeah, me too. When I find myself completely oversensitive and over-reacting, the chances are I am one or more than one of those things. Then it's time to go back to basics, and halt.

Throughout rehab, all I heard was, 'Recovery has to come first.'

Made sense; I could totally see the logic, so I took it on board. But I never expected that I would have to put my learning to the test so soon.

I thought I was going to Clouds for six weeks, that I would return home and everything would be fine. Towards the end of my six-week stay, however, I had some really difficult conversations and realisations with Lovely Jo. There were concerns that if I were to return to Kirkby, to the bedroom I had spent so much of my time in, to the family that needed to heal, to the streets that had caused so much panic, that it would be a recipe for relapse. The decision was mine and mine to make alone: would I choose recovery, or would I choose my family?

For many this would be a no-brainer: choose recovery. But for some of us, the thought of our family coming second is alien and completely wrong. After a lot of soul-searching and talking my options through, I decided that I *had* to continue on this path, the path of recovery. Without recovery how long would I have a family for? I know recovery is all about doing it for yourself, but the thought of relapsing and them having to go through hell once more was appalling to me.

The easiest and most selfish decision would have been to follow my heart and go home. And it wouldn't have been the right one.

I put my faith in the counsellors and the experts and hoped for the best. It was then suggested that I continued rehab for another six weeks in a secondary-phase facility, in Camden. Erm, hello? I am poor. Again, I was up against one of the biggest barriers to treatment: funding. But my numbers on the lottery came up once again, as another charity was willing to support me: the Amy Winehouse Foundation.

I couldn't believe it. I remember my friends and I were sat in Ange's conservatory for a gathering when the news broke of Amy's tragic death. We were devastated. An icon, gone too soon. If you would have told me four years later that Amy Winehouse's legacy would fund my rehab place, I would have thought you were as high as a kite yourself. I'm all about signs and symbols: I had a job interview on my nan's birthday – that was a sign. My mum's peace lily that didn't bloom until I left the house and went to rehab – that was a sign. (I do a lot of people's heads in with my signs and hocus-pocus, but I find it comforting.) And let me tell you, since my involvement with the Amy Winehouse Foundation, I get a lot of Amy-related moments. If a song comes on the radio, I always say a little thank you.*

Leading up to leaving Clouds, I started to see some of my closest pals leave and head into the big wide world again. There was no feeling quite like it. The changes that take place in such a short space of time give you hope and, as cheesy as this sounds, it made me believe in miracles. You pray and hope that they are going to make it on the outside and you hope you'll stay in touch. There are also some people who you wish to never see again, but often they're the people who you learn the most from, so I suppose we ought to be grateful for them.

And then it was time to bid my farewell to Clouds. (You know the score by now, so I will skip over the tears.) I left with hope and insight into what I needed to work on and what I had to do to stay well. I

---

* I kid you not, and may the man in the sky strike me down, fifteen minutes after writing this, 'Rehab' came on Radio X. Sorry, I just had to share that.

wanted to know about the counsellor's perspective, what it's like for them to watch someone successfully complete treatment; they are the unsung heroes in this:

I believe treatment works and I know it works, but it is not like selling someone a car. The client has to come to believe this for themselves, that this is going to work. That process takes time. The privilege of my role is to see those people, as we say, 'get it'. It can be like a light-bulb moment, some people display a certain confidence that we notice, a change in psyche that glows – it's magic. One part of our role is to create opportunities for people to feel a sense of hope and build their self-esteem. What we, the counsellors, do is try and keep the community focus on recovery, i.e. doing things differently. There is no feeling quite like it when we see someone 'get it', but we know that not everyone makes it – so our job is to do what we do 24 hours a day, 7 days a week, 365 days a year, to allow people to have that chance of recovery of life.

Michael Rawlinson

You could say a pink cloud carried me from Wiltshire to Camden. But, truth be told, it didn't last long; the pink cloud soon turned grey, and for the second time in six weeks, I found myself thinking: 'Toto, we are not in Kansas any more.'

The energy and feel in this new treatment centre was different: it was raw, it was real, it was rough around the edges and, I tell you what, it bloody toughened me up. I needed it.

The first few days were an adjustment. I had gone from a lot of space and a lot of structure to no space and not much structure. I had gone from as many phone calls as you like, to listened-to phone calls. The biggest change: I had gone from being trusted outside to having frisk searches and breathalyser tests. It felt horrible. It felt like I had gone back to a familiar existence – to being locked in. I didn't feel like a free woman at all.

I found it bloody awful at first. I wasn't welcome. That wasn't in my head – I was told it to my face. I wasn't welcome on the grounds that I used to be a teacher and my fellow inmates hadn't responded well to teachers in the past. It was going to be a long six weeks. But for all of how tough I found it, it made me more determined that I would stick to it; I would complete it and I would not back down (please read that with the theme from *Rocky* in your head).

The house felt quite chaotic, but this was one of the few services that would take on women with complex needs. As an outsider, today, I can see how the need for that type of service is essential. Addiction and mental health diagnoses are common, and therefore there has to be a space for people to be able to go to if they have complex mental health issues *and* substance issues co-occurring. But, as a resident, it was a lot, and I became desensitised to a lot of things. My tolerance for certain types of mental health episodes began wearing thin. I wasn't fazed by seeing self-harm, by psychotic episodes or thrown ashtrays. That became my norm.

Each day we would have a feelings check-in: we would choose a feeling from the 'feelings wheel' and say why we were feeling a certain way. Every day, without fail, one girl, who had the worst but best case of nervous laughter I've ever came across, would just say, 'I am completely … baffled.' And that would be it – I would be in tatters, laughing. Every day one of us would be suffering with hysteria, which would set the whole lot of us off. My closest friend in there was a proper East End girl called Nat. She was genuine, generous, a salt of the earth type, obsessed with bleach and the fierce type of woman who would do anything for her babies. Considering what she was going through herself, my god did she carry me through those six weeks. It may have been loud, noisy and with the crisis team on speed dial, but this was a female-only place and that's what was special. For a lot of us, forming bonds was difficult, maybe because of past trauma, trust issues or low self-worth, and it may not have been the easiest of places to live, but there was a certain unity and togetherness that came from being a group of women who have been through the wringer.

I thought that I had found humility in Clouds, that I had no more ego to lose. I was wrong. Each Thursday at this centre, there was a outdoors-based activity: a way for us to reconnect with nature. Sounds lovely, doesn't it? But this wasn't really horticulture or making bird houses. This was litter picking and heavy-duty gardening. It felt more like community service, if you ask me. It was the peak of winter, and we were provided with overalls and steel-capped boots. We had to walk from the treatment centre to the overground station in our work wear – it must have looked very day release. On our way back to the house, I would catch my reflection in shop windows and think to myself, 'What the actual fuck, Melissa? How the hell have you ended up here?' It was during one of these sessions one day, as we crossed the road somewhere in Camden, that a car sped past. It looked like a twenties-style car, something straight off the pages of *The Great Gatsby*. It pulled up at the lights and I thought to myself, 'What a dick.' Then I realised that it was only Jonathan Ross. I looked at Jonathan Ross in his car and I looked down at my outfit – my second-hand steel-capped boots and baggy overalls – and thought to myself, 'You have got no more pride to lose.' I made a promise to myself that day – that I would do whatever it takes to never, ever have to go to rehab again.

I am grateful for both residential treatment experiences, both of which taught me a lot and prepared me for the real world, the sober world. They gave me the chance to figure out what recovery meant to me, what I was made of, and how resilient I can be.

In those early days of sobriety, I didn't know whether I was coming or bloody going, and I certainly didn't anticipate the emotional rollercoaster that followed. It almost feels as if you are reborn (not in the Christian sense), and you are learning how to do life all over again. So, if you are new to this sobriety lark, or you maybe are about to start, be prepared to feel all the feels and then some. You may even question why the hell you even started it. It's a bit like when you begin clearing out the garage and after an hour you realise it's a bigger job that you thought but it's too late to turn back ... yeah, that's what starting recovery feels like. But just like that sense of achievement that you feel when you look at your garage and you won't let anyone mess it up now, you'll get a similar feeling and then some by sticking with sobriety, even if it can feel like a painful, pointless and overwhelming feat.

As you know, I had had bursts of being dry before: stints of being physically sober; but I don't think I could ever say I had been in recovery before. For me, sobriety is more than whether you have had a drink or not; it's about healing, learning and growing. During those early days of actual recovery and not just being a dry drunk, I know I laughed like I had never laughed before, but I also cried like I had never cried before. One day I would feel grateful to be alive, all very Julie-Andrews-spinning-on-a-hill shouting, 'The hills are alive ...', while the next day, or maybe just the evening of that day, I would be sobbing, cursing at the sky and hating myself for being an alcoholic on benefits. I'd say I was this way for a good year. Michael shared a common phrase in 'our world': The best thing about recovery is that you get your feelings back. The worst thing about recovery is, you get your feelings back. It's how we develop emotional resilience and manage these feelings that keeps us safe. Rest assured, as time progresses, things start to settle down and stabilise (thank god). So, please, if you're in this place, hold on. I'm not one for making grand promises, but I do know that the mood swings get better – anyone who you meet in recovery will tell you the same.

And the intensified emotions you feel in those early days aren't all bad; sometimes the emotions we feel when we divorce from the booze is pure joy. In my gang, we know what to be in the 'pink cloud' – the feeling of elation at the new you who is living life sober – feels like. You may be so impressed and so in love with it that you go through a self-righteous phase and start telling all people they should give up the booze. We've all been there ... it'll pass. (If it doesn't and its working for you, great. But if I'm allowed to be so forthright – don't be that person – don't be a dick.)

One of the most challenging things about finally getting sober is wanting everything to go back to normal as soon as humanly possible: wanting the job back, the friends back, the good times back, the money back. But if I had my rehab time back again, I would wish I had moved those wants and wishes to one side and just concentrated on myself that bit more. I'd put myself through a hell of a lot and I shouldn't have been rushing myself. As they say in AA, 'Easy does it.'

Rehab is a part of my story, but this is not the case for everyone. I thank my lucky stars that I was given the opportunity: my bursary-allocated place at rehab was a life win; I knew that the opportunity wouldn't come around again, so I took it and ran with it. I had nothing else to lose, and a lot to gain. But let me make this crystal bloody clear: *You do not need rehab to find sobriety.* It's just that for some of us, it is necessary. Quite a few of my mates in recovery didn't go to rehab: they got sober in the community and I applaud and respect anyone who found and maintained sobriety and recovery without residential treatment. Again, you have to find out what works for you.

When I went to rehab, I had already detoxed and stayed off the drink for six weeks so, I'll be honest, I had my reservations. I knew there had been a shift in my thinking and I had never felt so certain that I was ready for it, so why did I need to still go? Even fellow rehabbers questioned why I was there. But if 2017 taught me anything, it's that my addiction left untreated is a ticking time bomb. I had to get it treated, and I did.

Takeaways

- **When you stop drinking, your emotions will be all over the place (good and bad). It's normal to feel like an adult baby when you sober up**
- **Not everyone needs rehab**
- **Recovery isn't doom and gloom – laugh!**

- **By putting the drink down, you can learn about your behaviours and see that drink was a solution to a bigger problem**
- **Cravings are painful, but know that they will pass, and you can find tools and tricks to combat them**
- **Figure out your triggers**
- **You might start eating like a horse**
- **Recovery has to come first, nothing else.**

Chapter 6

Find yourself a support network

I need a *what*? A support network? Really? I am a perfectly capable grown adult, I do not need my hand holding …

Familiar? If so, in the kindest possible way and without causing you to throw this book against a wall … you do.

I cottoned on pretty quickly that for me to really get into this 'new way of life' lark, I had to do the complete opposite of what I did before rehab, and that meant having people in my life who knew how my mind operated; folk who I could call on in the hour of need; and folk that wouldn't reach for the house and window keys if I was having a wobble. Only an alcoholic would understand me when I described my state of mind as 'feeling like all my socks are out of the sock draw and they aren't in pairs and I don't know how to put them all back in'. On these grounds of lunacy, it was clear that I had to make new connections, and new friends in a new way … god help me.

There is a whole heap of reasons as to why, when we quit the booze, the sugar, the betting – whatever the vice that's in your way – having support from people who have been there, done it and worn the T-shirt is a good idea. If you are the type of person who loves the technical and a bit of theory, these life-saving friendships forged out of despair are known as 'peer support'. I could try and come up with a definition in my own words, but Mind, the mental health charity, puts it better than I ever could (and without swear words):

> *Peer support is when people use their own experiences to help each other. There are different types of peer support, but they all aim to:*
> - *bring together people with shared experiences to support each other*
> - *provide a space where you feel accepted and understood*
> - *treat everyone's experiences as being equally important*
> - *involve both giving and receiving support.*

I mean, come on, who doesn't want in on that? Peer support isn't just reserved for mental health or addiction; there are groups for new mothers, grief, cancer, weight loss – the list goes on.

When I think about my own opinions on why it works, it comes down to 'a level playing field'. In this type of set-up, no one is on the outside looking in, as everyone is in that same boat trying to make it back to shore.

Mind's definition points out that peer support is about giving and receiving. When you're in recovery, to get out of your own head and to stay as well as can be, you need to help others. Addiction is notoriously selfish: we're used to it being all about us, about what we can get out of life or why we are owed something. But helping someone out not only stops me from being a selfish mare, it also allows me to be of use and subsequently take on board my own advice. If I didn't have access to peer support, I wouldn't be hearing the recovery patter, I wouldn't be reminded of the little alcoholic-in-recovery life hacks; I'd find myself isolated, with my addictive brain working overtime. Don't get me wrong, I have had my moments when I question, 'Will this be it forever – having to be reminded of drinking? Surely I can move on with my life and just be a non-drinker and stop with this "alcoholic" spiel?' But then I stop and really think about it. Would I want to lose this gift? Would I want to be a lone wolf again? Would I want to forget that alcoholism is a chronic condition? And it is after that third question when I think, 'Yeah, you'd better stick with this recovery lark, you self-sabotaging tit.'

But where do you even start? It's not like you can put an advert on Gumtree:

> *Alcoholic with mental health diagnosis seeks to appoint kind and understanding support network. Preferably female and non-murderous. Must be comfortable with tears and catastrophic thought processes. Dark sense of humour and history of compulsive drinking is essential.*

Could you imagine? Unfortunately, as with everything when it comes to this game, we gotta put the action in and put our fears to the side and make connections with people who you look at and think, 'I want what they've got.'

On the cusp of turning thirty, I had just completed twelve weeks of rehab and I was still recovering from the painful decision to leave everything I knew behind in Liverpool, to start a new life in London. The move wasn't as mad as it sounds – it was hardly a Dick-Whittington-type scenario – as I was moving into what I jokingly called a house for wayward girls (it's really not that). My new pad, brought to you by the Amy Winehouse Foundation, is what's officially known as 'supported accommodation'. I know what you're thinking: 'What, she had *carers*?' It didn't feel like supported housing in the slightest and no, I didn't have carers: we had key workers – recovering addicts who were there to support us until we could support ourselves. Amy's Place is a space for women aged eighteen to thirty who are fresh out of treatment and need a safe place to live to rebuild their lives. It's one of a kind in that it's female-only and it is self-contained living. It's a part of Amy Winehouse's legacy, and without Amy, the Foundation and Amy's Place, I wouldn't have the life I have today. I wouldn't have the chance to talk to you in these pages. Relapse risk is high, so recovery housing such as Amy's Place is essential for people like me. There are recovery housing services across the country, they are often mixed-sex and operate on a 'one strike and you're out' basis. Amy's Place is person-centred and therefore, if someone does have a slip, they will be supported and signposted to the relevant services to get them back on track. Compassion is at the centre of Amy's Place, always. If there are any people in high places reading this, come and visit Amy's Place – look at the work they do, the women they have helped, and see what can be achieved. We need more.

If I had returned to Liverpool after treatment, I don't know what would have happened. I needed more time and the space to recover. It's a bit like riding a bike – I was learning how to ride one but I needed some stabilisers, and that's what Amy's Place was: a set of training wheels until I was able to ride safely on my own. Amy's Place is not rehab. Sure there are in-house services you can access, like daily check-in, relapse management, counselling, holistic therapies, nutrition workshops and even exercise classes. Although bonds are forged and there is a strong sense of community, it's not got that 'we're all in this bubble' vibe of rehab. You are free to come and go as you please, and do you. It's very much a bridge to independent living; a stepping stone.

When I waved goodbye to the secondary rehab, I was given a Paddington Bear cake. I wish I could say this cake was one of those blunders when you can't be arsed to buy a celebration cake in good time, but this farewell cake wasn't chosen out of desperation, it was intentional. Because that's what and who I resembled. I had a duffle-style coat, a fur hat and a vintage suitcase that I bought in the village of Shaftesbury from my time in Costa del Clouds; I even had a brown label on my suitcase (swear down). There are, however, differences between Paddington and me. Unlike my Peruvian namesake, I no longer had an unhealthy obsession with fruit-based concoctions and didn't stoop to concealing bottles on my person. (If you ask me, someone should ask Paddington if he's OK … seems a bit excessive. Jars under his hat? Unable to survive without a constant supply of marmalade?)

Although I don't hail from darkest Peru, London was a new land and wired so very differently to Kirkby; it was a shock to the system, particularly when newly sober. I looked and felt lost but, at the same time, was mesmerised by what I was seeing: red buses, Tube stations, palaces. I couldn't quite grasp that no one in London seemed to give a flying fuck … about anything.

My previous experiences of London were, at best, fucking disastrous. My earliest trip, when I was around five years old, was visiting my Aunty Sandra and Uncle Paul. Thanks to a *Spitting Image* exhibition, I was traumatised, and lost many nights of sleep thereafter thanks to the exaggerated features of the rubberised Margaret Thatcher. My other London encounters were of a drunk and disorderly kind; the last jaunt, I believe, was in 2014. In a nutshell, I pissed myself in Finsbury Park 'watching' the Arctic Monkeys and ended up in a Chinese restaurant accusing people of talking about me. A phrase was born out of this night, one that is still in circulation today: 'It's been going around the lazy Susan that you have a problem with me.' Oh god, lest we forget, on that night I was thrown out of a bar for having my own bottle of Jack Daniels in my bag. Classy.

I didn't appreciate just how ballsy moving to the capital was. Although, technically, you could say I was on my own, I knew I wasn't; there are alcoholics everywhere, especially the recovering kind. As the new girl in a building of sixteen women, it was all rather intimidating. You see, in rehab, I had begun to peel back the layers; and it turns out that making new friendships, nurturing friendships and even reaching out to people was a hell of a lot harder for me than I had thought it would be. On the surface, I can talk to anyone: fellow disgruntled passengers who are waiting on the Euston concourse cursing a late train, or people in the waiting room of the clinic at Aintree Hospital sharing war stories involving type 7 shit on the Bristol Stool Chart. But when it comes to reaching out for help on anything deeper or, the worst, suggesting going for a coffee, I can shut up shop faster than a store at 5 p.m. Christmas Eve.

Most of the friendships I had in my twenties started in the

workplace and developed on the dance floor, or in a toilet cubicle; chatting absolute bollocks and telling my once-colleague-now-best-friend how much I thought of them. In fact, a lot of my nights out were spent in the toilet talking to strangers and checking on the well-being of toilet attendants. I wasn't alone on my Sambuca Samaritan routine. My friend Cat would also accompany me on the Saturday night outreach work. Our clients' needs were varied: whether they were having a hair and make-up emergency, struggling to adjust their Spanx, moaning about their fella or had had a falling out with a friend, Cat and I would have your back. We'd provide our unsuspecting clients with support, positive affirmations and, as always, unsolicited advice. I'd like to think we made a difference to all we met in the toilets and smoking areas of Liverpool's finest watering holes … and I won't have anyone tell me otherwise.

Bonding on frequent nights out often evolves into friendships, but without booze, bars or beak (Scouse for cocaine) for rapport-building, what the hell was I supposed to do? I may have been recently released from a stretch in rehab, without a job, but I still had some stubborn residual pride left and I didn't want to beg for friends. I was shuffling around Amy's Place for the first couple of days, giving a load of big smiles and false hellos, but inside I was thinking, 'I don't fit in here. I don't fit in at all,' and saying to myself, 'What the hell have you done, this ain't normal, who are these people?'

Then, on the fourth day, god said, 'Let there be another northerner.' (I know I shouldn't be affirming the north–south divide, and for that I apologise, but I *really* needed a northerner.)

I was downstairs in the basement – that's where the laundry facilities are, and where the office is. When you first move in, you spend a lot of time in that basement, dumping all of your woes on the staff. After yapping away (probably moaning) to one of the key workers, I said my goodbyes and then I heard a voice, a voice that was so far away the southern accents I had been hearing: 'Are you from Liverpool? I'm from Sheffield.' I never thought the sound of an angel would be that of a Yorkshire lass from 'Steel Ci'eh'; her name was just as holy too: Magdalena (Mimi). She was a bit of me: she was Yorkshire brew in a sea of matcha lattes. There was no talk of 'shifting energy' or 'I'm just taking my time to heal from within and align myself with positive energy on my spiritual journey'; she spoke plainly, but there was nothing plain about our Mimi. Her eyebrows pencilled and powdered to perfection, she stood head to toe in one brand of gym wear (because god forbid you mix and match your brands), acrylic nails (talons) that you had to look at and ask, 'How do you put your knickers on wearing those?', a cracking set of gold hoops and, most importantly, a smile that could light up a room and make you feel at peace.

We did the awkward number exchange and, me being me, I thought the girl was too cool for me, and that she wouldn't want me tagging along. But I did text, and I went to an NA (Narcotics Anonymous) meeting with her. And, just when I thought my attraction was based on a booming Yorkshire accent and northern aesthetic, I discovered that she too was in the same gang as Jade (podcast co-host) and me: 'public health professional girls gone bad'. I couldn't believe my luck. Someone who understood the north/south thing, someone who had drunk litres of vodka, someone who was kind, a social care worker, a young woman who shared the same intense level of shame and regret ... from that moment on, I not only had an ally in the building, I had a friend. We had nothing in common but everything in common: she taught me about grime, I taught here about nineties grunge; she fancied men with muscles who loved protein, while I fancied skinny men who loved documentaries; I didn't stop crying, she didn't cry once. (In three years of knowing her, I have yet to see a tear form. One day I will make this girl cry; who knows, this book might do the trick ... *result*.) As cheesy as it sounds, that's the beauty of recovery: you meet people and forge bonds you would never have entertained if you were still on the sauce or on the bag (drugs) because your connection is deeper than the surface-level stuff; you connect because you have been in the same dark place and shared the same pain.

My friendship with Mimi is a special one. There are no secrets, no agendas, no filter; we nurtured our friendship using the tools acquired and lessons learnt in rehab: clear communication and boundaries (more of which later). I wasn't used to having conversations that would open with, 'I feel so low today', or 'I couldn't face getting washed.' I was used to avoidance and deflection with humour, not this vulnerability lark – that takes practice. For hours and hours we would sit and ponder where it all went wrong and we would listen to each other – really *listen*; there has yet to be a conversation where there is even a whiff of judgement (we don't even put the telly on in each other's company!). We created our own little safe space to be authentic, to be broken and to allow someone in to help in our mending process. This friendship helped me see that I wasn't a bad person or a bad friend after all. When we lose people, it's so easy to assume that we are rotten to the core; that we must be, otherwise people wouldn't drop us. But when we work on ourselves and allow others in, we start to see that, maybe, it's not just about what's wrong with us, it's also about our choices and who we invest our time and energy in.

This new friendship has set the precedent for how I should approach all my friendships, going forward. Without it sounding too much like a science experiment, when it came to reconnecting with people from my past, I approached the rebuilding process with the same mechanics: honesty, boundaries, understanding and love.

Recently, I met with Mimi, who has now returned to a profession that was once deemed lost, as I wanted to hear her take on support networks and why they're so important. (I also wanted an excuse to chow down on her culinary delights – this girl has single-handedly developed my palate by a good 30 per cent. Although I still won't touch fish.)

Straight off the bat she came through with the goods:

One of the main positives about having a support network is running your ideas past someone. In addiction, we are so used to living in secret and by yourself. Even if you are not completely by yourself – because I did still hang out with people – we are still only answering to our self. I was so impulsive all the time. Bang! I'm going to make this decision. Bang! I'm going to get a tattoo! Bang! I'm going to get shit-faced. Now, just knowing that I've run something by people will help me to think more carefully about what it is I've decided to do: I don't just make better decisions, I make informed decisions.

She's absolutely spot on. In my drinking days, I knew best so there was no need for me to run anything by anyone. If I thought there was a chance of someone disagreeing with me or they had the potential to throw their very reasonable 2p in, I just wouldn't bother. Now, I'm very much of a, 'Look, mate, my head's battered over whether

I should do this, what do you reckon?' person. We talk it out, weigh it up, figure out what the fears are and why I'm in knots over it and then we all end up laughing at how bonkers I am. I know that I am regurgitating 'a problem shared is a problem halved' but, for me, an alcoholic, this hasn't come easily.

Naturally, Mimi and I went off topic. Then the timer went off on her swanky cooker and the Jamaican spiced chicken was ready and, while she dished up, our Mimi raised a cracking point that I had never really thought of before:

> When you're in regular contact with a support network and your friends are up to date with your life and know where you're at, when shit does hit the fan I don't have to say, 'Well, it all started six months ago and now I'm up shit creek …' The prospect of having to tell someone every single worry and detail is just too much and I'd probably prefer to use [drink] instead. Whereas, if someone knows what's been going on, they are up to speed and give you suggestions straight away, without you having to bare your soul and feel exposed.

How could I have missed this point, when so much of my life was spent with suppressed emotion and pent-up fear? The number of people who knew me in the glory days and who have heard the podcast, and who have reached out and said, 'I had no idea you were having such a bad time; I wish you would have told me, I could have done more,' is ridiculous. I never want to be in a position again where I keep things to myself.

Which is not to say that I haven't tried to pull the wool over Mimi's or Jade's eyes and pretend I'm fine when really I'm not. I'm only human. Which brings me nicely to my next point – that having fellow sober people or people in your life who have been through the same stuff means *you can't get away with anything.* You really can't kid a kidder. As fucking annoying as this can be, it can also be a life saver.

In August 2019, I had a period of intense anxiety. I was in a situation that I had no control over – out of respect for the persons involved I won't say too much, but it was a knife-in-the-back situation that I was completely powerless in, and clueless about what the outcome would be, and I couldn't see the wood for the trees. I was a mess, the sort of mess I hadn't been since 2017. I thought I had it under control, however. One evening, Jade rang me, and although I was a rambling bag of nerves, I told her I was OK; that I had been taking all the necessary steps to stay present (distraction methods, meditation (deep breathing), helping someone else, going to an AA meeting). Billy bullshit. I was sitting in a nighty, unwashed, unfed, knickerless, rocking to and fro, playing out the worst-case scenario in my mind. I was terrified. I was in a state of mind that was so familiar, a state of mind that in the past I had drunk to fix.

I genuinely thought that I had gotten away with it, that I had thrown Jade off the scent, when there was a knock at the door. It was Jade and Mimi. They had travelled from north to east London, in their PJs, near our grandma bedtime (the joys of sobriety) to come and check on me. The guilt I felt that they had had their night disrupted by me having a Jean Slater episode was unbearable. When I said this, I was just told: 'Don't be so fucking stupid.' These knights in pyjama-armour sat with me, listened and held me mentally and physically. I don't know if I could have drunk that night, but I wouldn't like to think of what could have happened if they hadn't shown up. We like to call them 'wellness checks'. It takes real love and guts to say to yourself, 'Nah, she ain't OK. Mimi, get your coat on, we need to go to hers.'

If I hadn't had peers in recovery with the same head as me, then maybe that episode would have been dealt with differently. I could have been babied, or maybe the person trying to help might have gone into fixing mode. The chances are, I would have received a lot of sympathy, which probably would have given me the green light to go into victimhood. I certainly wouldn't have been reminded of the ways to cope with addiction. You see, support networks, peers, friends in recovery or whatever you want to call them, they share their experiences of feeling similar and the ways they got through it. You are instantly reminded that you aren't special or different, that you're an alcoholic, and that what you're experiencing happens in recovery and that you need support.

When it comes to wellness checks, they don't need to be dramatic late-night bangs on the door. The majority of checking in on a mate is a subtle affair: a cheeky WhatsApp voice note, a phone call or a text. If I think that something is going on with a friend, I have no issue any more with saying, 'You don't seem yourself, are you all right?' The way I see it, if I keep that stirring feeling that a mate isn't themselves to myself, have I been a good mate if I haven't asked the question?

These days, we all know the importance of reaching out to people; there are far too many social media outpourings during Mental Health Awareness Week for us not to. 'Don't suffer alone, my DMs are always open.' As much as it's a lovely thing to read, how genuine is it? How many times have you been on Facebook, seen one of those posts and thought, 'That's rich, coming from you?' If that is the case, forget about the fair-weather bullshitters and find the people who understand you, who will support you and, above all else, who you feel safe with.

You gotta find your people.

When it comes to recovery, or even life, you *have* to find your people; to find a place where you belong – aren't we all looking for that? It just so happens that I belong with people who had pissed or sniffed their life up the wall. I never wanted to belong to this club, but by this point in my life, I have accepted it and today I wouldn't want it any other way. Ever.

I desperately wanted to hold on to that sense of belonging and relief that I found in Clouds and the only way I could do that was to continue to follow the work I had started in there … through Alcoholics Anonymous. In rehab, I absolutely despised the thought that I was in AA. I thought I was too young, too cool and, obviously, above it. I found the whole thing sickly sweet and had the audacity to think that it was a cult. But what makes a cult is when you are forced to hand over or sacrifice something, or feel like you can't leave. That doesn't happen in AA.

My original issues with AA came from my experiences of indoctrination and the Church. I misconstrued spirituality for religion and I assumed that AA was a bunch of god-botherers (I know, I'm awful). I remember saying to a fellow resident who had success with AA, 'Nah, feels like brain washing,' and you know what he replied? 'Don't you reckon your brain needs a good washing?' Who was I to argue with that? Throughout my time in Clouds, I would moan that I was now sentenced to a lifetime of broken biscuits and church halls. I even made a piece of art (part of my therapy) which depicted this. It looked more like a poster for a protest than anything else, but it was my way of passive-aggressively denouncing AA. But for the majority of us, it was our only choice left (and, depending on the meeting, the biscuits are a lovely touch – especially if there are Twixes).

This resistance is common among newcomers. I had experienced AA once before in 2016; in fact, it had been used as a deterrent. My mum escorted me to a meeting and pointed out that this was where I would end up if I didn't stop drinking. The meeting took place in – you guessed it – a church hall. We chose a meeting in a neighbouring town to Kirkby; we chose not to attend the closest meeting in case we were spotted or knew anyone there. (What's laughable about that self-obsessed rationale is that if we had been seen by someone we knew, that poor bugger would have been there for the same reason, so what benefit would they have had to be the town crier?) We knew nothing of the importance of anonymity at the time. You could say AA is a bit like Fight Club. (The first rule about Fight Club: we don't talk about Fight Club.) But I realise I have to tread carefully here: the last thing I want to do is to reveal its secrets or break principles that have allowed millions of people to get well. But it would also be rather weird and disingenuous if I were to leave out the fellowship to which I attribute maintaining my sobriety and having the life I lead today. The lessons I learnt, my outlook on life and the new ways to cope? All AA. All of it.

I continued with AA because I was so terrified of relapsing – there was no way that I wanted to go back to rehab. As much as my ego was bruised by being twenty-nine and in AA, the stories I heard and

the literature I read were too close to home: there has been many a
time, especially in the early days, when my old paranoia of believing
I was in *The Truman Show* returned – it was as if these people sharing
their truth were living in my mind and, for a few seconds, I would
be convinced that they knew someone from my past and had intel.
(I can confirm that these people were not actors and did not have
access to my mind or film footage from my active addiction days;
they were simply alcoholics and I was one of them.) I was in the
right place.

To go back to the earlier waffle about peer support, in groups or
fellowships like this, we find identification and with that identification
comes connection and a certain comfort in knowing that you aren't
the only batshit lunatic who decanted your vodka into rinsed-out
bottles of Flash (you read right – bottles of Flash). I was at the point
where I had to conceal in my drink plain sight. The cupboards, the
garage, the soil in the garden were too obvious; an empty bottle of
cleaning product that sat under the sink was ideal. I thought I was
the only one, and then a beautiful woman in my life shared she did
similar with bleach. Feeling less alone is important in recovery from
any addiction. I was recently speaking to a very dear person in my
life, who has a gambling addiction. (He is comfortable with the word
'addiction' but I appreciate that there are people who prefer to say
'gambling disorder'.) I wanted to talk to him about the importance
of support groups, to show that although the vices may be different,
there are similar ways to treat them:

> It was suggested to go to Gamblers Anonymous and I did. For the
> first time in my life I could tell people what was going on in my
> head and not be judged. I also heard stories from other gamblers

which I could relate to, but the main thing it showed me was that there's a life to be had and enjoyed as long as I didn't place that first bet.

I refrained from gambling for a long time but I was still the same person, getting up to no good, lying and stealing. I left the meetings to go back to doing it on my own and it was only a matter of time before I was back gambling and I was, but this time it was worse than ever. They say it's a progressive illness and I agree with that. My thoughts were now getting darker and I loved playing the poor-me card – I'd blame everyone but myself for the situations I'd find myself in.

More years of pain were had and even having a young family I couldn't stop gambling. I needed help before I lost them or my life because that's where it was heading. I'd tell myself, 'They'll be better off without me.' My life was now well and truly out of control.

I knew only one place had worked for me and I had to swallow my pride and go back and I'm so glad I did. I went back and I listened for once, instead of thinking I had all the answers; to this day it's one of the best decisions I've made in my life.

What strikes me most about these groups is the love and kindness that is so freely given to people like me, people like my very dear person. Even if we go astray, the door is always open. Especially if we go astray, in fact. I was always so suspicious and found it so bizarre that strangers would offer me their number, pull up a pew and chat to me. As Brits we are a cynical bunch and naturally my head would come up with all sorts of nastiness and questions:

- **What are they after?**
- **Do they think I'm some kind of charity case?**
- **Why are they giving me their number?**
- **She's nuts.**
- **Why are these people so happy?**
- **They're deffo still drinking.**
- **Oh, here we go, a do-gooder – concentrate on yourself, love, and leave me alone.**
- **You don't know me, fuck off.**

I couldn't bear it: with each conversation I wanted to tear my skin off or shrivel up and die. I was never rude – I was still a people-pleaser, after all. I just couldn't for the life of me understand how or why people cared about me, a stranger who had fucked up so royally. Or, how these people seemed so happy and content when they were bloody alcoholics. It's clear to me now that, back then, my self-worth was nowhere to be seen, and my reactions came from a belief that I didn't deserve support, and I certainly didn't know how to receive it. But the more I kept my bum on the seat and the biscuits in my belly, the easier it all felt and the more I was able to let people in.

Walking into any support group meeting is daunting, emotional and bloody terrifying – of course it is. It's a symbolic acknowledgement of 'This is where I am at'. Although in rehab I was immersed in AA, I had never walked into a meeting completely on my own. My first London meeting was in Kentish Town. I was still in rehab – the female-only one in Camden – and I was itching to get to a meeting, as the Camden rehab wasn't based around AA or NA, so I didn't have a daily dose of it. As a result, my motivation and mood had started to decline. I knew I had responded well to AA and I begged the staff to get me to a meeting – something I never thought I would ever beg for in my life.

This would be the first Christmas that I had ever spent away from the family. All the women that I was living with then were struggling with that fact in some way: there were mothers unable to see their children, those without any family, and those like me who would do anything to see their family.

As I was due to be released from captivity in the next couple of weeks, I was finally allowed to go out on my own. This new freedom was a lot to handle: I hadn't been allowed anywhere on my own for a long time (and rightly so). But I was a big girl now, a sober girl, so I filled in my request form and found the closest AA newcomers meeting.

I set out with my permission slip, in my green coat, using a smartphone for the first time in god knows how long, trying to navigate my way from Camden to Kentish Town.

Apart from feeling wary of the dark and mentally holding onto newspaper headlines of London stabbings, I was doing OK. It didn't last. Walking past shops, pubs and special offers on Bailey's I was totally fine with, but then as I went down a residential street, I started to hear something. It was a Christmas carol – not just any carol, but the carol that I had taught my old class, back when I had been working as a teacher. 'The Angel Gabriel.' I tried to ignore it, but it was getting louder and louder and I looked across the road and there it was: a school putting on an outdoor nativity play. I should have just walked straight past it. But I didn't. I crossed the road and watched. I watched the teacher mouthing the words and trying to keep the naughty ones in check. I noticed the younger ones, who are usually cast as some kind of animal, pick their nose. I couldn't laugh or muster a smirk; not even a shepherd with the classic tea towel on their head clutching a Shaun the Sheep teddy could make me smile. Instead I sobbed; my god, I sobbed. My wounds had barely scabbed and my heart was still in pieces. I was so angry with myself – *I* still could have been mouthing the words to kids, but I wasn't. I was just an alcoholic who had lost it all.

I'll never forgot that feeling of hopelessness and loss.

Thankfully I turned up at my meeting in one piece. It was a busy meeting and I had no fight in me to be anything but a crying mess. I went in there without any intention of opening my mouth, but something in me led me to raise my hand, say the words: 'Hiya, I'm Melissa and I'm an alcoholic' and off I went. I shared about the nativity, about being frightened of London, being in rehab and, as you can all imagine, I shared about missing Liverpool. At the end of the meeting, someone came up to me with a little AA book (a daily reflections book, with a different quote to read and reflect on for each day of the year). His name was Ricky. I just remember him telling me in his broad, London geezer accent: 'It's going to be all right, darling. You're in the right place.' He was right. I have been attending that meeting ever since. It's my special place, filled with familiar faces and a real sense of community. Ricky and his wife, Linda, took me under their wing as one of their own; they have opened their home and hearts to me and, throughout the ups and downs of London life, I feel I have the closest thing to family here as I can have. The love I have for them knows no bounds.

Every month, I picked up my 'milestone' medallion, and could never believe that I had another month of sobriety under my belt. Everyone in the room is always genuinely delighted to see you stay sober for another significant period of time. When it gets to twelve months, the medallions are yearly (oh, how I miss the monthly claps). One of the highlights of my recovery was when my mum came to see me get my one year chip; when I picked it up and received my obligatory hug and clap, I went over and gave it to her. She keeps the medallions and, as much as the décor in my Kirkby home has no room for trinkets or sentimental items that aren't grey or white, there's a kitchen cupboard that's filled with photos, cards, drawings and, now, my AA chips.

After a few months, I started to understand the phrase I heard so often: 'People love you until you can love yourself,' and I knew I had to trust in the programme; trust that one day I would be as serene as all of these other recovering alcoholics. I had to do what was suggested and not analyse, intellectualise or pick it apart. I thought AA was just about staying off the sauce; I never really knew what was offered – healing, and a way to live your life. My mate from Clouds, T, explained recovery to me so simply: 'Recovery is about not being a shit cunt.' Don't really know what to say after that, really, other than the drink and the drugs is obviously a part of it, but recovery is about learning how to do things differently – selflessly, honestly, lovingly and respectfully.

AA allowed me to plant my roots, and it opened my world to a host of people who I could call on in my hour of need. But you have to remember that you aren't going to like every person you meet – there're arseholes everywhere, including mutual aid groups. It's in these meetings that I learnt that you don't have to like everyone and likewise not everyone will like you (who knew?). Just because you're sober doesn't mean your values click. In my beloved meeting, I had a few months where it was my responsibility to serve the teas; having a responsibility keeps us accountable, responsible and showing up. I shared this commitment with a long-running AA member, and each week we would chat about what had been going on for us (it's not just the actual meeting where you find support, it's the conversations you strike up before and after). One Wednesday, I must have said the classic Melissa spiel of, 'I don't think they like me,' to which she replied, 'Well, you can't be everyone's cup of tea otherwise you would be a mug.' I held on to this pearl and when it came to making friends, I didn't have to be liked by every person I met. I was friends with people who I connected with.

You will probably have heard the word 'sponsor' before, so I just want to explain a bit about that. Very lightly. Nothing in the twelve-steps meetings is forced upon you; there is no right or wrong, any advice is a suggestion and it is up to you whether you want to take on board that suggestion or put it to one side. I always thought I didn't want a sponsor; that I didn't want to have to be responsible or answer to someone. I had been a child for twenty-nine years, so there was no way I wanted another adult in my life to tell me how to live. Well, that's not what a sponsor is. A sponsor is someone who takes you 'through the work', someone who you confide in and share the things that you struggle even to tell your best gal. A sponsor is a constant and consistent fixture in your recovering life to whom you can unravel your fears and thoughts that are causing you pain. It's a beautiful thing, and its bloody free! *Result*. But finding a sponsor is just as awkward as asking someone out on a date – basically, you find someone whose recovery you respect and whose experience resonates with you and you ask them.

My sponsor is an incredible woman called Jo (I seem to collect Jo's). We met at a meeting and I heard her share about being locked in. As soon as I heard that, I was locked into her! There is never a time I meet her when I don't think, 'Wow, I wish I was that content.' Jo has known me from a girl in a green coat right though to a girl in the green room of BBC Breakfast, and has supported me through the good stuff and the bad stuff. There's no arse-kissing involved in sponsoring; if you speak to any alcoholic with a 'sponny' they will probably tell you that their sponsor has the uncanny ability of making you look at your own behaviour … much to our annoyance.

I think I had better wrap up talking about this because I promise I am not trying to sell AA – it's not the only sober community out there and, you know what, it's not for everyone. AA is where I was able to secure people in my life who help me in sobriety, but I also have friends who are sober and love life without the need for AA.

So what and where are these other sober communities?

There are so many online communities on Instagram. Now, I may not be social media's number-one fan, based on my previous experience of pretending life is perfect, but in its purest form it is a networking platform. There are so many online campaigns and accounts that unite sober people, and it is a beautiful thing. I have a gorgeous girl in my life called Vickie, a real beacon of positivity and one of those gals that empower you with their love of life. We started speaking after she heard *Hooked* and we clicked instantly. She found sober allies on Instagram and credits that online community with her happiness and sobriety.

Instagram has been the helping hand I needed to get out of my addiction rabbit hole. I had known for a long time that I needed to make changes to my relationship with alcohol, or rather, how it controlled me. The connections I have made through Instagram have hand on heart turned my life around. I was in a bad place and my actions due to alcohol were just getting worse. Coming across the Hooked *podcast and linking up with Melissa and Jade was really the step I needed to then find this Instagram community. I have made it now through ten months of recovery with willpower and my support network on Insta. What I love is that what we share with each other is not only the good, 'pink clouds' phase of recovery; it is the good, the bad and the ugly. The positivity that comes from being in recovery and knowing that you have been in places where you couldn't even see the light let alone aim for one at the end of the tunnel makes for a remarkable network of support. We share the days where you want a drink or drugs, where your mind is tricking you to say that just one is OK, and come together to encourage each other to push past those feelings and make it through just one more day. The ease of accessing support by messaging a group or a friend can change your outlook on the day and keep that sober streak going. The connections I have made – and I know I am not alone in saying – have changed my life.*

On Twitter there is always a strong community with the hashtag 'Recovery Posse' (#RecoveryPosse). Here, people from all over the world connect and share their triumphs and their struggles, and members of that community will always offer support and words of encouragement. The Recovery Posse lot always share those recovery life hacks, those one-liners and musings that get you thinking. It is a powerful and truly inspiring network of people; some remain anonymous and some are visible with their recovery. I have seen so many people tweet who aren't feeling themselves and who are struggling, and very quickly members of #RecoveryPosse will offer their experiences and good wishes – it's a truly beautiful thing.

In a similar fashion, there is a online community called Club Soda; again, an online community that provides a network of support for people getting sober. Professor Julia (from chapter one) highlighted the importance of these online groups, as they are a great tool for early intervention and for people to access support super early. I had the privilege of speaking to the co-founder of Club Soda – Laura Willoughby – for an episode of *Hooked*. As she explained, it's important for people to have alternatives to traditional methods (AA) and I couldn't agree more. The more pathways there are the more accessible recovery is, and one way is not superior to the other. Other non-AA-style support groups include SMART recovery (a CBT-style approach to problematic use), groups run by charities, sober meet-ups … The fundamentals and principles may vary, but one thing that all of these have in common is that element of peer support, a sense of belonging; that feeling of togetherness. Take Michael's word for it:

> *If we rely on ourselves alone, things become skewed and blinkered. A support network provides us with a different perspective. It is a vital component of recovery.*
>
> **Michael Rawlinson**

There'll be a fair few of you who'll be wondering how your friends will receive your decision to knock the booze on the head. (My gaggle of support isn't just made up of people who are divorced from the sauce and the devil's dandruff. I have my friends who were around with drinking Melissa, poor bastards.) Maybe you'll be wondering if they will still want to be your friend any more. Are you worrying that they will think you are boring now? Or maybe you are thinking that everything will be awkward now; that you may no longer be the friends you once were. These are all valid worries, and I had them all.

Making the transition from being the friend who had no limits with alcohol to being the friend who now limits their caffeine intake isn't as easy as it sounds. I think when we say ta-ta to the booze there is a grieving process, a bit of an identity crisis. Who are we without it? I always thought that it was alcohol that made me 'fun' – but that's codswallop. If anything, I think my mates much, much, *much* preferred me when I wasn't sloshed.

One day, post-rehab, I found myself on Primrose Hill. I stood at the top of the hill, and took a moment to look out at the skyline and read the information board (as a history nerd, I never miss an information board). I couldn't believe where I was and what I'd been able to do. 'I did it.' I had got sober. I knew I wasn't cured and wasn't in the best shape mentally, but I had completed rehab and was committed to recovery. This was huge. But I had no one with me to share this moment with. I took a leap of faith, pulled out my phone and clicked on Cat (my former Sambuca Samaritan). I didn't know if she would answer or what I could even say; I hadn't spoken to this girl for about eight months and even when she had tried to find out what was going on, via my sister, my family had closed ranks.

She answered her phone and I began to tell her that I had been to rehab. I then told her that I was living in my own flat in London. She was kind, she was gentle, and it was good to talk to her and get it all off my chest. Cat encouraged me to connect with our mate, Jonathan, as he also now lived in London (and is probably one of the most driven and successful Kirkby ex-pats I know). Cat and Jonathan had 'adopted' me in 2008 – when others had shunned me, they had taken me under their wing. We called ourselves Atomic Kitten and my wild ways were always the butt of the jokes.

After the call ended with Cat, I was on cloud nine. I knew there was a long way to go to rebuild trust but it was a start. Little did I know that the post-chat feelings weren't mutual – Cat thought I was pissed again. She rang Jonathan and said, 'Melissa has just rung me, she's saying Amy Winehouse sent her to rehab, she must be on something, we'd better get in touch with Becca.' I can't begin to tell you the amount of laughter this brings. I suppose to Cat, my tale of rehab must have sounded like a complete fabrication and also, she was probably so used to me egging the pudding and bending the truth that she had no reason to believe me.

I took on board Cat's suggestion of contacting Jonathan. (This is what I did now: I took on suggestions.) We met for coffee on Brick Lane, we sat down and you'll be pleased to know I held back the tears. I began by first of all apologising for my absence and went on to explain that I was an alcoholic and that I was now in recovery. You know what he said? 'I am proud of you.' He then likened my confession to his own coming-out story. I suppose it kind of was: the inklings and suspicions people had are validated and put to bed; there's no more secret life and, really, it's quite brave to finally say the word out loud. Atomic Kitten is the best it's ever been; like most nineties girl bands we are on a triumphant reunion tour.

Once you have told your friends you are quitting the drink or are in recovery, there's a period of uncertainty. Friends generally don't really know how much they are allowed to ask and whether or not they are allowed to drink around us; they may not even know what recovery is. The overthinking is on both parts: we, the drinker, could find ourselves upset that people don't seem interested, when actually our friend might be thinking it's better not to drag up the past and upset us. On the flip side, we, the drinker, may not want to talk about our drinking and the journey from hell and back, while our friend may have questions or want to know more about recovery. I could actually feel this walking-on-pins hesitancy in my relationship with Cat and Jonathan until one night, when I was invited for me tea (dinner) at Jonathan and his boyfriend Scott's. I'd never met Scott before, and I was worried about what he thought of Jonathan bringing an alcoholic into the house. (Turns out he was as stunning as his pictures and as lovely as Jonathan had made him out to be.) We ate our food and no one was really talking about what we all wanted to talk about – huge-elephant-in-the-room time again. It was time for dessert. Ever the host, Jonathan opened the fridge and in a very calm but serious tone said, 'Now, I am not blaming anyone, or naming any names, but *this* was full before.' He only pulled out a bloody empty bottle of vodka! For a split second I thought I had drunk it. Then poor Scott screamed, 'I told you not to do this, Jonathan, it's not funny!' I burst out laughing and, just like that, the situation was diffused, and the status quo restored. As gut-wrenching as our drinking days are, when a bit of time passes, there comes a stage when you have to laugh. Jokes like this and being comfortable enough to look back at yourself and laugh aren't about disregarding or glamorising alcoholism or addiction; they come from a place of acceptance and knowing that you are so far removed from that former self.

When it comes to reconnecting and having those friendships from before recovery, there is usually work to be done; well, there was for me, anyway. I had to take responsibility for my actions and hear them out – without interrupting or justifying. My actions had consequences and I had to hear how my behaviour had made them feel. The old me would have swept it under the rug, thrown a meme into the group chat and avoided heavy conversations. But if I wanted meaningful friendships in my life, I couldn't do that any more. It might be hard to hear and you may be surprised by what you are told, but that uncomfortable honesty makes room for trust and for a future.

When we have a support system in place, it's harder for us to hibernate from the world. I wouldn't be here without my support network, it really is essential. Do I have my difficulties? Yes. Iso-fucking-lation. Isolation is a huge issue for me even to this day. I don't know whether that comes from so much time spent alone in my active addiction, whether it's because I am used to being self-reliant, or whether it's because I've realised I'm actually quite anti-social. When I say I can go for days without leaving the house or speaking to someone and not even notice, I mean it. One of the hardest things I have found is staying connected: someone could text me, and in my head I have replied. Or maybe I say to myself, 'I should ring Jo – nah, I'll do it later, I know what she will say, anyway.'

I know I have some of the most supportive, empowering, loving and inspiring people at the end of a phone, both in recovery and out of recovery, but do I find it easy to stay in the loop? Absolutely not. Some weeks are easier than others and sometimes I have to force myself to pick up the phone (even if, mid-ring, I am hoping they don't pick up). But the beauty of having people in your life who know how you operate is that they know when you're isolating and they challenge you on it.

Peer support has allowed me to not only have friends, but to be a better friend to others.

Takeaways

- **Peer support helps you connect with others who have been there and done it**
- **Identifying with like-minded people helps us feel less alone**
- **Being there for others is just as therapeutic as receiving support**
- **There are all kinds of different sober support groups – AA isn't the only one**
- **Going from drinking to sober with your old friends can feel daunting – but if they understand, they will support you**
- **Don't isolate – human connection is often the treatment for addiction.**

Chapter 7

*The firsts are awkward as f*ck*

When you get a bit of a time under your belt and you are feeling confident, there are certain events in life you will go through, quite possibly for the first time, sober. Nights out, Christmas, holidays, dates and sex – if the thought of having to experience any of the aforementioned sober capsizes your stomach and puts the fear of god in you, then you're in the right place and you're in good company. I never once thought that I would have the ability and desire to do any of that stuff sober. What would be the point and why would we even bother?

Just because the contents of our glasses don't look or smell the same doesn't mean that we can't do these things.

At the same time, unfortunately, being a non-boozer in a boozy world means we just have to accept that we are going to be in situations where alcohol is. If we were to avoid alcohol for the rest of our lives, we would never leave the house, read a newspaper or watch TV. We have our boundaries. Sobriety for me is about freedom. I am free to go wherever I like and drink my Diet Coke without having to hide away. Come on, I cut myself off from the world when I was drinking, I don't want to be cut off from the world when I am sober … but feeling comfortable in drinking spaces, dealing with intimate moments without Dutch courage, or juggling family politics for an extended period of time without a blowout all takes some getting used to. So, for this chapter, I want to do things a little differently. I have chosen the most pertinent of 'firsts' and with the help of a few recovery friends, we will share with you the experience, where we went wrong, and how we manage the same experiences today.

Nights out

I didn't think sober people would be 'allowed' on nights out, never mind go to gigs, festivals and raves. I also thought that it would be a miserable time, watching people drinking and enjoying themselves, while making my soft drink last. Before I even contemplated a night out, I found myself a wee bit resentful and ultimately jealous of people who were drinking and loving life. Genuinely, I didn't want to drink: I was taught in rehab and in AA that, actually, I have an allergy to alcohol. What it does to me isn't what it does to most, so I am best not putting it in my system. Yes, I have accepted this allergy and know where one would lead me – as the NA saying goes, 'one is too many and one thousand is never enough' – but I would be lying to you if I didn't say to myself in those early days, 'You had to take it too far, didn't you? You ruined it for yourself.'

I waited about six months before I went on my first night out. That may sound extreme to you but bear in mind that for three of those months I was in treatment. Waiting a period of time isn't a bad thing. I wanted to be confident in my sobriety so that I could stand in a sticky-floored bar without hitting the 'Fuck-it' button. For some people this might be a fear-based approach; Jade, for instance, well, that girl used nights out to prove to herself and to others that she could be in a bar. She was testing her resilience. What can I say? Being risk averse is my jam.

By March 2018, I wanted to get back out there, I wanted a night on the tiles. I panicked at first, as I was wondering whether this desire to have a night out was a warning bell. No, it wasn't: I was a twenty-nine-year-old female with good rhythm and good hair and I wanted a good time sober.

Mimi and I decided to head to a club – I was grateful to pop the sober-night-out cherry with someone who was in recovery. Before we went in, we made a pact – if either of us felt like it was getting too much, we had to be honest and we would leave. Whether you are on nights out with boozers or not, it's always good to be with an ally who will support you (remember that).

What was most odd to me was that, out of the whole night, the most triggering part of it was the getting ready to go out. I didn't know what to do with myself: I had all the nervous energy and anticipation for the night out, without the glass of ale to calm the nerves and loosen me up. The worst decision I made that night was attempting to put on dance tracks that used to get me pumped: Kylie Minogue's 'Get Outta My Way' sent my body to a different era, but (thankfully) my mind was in the recovery game. I was out of sorts. My body was gearing up for a moment, a feeling that it was never going to get: shit-faced. I changed tactic and coloured my cheekbones to the soundtrack of *The Crown* and a slab of Dairy Milk. It did the trick (it still does).

We arrived at a club in Shoreditch: £22 entry. I couldn't believe it! Twenty-two bullets to listen to music way past my bedtime – what a fucking cheek! You see, since getting sober, I have more respect for money. One day I sat down and worked out how much money I had spent across the average year as an alcoholic – that cost alone would keep anyone sober. (I'd just like to point out, I am not a tight-fisted person. In Liverpool we call such people 'mingebags' and being a 'mingebag' is almost as bad as being a grass … and no one wants that.) I grudgingly paid the admission fee and here it was. A momentous occasion. This was my moment to finally have my bag searched and not have to sweat about if they spotted a baggy or took the time to notice a bottle in my trousers. I proudly opened my Primark bag (times were hard), and let them rummage away. It felt great.

We went to the bar, and I asked for two lime and sodas. The look on the girl's face was a picture. I bet she thought we had our own handbag vodka. So off we trotted to the dance floor, a sea of swaying people looking absolutely … awful. Everything was in HD and I didn't like it. At the risk of sounding like a cliché: was this how I used to look? Is this what goes on in clubs? I finally knew what I looked like on a night out: the vacant eyes, the dilated pupils, the out-of-time dancing, the swinging jaw … and then I spotted this one girl. She was emptying the contents of her bag onto the floor, frantically searching for something; she had a dopey look in her eye and was in a world of her own. She was me. My paranoia always had me emptying my bag out onto the floor, looking for keys, lighter, my Mac lipliner, my money and, if it was 4 a.m., I'd be looking for my sanity too. But I wasn't that girl any more. I knew exactly where my items were, I was in control of my decisions, I didn't look like any of these people … and it felt good. Dare I say, I felt powerful.

It was a healthy smugness: I didn't feel jealous in the slightest, as I knew that I was going to wake up without regret or with my head down the toilet.

There's also something quite liberating in dancing sober. I know a lot of people hate it. I am not those people. Dancing sober taught me I didn't need a drink to enjoy music, that it wasn't the drink that turned me into total tit when ABBA comes on – I am just a tit. Your ability to cut shapes without chemicals can be rather perplexing for some people, especially if you are out with people who are drinking. Prepare yourself for people saying: 'I just don't know how you do it. I think it's amazing.' As annoying as your sobriety being made into a 'thing' may feel … own it. Be proud that you can do what some people couldn't or wouldn't dare to try: letting loose sober.

One of my biggest fears about nights out was having to tell people I didn't drink. The first few nights out, I used to tie myself in knots about this, resulting in all sorts of overshares. I would end up justifying my decision not to drink and recalling parts of my rock bottom in the middle of a bar, knowing full well that I was never going to see this person again. It would make me feel 'less than' and embarrassed, and the rest of the evening would be spent wondering what they thought of me. But here's the thing. *We don't have to explain our decision to anyone.* So now if people ask why, I shut that shit down with a, 'I just don't drink.' If that's not enough for someone and they continue to probe, I throw it back on them and get quite sassy: 'Don't be worrying about me, I don't need a drink for a good time. Enjoy your drink and have a ball – I am.' This line of defence seems to do the trick. Remember: 'My drink, my choice.' And if someone is being a dick and just won't let it go? Walk away.

I know for some people these types of interactions are not as easy as I make it sound. For many people, buying a drink that looks like an alcoholic drink does the trick. On an episode of *Hooked*, Michael shared a tactic that involves white lies. I know what you're thinking – surely Michael wouldn't promote dishonesty! But think about it, if we aren't ready to say why we aren't drinking, telling a white lie of being on medication can be an effective strategy, one that requires little to no thought or resistance. Lots of people have shared with me their hacks. I got a lovely message on Instagram once from a lady who orders soda water with fruit, and asks for it in one of those gin glasses that look like you could raise a goldfish in it. For her, that helps her keeps the awkwardness at bay. In fact, there are many non-alcoholic beverages that do look and are served similarly to alcoholic beverages, and rightly so. We are a growing bunch and we deserve a seat at the bar. Normalising non-alcoholic drinking in bars is a movement that's on the up. I don't really bother with mocktails or alcohol-free wines etc.; it's less that I might be tempted by the taste and more that I don't want anything related to alcohol – including alternatives to alcohol – in my life. As always, it's very much an each-to-their-own situation, but I am here for the alcohol-free uprising. It's just not for me (I like my soda cup emoji and that's OK).

Actually, thinking about it now, I have had a moment when I simulated an alcoholic beverage. I was on a night out with my friend Sarah and a few other Glastonbury folk. I took myself to the toilet and on my return there was a tray of shots filled with what looked like Sambuca. I was totally fine with it but then they passed me one. I looked at it in horror and then Sarah demanded I smell the shot. It was water. They didn't want me to feel left out (god bless them), especially knowing that shots of Sambuca were once my thing, so had asked the barman to polish up a shot glass and fill it with the finest tap water. I could have cried over their thoughtfulness.

Knowing my limits has never been something I did well – I wouldn't be writing this chapter on my second pack of custard creams if I did. But when it comes to knowing limits on sober nights out, I am ruthless. There's always a bit of a temptation to stick around until the end of your nights with your mates; you know, so you don't miss out on anything. But believe me, the only thing you're missing out on is a decent night's kip. At the beginning, I did go on a few nights out and thought the polite and proper thing to do was to stick around. But who was that 'polite' to? Certainly not my recovery. I'm perfectly all right being around drinking mates for the first few hours, before the 'turn' … There's always that pivotal moment on nights out when it goes from fun to sloppy and, being sober, I am completely in tune to this turn: I have a highly sensitive barometer that knows exactly when the atmosphere changes. So if I hear the same thing twice or I am struggling to grasp the thread of a story, it's time for me to go. After all, if someone doesn't remember that they have told you that story already, then surely they won't remember what time you decided to go home? My rule of thumb is usually 12 a.m.; there's nothing for me to gain from a night out after midnight. I never thought going home early would be something I enjoyed – I was always the gal who didn't want the night to end. But my values have changed and my understanding of fun has certainly changed – for the better. I don't think there has been one night out when I left and regretted it.

As important as it is to not be afraid of nights out and to enjoy yourself, sometimes there can be a danger of being around 'it' a bit too much. There's a saying in recovery: 'If you stand in a hairdresser's long enough, you're going to get a haircut.' So when it comes to nights out and being around the booze, I have to make sure that I am still keeping up with the recovery stuff: my meetings, and connecting with recovery people, to avoid the old 'Look, I am totally fine. I can have one – no one will mind.' It's important to check in on yourself after your nights out: has it brought anything up for me? Do I feel sad? Has it made me miss a drink? I know this sounds a bit extreme but sometimes I experience what I like to call a 'fun-down' – the sober version of a come-down. After a big night out of sober fun, I can sometimes feel low and a bit shit and maybe I want to chase that buzz again. So what I do now is plan some non-drinking-atmosphere-related fun instead – usually something food-based.

Christmas

How does that song go again? 'Christmas time, mistletoe and wine.' Nice one, Cliff, thanks for that. Just what I want to hear blasting all over the shop floor every fifteen minutes … If there was ever a time of year where you do nothing but push your body towards gout, it's Christmas. Two weeks of mindless eating and drinking your way through forced family togetherness. A time when Christmas 'spirit' means actual 'spirits' and there is no social etiquette around what time of day you get into the festivities (surely this is what Jesus would want?). This time of year can be an absolute nightmare for the recovery lot, and therefore extra precautions are required.

I'm a bit of a self-confessed Grinch, to be honest; not because I can't have a tipple, but just because I always feel like a fraud. Every year there are so many people jumping up and down and shrieking how much they just love Christmas, and I'm just feeling like there is something wrong with me for not resembling Will Ferrell's character

Buddy in the film *Elf.* The best thing about Christmas for me is the pigs in blankets, hands down. I love a hot pig in blanket and I even love eating the leftover ones on the days thereafter (there hasn't been a Christmas when I haven't said the words, 'Mum, are these still OK to eat?'). I'm probably being a bit harsh here, as I do enjoy seeing my family, and I especially love seeing my nephew open his presents. But it also brings up a lot of shit. It's as if the Ghost of Christmas Past turns up with a whole load of bad memories, and the Ghost of Christmas Future doesn't help much, either. I'm not alone in feeling emotional at this time of year, I know – for people who have lost loved ones, Christmas can feel especially painful. For people who are unable to see their family, Christmas can feel a lonely time of year. Even the pressure of everything having to be right because it's Christmas and it must be special can get the better of people. Whether you're drinking to cope or drinking for fun during this time of year, the amount consumed is gastronomical – fact. With all this booze around, it can feel quite isolating, particularly the first Christmas sober.

From the age of seventeen through to twenty-six, it's safe to say I ruined every Christmas Day with a hangover. Christmas Eve was hands down my favourite night of the year. In Kirkby, there is a pub crawl called the 'Kirkby Mile': a series of five pubs in one straight line. Oh, it was glorious. You would start out in the Carter's Arms – it was vital you got there early for a seat. You'd be turned out in your best winter woollies and the juke box would play all your Christmas classics. There'd be singing on the tables and the who's who of Kirkby would be out in force. You'd then make your way down the road, hitting each pub in turn.

Not everyone committed to the full mile experience: some people actually respected their mother's efforts of preparing Christmas dinner. Not me. I would return home pretending to be less drunk and wired than I was, and hope to god that I wasn't told off the next day. It was a bit of a tradition, which is quite sad: I had a tradition of being fucked on Christmas Day. And, of course, after Christmas Eve, there is your Boxing Night, but then after that there is the dreaded Christmas Gooch. (For those of you who don't know, a gooch is that weird bit of anatomy between a man's privates and back passage – I am so sorry. No one really knows what the gooch is for, or what it even is, it's just that really awkward nothingness that no one knows what do with.) That to me is what the 27th to the 31st of December is: five days of not knowing what day it is, what date it is – what you are to do with it. For me, it meant five days of filling your time with random pub drinking.

With all of that out of the picture now, how was it ever going to be possible to navigate Christmas, the Christmas Gooch and New Year? Could I get through the period relatively happy and remain sober?

My first sober Christmas back home was a weird one. I still didn't feel quite right being seen in the home town, and there was still that whole tiptoeing behaviour around me, regarding my alcoholism and my mental health. You'll know yourself if you've ever had a bad time – your extended family will go into overdrive with the compliments: 'You look *so* well, it's the best I've seen you.' (To me, whenever I hear the phrase 'You look well' I hear 'You look fat.' I probably need to work on that.) But I suppose it's better to be called 'well' and avoid having to go into the ins and outs.

My mum is the host of all hosts: she usually has twenty-plus guests. We don't live in a sprawling estate with a banqueting hall, but we do have a conservatory and folding tables. How that woman keeps all the food piping hot is beyond me. The attention to detail is ridiculous: each year we are served our dinner on my nan's Johnson Brothers dinner set – Eternal Beau.

I kind of like the chaos at Christmas: having a busy house on Christmas Day keeps me distracted. The supermarket trip is a nightmare. It's usually a 5 a.m. job. I have only done it once and I will never do it again, and this first Christmas back sober was no exception. I had the perfect get-out-of-jail-free card. Nothing to do with recovery or Crohn's – Ange knew there was no way she would wake me up as my trusty mirtazapine (an antidepressant) is a sedative. Winner winner, Christmas dinner. When she got back I spotted all the usual suspects: profiteroles, stuffing, half of a small abattoir, tubes and tubes of Pringles, mince pies ... but no booze.

Usually we keep the booze in the garage: cases of beer and a couple of bottles of Asti, white and rosé wine. But this year there were none. Once more I had ruined Christmas, not for me or for my mum, but for everyone else.

I can understand my mum's decision not to buy any alcohol; she had watched her daughter go through hell and back, and didn't think it was right to serve it or even want to keep it in her house any longer. But for me, this decision didn't give off the right message. It kind of made me feel like we were now like those ultra-prohibitionists, when actually I was perfectly all right being around it.

For me, Christmas is probably the only time of year when I feel somewhat excluded. Sure I will go on the odd night out, and it's not that I can't go on every night out: it's that I don't want to. So it was time to look once more at that calendar and rebrand Christmas so that I wouldn't feel 'left out' and I wouldn't get FOMO. My suggestion:

don't just wait for your mates to suggest something that is less booze-heavy (as you could be waiting for a long time): organise something yourself. Choose something that makes you happy, reclaim your Christmas. For instance, we have an Atomic Kitten Christmas event: we book a restaurant, walk around Christmas markets or even go to the cinema to watch a Christmas classic. I also book in gorgeous, crisp, morning walks with my friend Sam: we'll have some type of American breakfast and hit Crosby beach. I actually make an effort to do something nice with my mum, our Becca and my nephew too. For so many years Christmas wasn't about them, it was always about my nights out. And although the novelty might wear off before we even get out of the car, making memories with my nephew is worth more than any stumble down the Kirkby Mile.

You may adore your family or you may have a strained relationship with them – for a lot of us, spending a concentrated amount of time with our family and out of our routine can feel a bit overwhelming. My first Christmas in L32 (Kirkby's postcode) at points felt stifling. I would find myself feeling irritable and just wanting to take a break, but rather than communicate this and get my needs met, I opted to persevere and then, as always, my feelings would simmer and bubble over like an unwatched saucepan. I don't do that any more. If I need to take a time out, I take the time out. I don't storm off or make it into a bigger issue than it needs to be: I let the family know that I need a minute and I head out in the car or take myself off to my room and unwind. At first I found it really difficult to admit that I needed a time out; I felt like I was causing worry or worried that I was letting Christmas down. I wasn't. Whatever time of year it is, your head comes first and whatever you gotta do to keep the head well … well, bloody do it.

For me the most important festive tool is to stay connected. There is a temptation to forget everything and just get lost in tinsel and Quality Street, to put our daily routines and mental health maintenance to one side. Unfortunately, there are no holidays from sobriety or recovery, and as happy and joyous as I may be feeling, I won't cut off from the likes of J or Ricky or Mimi or Jade. I can't choose a *Gavin and Stacey* Christmas special over an AA meeting – I have to keep connected so I can communicate my emotions and talk about what's pissing me off, and I keep connected so that I can support my mates if they are struggling.

Dating

Female, thirties, single – and sober. Is there anything more tragic? More sad 'on paper'? In a time where we base compatibility on what people appear to be 'on paper', how the hell do I stand a chance? I am an alcoholic, with Crohn's disease and a matching ileostomy bag. I have anxiety and depression, and my reputation in my hometown isn't great due to many a scandal. In the not-so-distant past, I was a very wholesome-looking primary school teacher (who fell from grace) and I have been institutionalised for my drinking. I mean, if I was a dog, many an owner would have put me down as an act of love; a mercy killing to prevent a life of sickness and distress. But although all of the above is my truth, I am the happiest I have ever been.

Trying to convey my truth as well as getting a 'swipe left' is like walking on a tightrope, however. How do you even go on a date without a drink? Added to this, I had never really done the whole 'dating' thing before. My previous relationships hadn't required online apps. You necked (snogged) someone drunk, kept doing it over a few nights out and then, boom, you've got a fella. Recovery revealed that I would always lose myself in them, and then I'd end up ruining it to escape the situation.

Once I was sober, it was recommended to me to wait for a year before dating. I had never had a relationship with myself, I didn't know who I was or how to love myself. I had just came out of a thirteen-year relationship with alcohol, a relationship in which I abused myself. I had no understanding of treating myself kindly or lovingly. My understanding of a healthy relationship and even love was pretty warped, so it was important that I learnt how I was in relationships and addressed my repeated patterns of behaviour (mainly co-dependency, which I will touch on in another chapter). So, before I let someone into my heart, I had to be in love with me (cheesy, I know). If I were to have dated just a couple of months out of rehab, it would have been a good distraction – a way for me to avoid sitting with myself. I didn't want to risk recovery so I took on board that advice, and waited.

Alcoholics are sensitive beings, ones who have been through a lot, and dating taps into the big hitters: rejection, self-esteem, feelings of inadequacy. But after a year and a half of building a much-needed relationship with myself, I thought, 'It's time. You got this, hun.' What man wouldn't want a woman who knew herself, had overcome adversity, was able to laugh at her own misfortune and have an absolute hoot without making a show of herself or calling someone the c word? Turns out, quite a few. Putting yourself out on the market having been through some real, life-shaping mental health and addiction issues is daunting. I spoke with my friend Rob after I had a few awful dates, and he gave me great advice: 'Just be true to you and remember your recovery is a gift.' He has had his fair share of dating disasters but insists that dating is a good teacher, and that each blunder reveals what you need to work on.

At first, my online profile didn't state I was in recovery; although I am proud of my recovery, I just wasn't willing to put it *way* out there, like, 'Here you go, and would you like ice and a slice with that honesty?' I feared judgement. I was at a point in my recovery, in life, where I didn't want it to define me (pre-podcast, obviously). Like with any label, whether it be positive or negative, you are at risk of being synonymous with everything that comes with it, depending on an individual's interpretation of the label in question. In my case, Joe from Surrey could believe that an addict is unhinged, weak and a liar, while Mike from the Midlands may know a fellow who knows a fellow who has been off the sauce for a while and is a rather lovely bloke. So you see, letting *the* cat out of the bag so early on felt like too much of a risk for me. I mean, if I hadn't had the privilege of an awkward first encounter, how would I be able to determine whether this match on Hinge was a cat person or not?

The swiping and laborious small talk were underway; my best pics, no Snapchat filters, I let my sense of humour and choice of TV shows do the talking. I thought it was a winning combination at first, and, dare I say, rather brave, considering that for a long time I kept my love of Lucy Worsley just as much a dirty secret as my penchant for half a Glen's.

With the vetting procedure complete, there it was: 'Do you want to go for a drink?' Panic, sheer panic, my hands cold, trembling; ironically, the same shaking, perspiring hands one had during alcohol withdrawal. What the hell do I say? The first time this question came up, I needed guidance, advice. Should I say yes to a drink and then when at the watering hole order a Diet Coke? Or did

I just announce it there and then: 'I don't drink'? If I did the latter, would I be making it a 'thing'? I have tested out multiple methods. Let's break this down.

Method: Say yes to the drink and then just order a Diet Coke
Awkwardness: Solid 9/10
Well received?: 1/10
Follow-up date: No
Self-esteem post-date: 3/10

For the purpose of anonymity I am going to call this person The Kiwi.

In the words of Lana Del Rey, 'Done my hair up real big, beauty queen style, high heels on, I'm feeling alive.' The prerequisite chat was on form, we had things in common – David Brent and Malcom Tucker quotes were a-blazing – what could go wrong?

I went to the date, I sat down, he was a good-looking chap and very chatty, and in no way was he a height-fish (someone who says they're 6' and are clearly 5'9"). The waiter arrived: 'What would you like to drink?' The Kiwi confidently suggested that we share a Merlot. To which I said, 'I don't drink, I'll have a Diet Coke.' His face did the exact same perplexed contortion I pulled when someone once told me that they were a flat-earth believer. It occurred to me: 'Maybe he feels bad for suggesting that we go for a drink if I don't drink?' I began to feel guilt for approximately 45 seconds, and it was on the tip of my tongue to apologise until he came out with: 'It's not like you're a fucking recovering alcoholic, is it?' (Please insert a New Zealand accent for comedic purposes.)

Flirtily, I replied, 'How do you know I'm not?' accompanied by a cheeky, sexy eye glance and a giggle. (Apologies, I feel like I have taken females back fifty years typing that.) He continued: 'Urgh, I lived with a secret alcoholic. It was fucking horrendous – thought he was missing, but he was locked in his room for days, unconscious. We threw him out.'

At this point my back was well and truly up, but to counteract the ignorance I simply said: 'That poor lad, I hope he got the help he needed. How sad.' I thought my approach might bring out some compassion in him. It didn't. Strike 1 and 2. I wish I had ended the date there and then, but I didn't.

For reasons unknown, the conversation moved on to Brexit. Jesus wept. Fair play to him, he was interested to know my thoughts, but brace yourself … 'I know you northerners think Margaret Thatcher is a *c word*, but she's a personal hero of mine.' I didn't know what to say, how to act or what he wanted from me. I just knew that the date was over.

The bill was paid. I purposely told him that I was going in a different direction just to avoid any more torture.

That was fifty-five minutes that I will never get back, fifty-five minutes of me sitting with a Primark £8 label hanging out and not being one bit fazed.

> **Method: Say you don't drink but still agree to
> go to a bar.**
> **Awkwardness: 6/10**
> **Well received?: 4/10**
> **Follow-up date: No**
> **Self-esteem post-date: 6/10**

Boy, oh boy. Where do I begin? This lad – let's call him Millwall FC Mike – I felt more comfortable with – weirdly because he said he liked a bet. Could it be someone who had a vice just like me? What was wrong with me? I was attracted to someone because they admitted to a rather unhealthy habit. Maybe it was because it made me feel less like a fuck-up, or maybe it was because my dad loved a bet and in some weird, Oedipal way I wanted a sense of familiarity. Whatever it was, whether it was perverse, thrill-seeking or even a rescuing mission, it was certainly not a 'good shout'.

I turned up to the date; again, too overdressed: the northern genes are strong and I disregarded the Shoreditch minimalist memo. The awkward hellos were fine, and he was pretty good-looking too, but I quickly realised this kid was absolutely sloshed. I knew he had come straight from watching 'the match'. I was down for 'the match', I was 'here' for 'the match'; it reminded me of home. A match-goer was a-OK with me; a pissed one, not so much.

I had to quickly check my wants and my needs: I had told him via text that, even though I didn't drink, I was fine with people drinking around me – so why was I so bothered that this lad was tanked? It would be arrogant of me to believe he needed the Dutch courage more than I did; he was a seasoned pro at this, for sure. I don't think he had ever been sober and sat with someone so drunk before, and didn't realise how annoying it is to be sober and sat with someone sloshed. Or he did know how annoying it was; he just didn't give a shit. You have to applaud his actions really, to be so confident in your ways and behaviour that you don't slow your drinking down for anyone, not even a girl who doesn't drink and who spent forty-five minutes painting her face for your date.

Again, I don't quite know why I didn't cut the date short: I think I put his history-documentary chat and funny quips above his inebriated state. But before long I was surrounded by overpriced, half-drunk Diet Cokes (I realised that I somehow found myself drinking in rounds). No one can drink six Diet Cokes. No one. What was even more annoying was that I paid for three gin and tonics! Pfffft.

What I have realised is that often what people say and what they mean are different things. The first time this lad said, 'I think it's cool you don't drink,' I was happy; by the sixth, seventh and eighth time, it was pretty clear he wasn't.

**Method: Say you don't drink and do something
non-drink related**
Awkwardness: 3/10
Well received?: 5/10
Follow-up date: No
Self-esteem post-date: 8/10

In light of my previous experiences and somewhat in embarrassment at my recovery status, before this date I took a little break from the cut-throat London dating scene.

With my BBC experience under my belt, I had more things to talk about, to feel proud of. I thought to myself, 'I have turned this lemon that is alcoholism into a virgin margarita. Surely a bloke will be impressed by my efforts to help reduce the stigma and shame of addiction by bringing it to the masses?'

As always, discretion is key, so I would like to call this chap The Flapper. I don't mean a 1920s-jazz-scene darling; what I mean by 'flapper' is someone who absolutely flaps it, falls to bits, doesn't know what to say, nervousness ... basically, me. I was on a date with my male counterpart. Never did the phrase 'two wrongs don't make a right' make such sense.

I thought we were suitably matched, if the weird prelude to the date was anything to go by: similar sense of humour, similar outbursts of honesty and similar apologetic tendencies – apologies for the delay, etc. Like I said, I was more confident within myself and I was actually rather looking forward to this date. We agreed to go to a museum (tick). Although there was no sexual chemistry involved, the chat was great. We spoke about all sorts and because there was no ale in sight, there was no real reason for it to be an issue. When you are in a venue that isn't booze-related, your choice of drink doesn't really matter. It would be weird to walk around the museum with a can of Stella, but for me to get the steps in and absorb some history with a coffee was perfectly legit.

I left that date happy, probably happier than I have been after pub dates. I do often think about The Flapper – I do hope he's doing OK.

I could probably write an entire book on awful dates and different combinations. My experiences with dating may not have led to anything more serious, but they have given me confidence and helped me realise that I don't have to prove to a date that I can be around booze. When I started out dating I was almost apologetic for my past, overthinking the outcome a bit too much. Now I know my worth and know what I do and don't want from a date. I don't want to watch someone sink eight pints while on Diet Coke numero uno. I do think it's rather sweet when someone acknowledges my sobriety when suggesting a date. I don't want to date someone who goes out on three-day benders and just wants a come-down cuddle partner.

I do want someone who is supportive and impressed by sobriety. I won't compromise on that. God, I sound like a right bossy cow, but it's important we know what it is we want from someone. Why settle or make exceptions to our own rules just because someone shows interest?

It took me a good year of dating for me to realise that I was a fucking catch. All of those dating mishaps, blow-dries and hours of painful small talk led me to a healthy place of self-love. For the first time in my life, I wasn't looking for a relationship to save me, I wasn't desperate for male attention and I didn't hate being alone – miracles within themselves. My happiness doesn't depend on being 'on the arm' and ordering a takeaway every week. I create my own happiness and if I do feel that yearning and want to go on a date or do something nice and there's no one to go out with, I take myself on a date. I get myself dolled up, choose an activity I want to do, find a nice café, order a latte and a piece of carrot cake, buy myself some flowers, come home and cook myself something from Waitrose. Now to you that may sound absolutely pathetic – 'Ahh, bloody hell, she's taking herself out on a date, god love her' – but don't worry about me, I'm loving life. In fact, I'd encourage anyone to do it.

When the right person comes along, the right person will come along. No match on a phone app is worth any self-doubt. If someone decides to ghost me, I don't question it any more. I respect the ghost and move on, because I know there is nothing wrong with me; I'm 'sound', and one day there will be someone who is able to share in my love of dark humour and nerdy ways. I am enough, I'm not too much or too little, and if someone thinks otherwise, then it's not meant to be. That's not to say that ghosting doesn't feel shitty, of course it does. I got ghosted after telling someone about my stoma surgery. We'd had three screen dates and on the third and final date, it felt the right time to mention it. Never heard from the twat again. I had a little cry into a burrito with Jade, but then I was like, 'Hold on, what does that say about *him*?' Dating is about learning, and I'm glad I put myself out there to be open to finding someone, rather than starve myself of affection or the chance of happiness.

Sober sex

There's no point beating around the bush (no pun intended): I am yet to have sex sober. You read right: three years into recovery, and I still haven't had sex. So I have invited a friend to share their experiences of sober sex. But I suppose my experience (or lack of experience) can be of some use.

When I think of my sexual encounters over the past decade, I'd say they were 70 per cent under the influence. I think I relied on alcohol to let my guard down. I was by no means a prude and I didn't hate sex, but it was always easier if I had a drink down me or still had drink left in me from the night before. When I really dig deep and think about my poor relationship with sex, I think it comes from a poor relationship with my body. There're scars here and there due to various surgeries, largely related to my Crohn's. I've never been the body-confident type; I'm all for body positivity and applauding women who are confident in their own skin, but I've never really been like that and drink, for all its flaws and toxicity, does help with losing your inhibitions and getting the girls out.

I wouldn't say I have avoided sex in sobriety; it just hasn't happened, and that's all right. It's known that mental health meds can affect your libido … Plus my body has changed a lot: I have this bloody stoma bag to think about now, which adds a whole other layer of complexity. Or maybe I am just not willing to jump into bed with any Tom, Dick or Harry any more.

Like me, Steph (not her real name) waited a while after she got sober and took the time to know herself before jumping into what can feel like a pool of sharks. We spent many a girly conversation laughing about ridiculous sexual encounters and ones that we wished we could forget but knew were important to talk out.

Ladies and gents: Steph.

> *They say coming into recovery you will get back all that you have lost in active addiction. I didn't know that would include my virginity!*
>
> *After two long years of celibacy I decided the time had come to have sex before I completely forgot how to do it. I wasn't too bothered about being in a loving relationship, although for some this is of great importance and I respect that. For me it was important to find confidence first, so I achieved that through sexting. Yep, sexting. I found myself receiving Snapchats of male genitalia in their most rigid form. At first, I panicked and felt slightly embarrassed, but for me it was a way to get back on the horse and dip my toe into the world of sex. My virtual encounter was a revelation; I was relieved to learn I could still orgasm! In all honesty, I don't really remember many of my sexual experiences pre-recovery. It was just something I 'did'; it was transactional and less about me and more about the person with the willy.*

Having sex for the first time sober was a very surreal experience. I was exposed, self-conscious and completely aware of every movement. Every awkward one at that. I didn't even know what to do with my hands! I felt extremely vulnerable but at the same time I felt in control. It really was like being a virgin again, but this time I remembered it. The feelings that came afterwards weren't something I was familiar with. I thought I was immune to feelings after sex, but it turns out being clean and sober I'm quite a different person. I had never emotionally connected to sex, with intimacy – addiction for me is all about a lack of intimacy with anything – and sex was no different.

I wanted to know why he hadn't contacted me (as quickly as I would have liked). Those feelings of self-doubt were tenfold. Was I good enough? Did I do it right? Was my body OK? Don't worry, though, I got into the swing of it soon enough. But that in itself came with problems – I was like a child that has been let loose in a candy shop. I wanted more! Sober sex is much more daunting but also much more invigorating and empowering. How wonderful it is to wake up and remember who I had slept with and how it went.

Holidays

Us Brits love a boozy holiday: whether it be a ten-day resort holiday with your fella or city breaks to Amsterdam with your mates, the one common denominator that links these varying trips is booze. Holidays are a chance to unwind, to let our hair down and to put two fingers up to the British weather. But are they the same when we are sober?

I remember being in rehab, talking about holidays and the risks of airports, etc. Before I got sober, my holiday would officially begin when I was in the terminal having an overpriced Burger King and a pint. While we were sitting, talking (almost salivating) about airports and holidays, the most educated fella in the community contributed to the discussion. He didn't share our fears of the duty-free purchases, the twenty-four-hour pub in the departure lounge or the drinks trolley shoved in your face mid-journey; this fella had genuinely convinced himself that if he drank while flying it didn't matter; it didn't count. We all laughed, and wouldn't let him live it down. He was being deadly serious, and he struggled to see why we thought it was all so laughable.

But the more I thought about it, the more I thought about my own old, illogical rules and I had a bit more compassion. I had booked many a flight when I was drinking, hoping to run away (only to realise that my passport was confiscated). You see, I had been convinced that if I moved to Dubai or a country with strict rules around drinking then I would live a happier life, free from carnage, and that the risk of imprisonment would keep me on the straight and narrow. I even managed to get an interview at a school in Abu Dhabi once ... In recovery, we call that a 'geographical': we convince ourselves that if we moved to a new city, country or culture our problem wouldn't get through Customs with us. Horseshit – of course they do.

But when it comes to going on holiday in sobriety, there is sometimes a fear of the opposite happening – that our sobriety (our solution) gets left in Heathrow Airport's departures lounge unattended as we're thousands of feet up in the sky.

I have a friend who went on holiday with the best of intentions and sadly relapsed. There's no shame to be had in relapse; remember, addiction is a relapsing condition. But for her, the holiday and all that it reminded her of was just too triggering.

I was used to going on holiday to beautiful resorts, usually all-inclusive. When I booked my trip to Mexico, I booked the same resort I had been to so many times; upon reflection, I should have realised that me booking this hotel wasn't going to end well. I was still relatively early into sobriety and while I thought I deserved a bit of R&R, I think I was trying to replicate my old holiday minus the drink. I felt confident about going away, I spoke with friends and my sponsor, and I know how important having a plan, having boundaries around drink, was. But I booked an all-inclusive hotel, one where I knew how good the espresso martinis were. I packed a load of books, I had activities all lined up for my trip and I was glad to be sober.

It was about day two or three that I was starting to feel uneasy. The sun was shining and theoretically this should have been bliss. I found myself watching others sip their cold Desperados in the 38-degree heat and there I was, with my water and a book that I could barely read, obsessing over drink. Looking back I should have picked up the phone and spoken to another alcoholic, but I didn't. I was torturing myself. The voice in my head started to say, 'No one knows you here, you're on holiday, it's all-inclusive, you'll stop again when you're home, it's totally fine.' So I drank, and I drank. I panic-drank. I was guzzling away, making sure that I got my money's worth, and binged for the rest of the holiday. I don't remember much of that holiday and it showed me how powerfully triggering holidays

can be. After sobering up, I waited a while before I went away
again. Now, when I go on holidays, I do try to avoid all-inclusive
resorts and I try to choose places where I know there is more
to the holiday than lying around with a drink. I try to plan in
advance and make sure that my holiday is meaningful and fits
with my recovery. I make sure that I am in regular contact if
and when I need it. Running, praying and meditation are a part
of my recovery and that's what I need to take with me when
I go away.

Dealing with difficulties

Originally, this subheading was going to be called 'first crisis'. But
when I was chatting with Michael about this potential heading, he
raised an issue with using the word crisis for all of life's challenges.
He pointed out to me that the language we use to describe an
extremely difficult moment in our life can prevent us from 'right-
sizing' the situation. Although when we experience difficult times
there is no disputing that we feel that we are in a crisis, to call
everything a 'crisis' may not be the best use of language. Getting
sober doesn't mean that life won't happen; Jo often reminds me of
the AA way – accepting life on life's terms. For a lot of us, we drank
and used drugs on things like grief, bereavement, heartache, a family
member being ill, divorce or losing jobs. Most people do, in fact, but
when we are committed to recovery, we can't escape our feelings
or numb the pain. We have to process it, in the best way we can –
using the strength we have got and the resources we have to hand.
Michael and I spoke for a while on this subject; we have a terrible
habit of speaking a bit too much on topics, and he brought up
emotional maturity.

Drinking stops emotional maturity. When we stop and embark on recovery, that emotional maturity develops – we have to use new strategies, the ones that we used at seventeen [and drinking] won't help – in recovery we have to do things differently.

Michael Rawlinson

I wanted to chat with someone who, quite early into their recovery, faced extreme difficulty. I wanted to hear how they handled it and what it felt like to longer have the 'crutch'. So I reached out to Thomas Delaney, an addiction and recovery campaigner. When we started our chat, Thomas had just heard the tragic but all-to-real nature of addiction – a friend from his time in rehab had died. We spoke about this as two people in recovery, not as an interviewer and interviewee. For Thomas, this loss was not the first. He lives in Glasgow, which has the highest drug-related death rate in Europe; this wouldn't be the last either. This heart-sinking conversation starter really hit home to me why Thomas and I speak out in whatever way we can – addiction is fatal.

With our respects for Thomas's friend paid, we spoke about experiencing difficulty. Thomas shared about being in rehab when he got the news no son or daughter wants to hear – that their parent is extremely sick.

> *I'd just got to rehab, I hadn't heard from my mum for a while and I thought it was really weird. She had asked to see me and I could sense something. So my mum and my brother came up, and I knew straight away that something wasn't right. We got in the*

lift and she just said, 'I'm not well' and burst into tears, which made me burst into tears. I whisked my mum off to my room and we sat down to talk, and then my mum told me about her cancer and recent operation. So while I'm in rehab sorting myself out, my mum was in hospital going through this and I had no idea. I wasn't there for her. She shouldn't have even travelled to see me, and in that moment I felt so helpless, selfish, and I felt like a terrible son. I asked her the reasons why she didn't tell me, and I knew already what the response was going to be – if she would have told me, I would have left rehab. I cried, and you know why? Because she was right, I would have left rehab and I would have been by her side and I probably would have used drugs, because I would have needed the drugs to cope; to feel better. I promised my mum that day that I would complete treatment. It was the first time I wasn't there for my mum (who I love so much) – but saying that, was I ever there? I was drugged up a lot, was I ever actually a son?

I asked Thomas what it was like going through that pain and not drinking or using.

I'd only been clean for five weeks at that point and I was having a lot of using thoughts anyway. It made me realise how selfish it was for me to use drugs – I realised that I hadn't been loving my mum the right way. My mum was only allowed with me for a few hours, and she held my hand and I didn't want her to leave. Even when she left, instantly I thought, 'I could do with a gram, that would fix this.' But I didn't act on it, I put my mum first, her situation first and I had to 'man up'. I had to be there to support my mum. It made me realise how important it was for me to stick out at recovery so I could be there for her and my brother. In hindsight, we can learn from everything – even though it was an early stage of recovery, I got through it and I didn't use on it.

Our chat was virtual (such is the way of the world these days) but if I could have, I would have jumped through the screen and given Thomas one of my infamous awkward hugs. We spoke more together and both shared the belief that whatever happens in life, however painful it may be, a drink or a drug won't fix matters. It might numb for a few short hours but it would cause more damage and heartache than the original pain we are feeling. I have friends who have lost their parents, been diagnosed with illness, lost jobs, lost homes and, through it all, they have stayed sober and held on to their sobriety. It goes without saying that their heads took a battering and their hearts were crushed, but they did it, bit by bit and day by day, and I take strength from that whenever I am faced with any difficulty. I learn through listening to the experiences of others. It's very much an 'if they got through that, I can get though this' scenario.

Success

Feeling confused about why the first bit of success needs a bit of exploring? Experiencing success is often linked to the need to celebrate, and celebration can let thoughts of a drink, a drug or a bet back in. When life starts to look good and we get back on track that feeling of joy can stir up old memories. A very good friend of *Hooked* is a chap called Chris Gilham. When I first met with Chris, he was anonymous on Twitter, but his support for all things *Hooked* really meant a lot and I asked him if he would like to share his story on our show. Although Chris is in my gang (AA), he is also in Gamblers Anonymous and has gone on to co-found his own podcast called *All Bets Are Off* and a non-profit organisation called TalkGEN, to help guide gambling-harm prevention strategies, and I couldn't be prouder. He is helping so many find recovery and live a happier and healthier life. I remember Chris sharing with me how experiencing good times led to bad times and I wanted to explore that.

With gambling, you're left with nothing, both mentally and financially. Working hard means you can get back in a stable financial position, but this means you're in a position to gamble again. With drinking, hopefully you'll never have to fill up that glass with alcohol. With gambling, it's your money and it will come back. 2015 to 2017, I got my finances in order, things were great – I had debt to family but my debt to creditors was gone. I had received some help for my gambling at the NHS Problem Gambling Clinic in London. We were remortgaging to get the house done – it should have been an exciting time. It took us two-and-a-half years to get to a good place and be in this position, to build a better house for our family, but the gambling creeped back in. In a few short binges, I had lost a year's salary, spent the money for the building work and made the decision to take out a £25k loan in an attempt to win back the money I lost. Within two hours, I had spent the £22,500 in the online casino and I was ready to end it.

When the remortgage was going through I had a feeling of 'Done it, I've got it, what now?' I read a book by Jonny

Wilkinson, the rugby player, and he said that, once he hit that drop goal, he should have been elated but all he thought was, what next? I've achieved my goal. I could relate to that, that time when I stopped gambling and was in a position to remortgage the house. I felt like I'd achieved something and the problem is, when I achieve something, I want to knock myself down and I had the ability to do it — money.

I asked Chris if he had similar experiences but with drink. Were there any times that life was good and he picked up a drink? In a similar vein to myself, since Chris came into recovery he has yet to pick up a drink. But prior to AA, he had periods of sobriety and did have experience of drinking when life was on the up:

I remember I hadn't been drinking and we were invited to my brother-in-law's wedding in Italy. I was feeling great and everything was going really well. We were staying there for a week or so with the wider family. My sister-in-law said, 'It's a shame you can't drink.' My response was, 'Well, I haven't drank in a while, so I can have a drink.' When I think back to that, I was just waiting on an 'in'. Slowly but surely, the drinking increased and as alcoholism does — it only gets worse.

When life is really good is when I need to double up on what I do [recovery]. I ask myself, why is life good? Is it because I have been drinking or gambling, or is it because I have done neither of these things? Let's be honest, life is good because I have done neither of those things. Life's good because I have done the sensible stuff — meditation, keeping it in the day, speaking to another alcoholic/gambler.

For me, Chris hits the nail on the head – when life's good, look for the reasons why.

Takeaways

- **Learn from others – listen to how others coped in these situations**
- **Stay connected to your recovery network and talk about your fears and worries**
- **Plan, plan, plan – have your responses prepared and an exit strategy if you need one**
- **If you feel uncomfortable in a situation – bar, pub, Christmas do – you don't have to explain or stick around longer than you have to**
- **Get to know yourself and build a relationship with yourself**
- **Sober sex is there to enjoy**
- **In difficult times, ask yourself how would a drink or a drug improve a situation**
- **When life is good, remember why it's good – there's no drink or drugs around!**

Chapter 8

You are not your past –
it's time to forgive and move forward

Someone told me early into my recovery (I can't remember who – I was probably in my 'I don't want to let AA people in' phase) that putting down the drink is the easy bit. Easy? You taking the piss, mate? But as days turned into months and the AA medallions went from months to years, I got it. I really fucking got it. With the drink out of the picture, I was left with all kinds of pain, consequences, harmful thought process and, of course, shame. I may have found freedom from alcohol, but I still had the '-ism' – the dark, uneasy stirring inside. To find that freedom, that holy grail that I would fill with Pepsi Max, I had to let go. The main things I had to let go of (or at least try to):

- **Shame**
- **Ill-feeling towards others**
- **The past.**

Christ on a bike with Our Lady on the handlebars – how was I going to do this? Letting go doesn't come naturally to me; I can't part with anything. I still have going-out outfits from the age of eighteen that are collecting dust in my mum's house. Bearing in mind that I will never fit in them again (I developed tits in my thirties – I think that's due to the choc-chip muffins) and I wouldn't be seen dead wearing them in public anyway, I still can't let them go. I even have my childhood doll, Slaphead. She is the ugliest-looking doll you have ever seen but there she remains in Kirkby, with her half-opened eye and biro scrawling. (I have spent far too much time thinking about whether Slaphead should get buried with me or whether I should leave her to someone in my will to terrify children for all eternity.) I'm not just a hoarder in the physical sense; I am an emotional and behavioural one. By default, I go through life carrying each shitty experience, painful memory and bad word that's ever been said about me. I collected resentments and grudges like Beanie Babies. (Again, I have a bag filled with Beanie Babies in me mum's garage that have yet to be binned. Still waiting for them to turn into collectors' items – absolute con.) I carry this negativity on my back, and every new scenario I find myself in, the contents of this 100-litre backpack either spill out or weigh me down so much that I need to take a break. My past and my shame are closely linked – of course they are.

I did things that didn't make me feel proud, over and over again. I lied. I manipulated. I stole. I hurt people. Even for all of the good things I did and the nice qualities I had, I only held on to the shame. Wouldn't it be great if we got sober and all those things were resolved and absolved the minute we stopped drinking? I suppose that's me wanting to do the least to achieve the most – classic Melissa. Since getting sober my biggest hurdle has been shame. In Liverpool, that's a staple of our unique phrases: 'Oh aye, I feel ashamed.' But I never truly understood the mechanics of this phrase that would roll off my tongue with such ease. There are many in-depth psychological papers that I could reference to explain shame and the impact it has on our mental health and the way in which we see ourselves, but I've always responded well to the 'get to the point' approach in life. So here is a description that sums it up and hits the nail on the head.

We feel shame when we violate the social norms we believe in. At such moments we feel humiliated, exposed and small and are unable to look another person straight in the eye. We want to sink into the ground and disappear.

Women are quicker to feel humiliated than men, and adolescents feel shame more intensely than adults do. As a result, women and adolescents are more susceptible to the negative effects of shame, such as low self-esteem and depression.

Professor Dr Annette Kämmerer

Nice one. We have all been in a situation when we want the ground to swallow us up whole. And it's not just reserved for the aftermath of alcohol binges or the cringe-worthy things we may have done when bladdered. I have felt great shame over silly things, like when I sing the wrong words to a song in front of people or I've been late for something. The way I use these instances to punish myself ain't right. Shame is a natural human process or emotion; if we didn't have the ability to feel shame or even guilt, then empathy would be non-existent and what a sad world that would be. Our shame is personal to us: there are things that feel awful to you that I wouldn't bat an eyelid over, and likewise there are things that I feel shame over that are water off a duck's back to you. Here's one for you: I feel no real embarrassment about being on antidepressants; like, I genuinely do not give a hint of a fuck that I am on medication for having a chemical imbalance. Maybe it's because I have a physical chronic condition that I medicate and I know that if I don't take medicine I get ill. However, I know I have friends that do suffer with the shame of being on medication and I would never, ever diminish their feelings. Their shame is theirs and it's not my place to tell them, 'It's no big deal' or 'Who's arsed, mate?'

But I did feel shame picking up my prescriptions. It had nothing to do with me picking up a high dose of mirtazapine and wondering what the woman on the till thought. The blow to the stomach was the 'Do you pay for your prescriptions?' question. For the first couple of times I paid for my prescription, even though I was entitled to free prescriptions as I was on benefits. I just couldn't bring myself to tick the exemption box on the back of the prescription. But when you have a repeat prescription that is more like a dossier, something has to give. I realised once more that I was refusing to accept the help I was able to receive because of my pride; I didn't want to be that person. I'd never not worked. The stigma attached to benefits is as real as it comes; it's unfair, and yet there I was feeding into that stigma. My shame around it was shaped by the family norms I had been brought up with – you have to work, you don't live beyond your means and you look after your money. With this being so ingrained, to be jobless and claiming (even though it was justified) caused that friction, that shame. After a few trips, I finally plucked up the courage and became willing to accept the position I was in: I had just left treatment after a form of a mental breakdown – that's what the support of benefits is there for. So each time I went to the chemist (the place where celebrity perfumes go to die), I worked hard not to feel that intense level of shame, reminding myself that I was entitled to support, that this wasn't for ever and that I deserved it.

Shame is such a shitty feeling, isn't it? But there are some uses for it – hear me out – if you think about it in the context of alcoholism. For many people the feeling of shame and guilt can push us to the point of change. Those uncomfortable feelings of remorse and the shocking realisation of our behaviour can lead us to say, 'I'm not that person, that's not how I want to behave or who I want to be.' Then we make the change and vow never to be *that* version of ourselves again.

But shame affects some more than others and even in recovery it can be rather debilitating (hi). 'Shame-proneness' is a term that I learnt when I was researching this chapter (finally, a bit of frigging validation, or is this just another label to add to the ever-growing list of things that make me eligible for a very awkward episode of *First Dates*?).

I have enough evidence that proves that I am more shame-prone than my peers and the average human – it really doesn't take much for me to reach for a massive stick and beat myself soundly.

I always thought that shame and guilt were one and the same: they both made me feel like my skin was on inside out, both make my toes curl up and hands feel all tingly, and they both send me into a right tizz. But they aren't the same. Guilt is the partner to shame. They are like salt and pepper – both seasonings, but with very different tastes and effects. In treatment it was explained to me very simply: guilt – I did something bad and it caused harm to another person; shame – I am a bad person and my actions are a reflection of who I am as a person.

Who would have thunk it? News to me! Now of course it's not as black and white as it seems, as I would say that there are many a shambles I've been involved in where I've felt both guilt and shame at the same time. A double hitter – feeling mortified by my own actions and who I was as a person, as well as feeling so terrible that I have hurt someone. It doesn't matter what I am able to achieve or do, my shame will hold me back and keep me down. Notice how I talk about it in the present tense? Well, that's because I still live with it, I have to manage it daily. (I would just like to point out that I did say in my introduction I didn't have the answers.) Some days the shame of my past will be so very loud and prominent that I'm unable to see and hear the positive things in my life. I get a new job – I won't celebrate it. The podcast is well received – I play it down. I sign a book deal – I don't tell anyone. To feel proud is uncomfortable for me because my shame and self-worth tell me, 'You're just a fuck-up,' and then my mind will proceed to reel off every reason as to why I am a bad human being who deserves nothing in life. So now, in those moments, I have to force myself to celebrate and push myself to say the words, 'I am proud of …' By saying this stuff out loud, it can stop my shame spiral to some degree.

Holding on to shame is not what recovery is about. Jo told me once: 'Melissa, there's only room on the cross for one.' Boy, oh boy, is she right. For me, recovery is about freedom – so does this mean that recovery isn't working for me? Nope. As with most things in life, it just takes time.

I am much better at managing this negative self-talk today and that's thanks to Shahroo Izadi. Shahroo works in Amy's Place and has sessions with the residents. She's one of those women who empower women – the type who, when you leave their company, you feel all sassy, confident and charged. She has written a book called *The Kindness Method* and it's brilliant. Within the book and throughout the sessions, the most valuable teaching was relearning how I talked to myself; basically, that I should talk to myself the same way as I would talk to a loved one. So in those frequent times when I talk to myself in such a harmful and damaging way, I just imagine what I would tell a friend if they were feeling or experiencing what I was going through and afford myself that same kindness.

Talking to myself with compassion is a wonderful tool for me. But to really rid myself of the guilt and the shame, I right the wrongs of the past. If I had a pound for every time my sponsor, Jo, said, 'The whole point of this stuff [AA work] is to walk down the street with your head held high,' I'd be in a position to buy Charlotte Tilbury make-up instead of Maybelline. For the first eighteen months of sobriety, I didn't walk around with my head held high, not in Liverpool anyway. Living in London meant everything was fresh; the slate was clean and I hadn't hurt anyone there. But when I got on that train to Liverpool Lime Street, the head would go down and I would shrink. The pride of being sober and overcoming the darkest hours was supplanted by the heaviest regret and the grubbiest of feelings. Don't get me wrong, while on those early visits to Kirkby I adored seeing my family and I'd still get all the Judy Garland 'there's no place like home' vibes. But that happiness was only felt inside the family home, and never beyond the garden path. Even then, the first few visits were difficult: seeing the broken wardrobe of 2017 and the holes in the wall that my mum decided to cover with birthday cards, and a cigarette butt that had been there from my locked-in days. I was confident in the new and improved version, but outside the walls of my mum's house, I didn't want to be seen, I didn't feel comfortable and I didn't feel safe. I wasn't strong enough to handle ghosts or postcodes of the past, I was just as ashamed of being in recovery as I was about being in active addiction.

I thought my family hadn't noticed that each visit I would mainly stay in the house, but Ange noticed – nothing gets past Mum. I remember she asked me to go to the local shop for a loaf. I couldn't come up with any valid reason not to – I didn't want to lie, I was past that. I wanted to be the daughter that did those regular 'help Mum out' things, but the panic of going to the shop, to see the shopkeeper who had served me with countless bottles of vodka in the past, was just too much. This didn't wash with Ange – she said something which she probably has forgotten by now, but it stayed with me: 'You have nothing to be ashamed of – who are they? You are not that person now.' She was right. Walking into that shop, seeing the shop assistants for the first time, *was* fucking awful. I picked up my thick white loaf (obviously) and two bottles of Pepsi Max. I don't know why I added the fizzy drinks to the shopping list; I think I was looking for a visual way to show the girl on the till that *this* was my new drink of choice and that she could keep her Kirov and her Glen's – this sober lady is not for turning. My eye contact wasn't great and my hands trembled as I went to get my card; she probably thought I was back on the sauce, to be honest. Then she said, 'Is that it, love?' and there was a bit of an *X Factor* pause and then I said, 'Yes, thanks, love.' She looked at me and pulled a kind smile; I think she was slightly relieved: there were no teeth involved in the smile – it was all in the eyes, and that meant a lot. But then, just when I thought that this was a special moment between the cashier and me, a moment that needed no real words or to acknowledge the past, she had to go and say the words no woman wants to hear: 'You look really well.' Nice one.

Those moments of facing the people, the places or the things that remind us of our past, no matter how small, are so important. They are the small victories that all contribute to building confidence and the shame-shrinking. I went back to Kirkby every six weeks for my Crohn's treatment (a wonderful drip that takes out my immune system, to stop my body thinking my digestive system is a foreign invader). Each visit I was able to tick off another place that I had faced up to.

It did take about a year to return to the local retail park and the Asda. This Asda and retail park combo was the epicentre of all things school-related. Parents from the school I taught at would frequent there, and to get to it I had to pass the school. I would drive down that road with my eyes averted, making a sound so that my head wouldn't wander. I would then wait in the car until Ange or our Becca had their shopping done. This wasn't a way to live, but I understood why I was the way I was. I hadn't made peace with the past, I hadn't processed or healed from the departure of Miss Rice. Today, though, I can walk freely in Boots, Next and Marksies; I can even queue up in the rotisserie chicken queue in the Asda. I don't look over my shoulder or avoid children in certain coloured uniforms. This ability to return to places and see faces only came about by letting go, and through forgiveness, of self and by others.

Before I went on the arduous but necessary quest of seeking forgiveness, I had to let go of being a victim. Although I would be the first to say that I was a bad person, I also thought I was a victim –

hard done by. There's no denying that people in my life have treated me unfairly and in a way that lacked compassion, but clinging on to this 'poor-me' way of being enabled my harmful behaviours. Bad shit happens – that's life, and in many cases people who don't deserve to be shat on get shat on. In my case, there were so many situations that did involve personal responsibility but as long as I was a victim, I could sit in my misery comforted by the fact that I was treated unkindly. Living life 'hard done by' would ramp up my self-pity and give me the green light *and* the ammunition to justify my drinking and self-loathing. My internal dialogue went a little something like this: 'You don't know what it's like, you don't live with my head, everyone hates me, you haven't got a dysfunctional bowel, you haven't got this head, if you felt how I felt you would drink, an' all.' I couldn't see past my own hardship and the resentment I had of people and situations. I blamed everything and everyone for why I was the way I was. And the more I blamed others, the less I was looking at my part in these situations and, therefore, I became powerless, as all of my life's woes were someone else's doing and not my own. Which is absolutely not the case. My actions caused consequences. I needed to drop the victim act, take responsibility, take back control and claim my past as my own.

Through the process of re-examining my ill-feelings and finger-wagging towards the world, its wife and its dog, I was able to look at my own behaviour in situations and almost always rebalance the blame. There were some instances that I had to take more accountability for, and also some instances when things simply were not my fault. Figuring out who you need to make it up to and who is simply living in your head rent-free is mind-blowing but, by figuring

this out, I was able to take the next step in squishing the shame –
forgiveness.

Building bridges and making amends … it's the part of recovery I
dreaded most, but it is also the part of recovery where the good stuff
(freedom) is.

In my head, I was convinced that every embarrassing encounter
was just as big in other people's heads as they were in mine (more
self-obsession). But if I held on to those memories – the wrongdoings
of my past – and avoided addressing them with the parties involved,
then they would remain huge and I would continue living in fear. I
had to right-size these memories.

'Sorry' is a word that I am familiar with (I have no idea why Sir
Elton John said that it seems to be the hardest word – I've never had
an issue with it). I can safely say that I exhausted the word and said it
over and over until it had absolutely no meaning – it was just a two-
syllabled noise that would come out of my mouth. Every person in
my life has heard me apologise repeatedly. I can even apologise for
things I don't have to apologise for. The heavens have opened, it's
lashing down and our outdoor walk is cancelled? My fault. How the
fuck is the weather my fault?

Being an alcoholic usually means that our loved ones, employers
and friends have 'heard it all before'. We mess up, we apologise, we
may try and make it right, and then we do it all over again. It's shit.
So how then, in recovery, can we make it right?

When I first got sober I was *so* very desperate to apologise – not
to everyone, mind you. I'll tell no lies – there were some people
where I thought to myself: 'I wouldn't piss on you if you were on
fire.' My resentment and pride were stubborn and resilient. I had a

lot of anger ... I didn't know it was anger, but the more I unpicked scenarios, the more anger I would feel. I was still so wounded and unwilling to consider certain people's reasoning that I point-blank refused to consider apologising. But I know now that avoiding forgiveness only causes me pain, while the person who I don't want to forgive probably couldn't give a shit if I did or didn't. I've realised forgiveness isn't a weakness and it doesn't let someone off the hook for the harmful things they have done. Instead, it's about me not holding on to anger, and turning that pain into something worth holding on to: compassion. Jo's words flood the space between my ears, 'Do you want to be right, or do you want to be free?'

I had to let it all out and I had to let it go. I had twenty-nine years of resentments I had to detox from. But it's not as quick as alcohol withdrawal: it takes time, and it happens only when you're ready for it. I think the most significant resentment was the one I had towards my dad. I was angry that he left us; that we were not enough. I blamed him for a lot. My resentment was all about how his behaviour had impacted my life, and I never once considered his thoughts and feelings, and his pain. When you're in recovery and you start to think less about yourself and more about others, you start to re-evaluate the people who you have written off as 'bad'. You start to put yourself in their shoes and think about their life and the experiences that have come before. I love my dad. In fact, I am more like my dad than people realise. For all his bravado he is a sensitive beast who has no issue with bawling his eyes out; he cares a great deal about what others think of him; and he's a man who loves to be loved – and deserves to be loved. He may be a nuisance and a pain in the arse at times, but he's my nuisance and pain in the arse. My dad has his own pain and I understand that pain now. This shift in my thinking took a good while, and I can honestly say that it was one of the most freeing and healing moments in recovery. Dad, I know you're reading this, so I will repeat it: I love you, and what's in the past is in the past.

When it comes to seeking forgiveness from others, I learnt that it takes more than words: it requires listening and action. There was no way that my mind could have handled the amends process in the first few months of sobriety – my only job in the first year was to stay sober (fact). In the same way that I had to wait before I could tackle past trauma, I had to wait before I could revisit the people of my past. I had to be confident enough in myself and my sobriety to be able to handle potential rejection or the 'stuff' (emotions) that would be brought up as a result of seeking meaningful forgiveness.

This process is about me giving someone the opportunity to tell me *how* my behaviour has impacted them, and asking them if there is a way that I can make it right. It requires me keeping my mouth shut (something that I am not that good at); I can't interrupt with justifications and excuses; I can't retaliate with a 'Well, actually, I may have let you down, but fucking hell, remember that time when you …' My old apologies were me saying what I needed to say for the sake of it and not even considering what the receiver felt or what they had to say. I'm not proud to admit it, but I would even force an apology onto someone. It wouldn't even enter my mind that the person might not want to hear it. As far as I was concerned, you *will* accept my apology or at least hear it and if you didn't, then that was that and I would retreat and deal with another relationship biting the dust. I may have even tried to carry on like everything was normal between us or, worse, I would beg you until submission. Very selfish and very manipulative – as you will see here: I tried to have the conversation with my granddad. I was dropping him off home and I saw this as an opportunity to open up. I began with: 'Granddad, I just wanted to talk to you about the worry I caused and the disturbance I brought to the house. A part of my recovery is about making amends.' He said, 'What are you bringing that up for now? It's finished, it's done, I don't want to talk about that, don't be worrying about yesterday.' I felt cheated. I was hoping for this huge moment and, nope, nothing. Then there was the time I tried to sit down with my mum – in my head this was going to be gruelling and ever so cathartic. But she didn't want to go there, either. I was in for another anticlimax: this process wasn't for Ange. Whether or not it was too painful to relive, or whether she thought that the way in which I chose now to live my life was enough, I don't know. So I got creative.

When I had been drunk one time, I had broken her reading glasses. She pays all kinds for her glasses because she requires one lens that's like the bottom of a milk bottle, and one thin lens – the glass-shaving process costs a fortune (she's going to kill me for outing that). When I broke her specs, I was that drunk I didn't even know she was there watching me break them. Now, sober and wanting to make amends, for her birthday I bought her a Specsavers voucher. She received the voucher, flipped her lid and transferred the money back into my account. I was firmly told that I should not live in the past or try making up for a pair of glasses.

Lesson learnt – don't force your amends.

Not every single person we reach out to will want to hear from us and that is their prerogative. When entering this type of process with someone I have harmed, it's not all about me; it's about the person feeling heard. And if someone does not wish to hear from you, then we/I have to accept it.

With Jo by my side, I made a list of all the people I had harmed and within that process I had to decide whether my apology would cause the person or myself harm. If that was the case then it was best I didn't do it. I have caused enough harm to others and to myself.

When I was nine months sober, an opportunity to reconnect with a friend from the past presented itself. His name is Sam. Sam was a part of the circle of friends that I lost when I pushed things too far in 2016. The shame that I felt around that situation was very intense. Even sober, I was still so embarrassed by my actions and would have done anything to avoid these people for the rest of my life if I could.

It had gone around Kirkby that I had been to rehab, which was to be expected, and, during this time, Sam would periodically reach out to my friend Cat to see how I was. She would tell me he had been in touch, but I didn't know where to begin with that, so I ignored it. Then it dawned on me that I was shutting out a person who I loved who was trying to reconnect; it didn't feel nice or right: my pride and fear were getting in the way of a meaningful relationship. I messaged him and met him for a coffee: it was in Covent Garden, worlds away from L32.

It had been nearly two years since I last saw him – everything had changed, but nothing had changed. We put our cards on the table, and to hear his perspective and take on what had gone down made me realise that for those two years the narrative I had created in my head was so very different to the reality. I had filled the gaps with my 'everyone hates me' spiel. I wouldn't go as far as to say my version of events were completely incorrect – the feelings I had at the time were real – but hearing another person's take on events, his rationale and reasoning, allowed me to apply his perspective to my own thinking, which resulted in things making more bloody sense. To him, I had cut them off; I had chosen to walk away. To me, I thought they had dropped me and I slunk away.

This reunion with Sam kick-started a feeling of hope for more reconnections. I've already told you about Fran, but there are more. My world began to open up the more I started to take responsibility. The fear in my head that no one would ever forgive me was just that, a fear.

For many people, myself included, the fear of the apology will prevent us from being willing to even attempt it. Every reconnection, reunion, amends – I have projected my own thinking onto them, and not once did I think they would be received well. Goes to show that I really do know nothing.

I wanted to talk to a male about shame, as I think there is a bit of a misconception that men don't feel it, and are less likely to harbour such damaging feelings of self-loathing. It's just not the case. I approached my mate Marc: he's known me from the start of my recovery and he's a cracker. On a bench in Archway (the windiest part of London, according to Marc) one day, we spoke all about it.

I didn't know I had shame. All's I knew is that I had guilty feelings and with those feelings I hated myself. I was five years into recovery when I knew it was shame. As a man, I just wanted to get sober, I didn't want to admit to stuff that made me feel weak, so I left it. I kept it in and I kept it to myself, but it was killing me. I had so much shame and I couldn't handle it. I had shame around cheating in relationships, the way I was on nights out – the disgusting feeling of waking up and remembering the stuff that deep down you didn't want to do but you did it anyway. Then you'd find me laughing about it in the pub the next day–? I thought I had to do that, I had to keep up the whole male bravado.

But the main guilt and shame I had was around the way I behaved when I had young kids. I would put drink and drugs before the rent, the electric, the nappies, the milk. Who wouldn't feel shame around that?

As we sat there in Archway, him puffing on a fag and me thinking, 'Oh, that smells lovely,' we took a minute. I shared with him my experiences of shame and then I asked him what helped him:

Each time my head would take me back, I had to remind myself that I wasn't a bad person – I was very sick person. I always thought I was a bad person – my whole life. I was always told I was a bad person and I was always told there was something wrong with me, whether it be police, judges, teachers, prison officers, Mum, Granddad, Nan – all of them would ask, 'What is wrong with you?' and I would just say, 'I don't know.' Because I didn't know, until I came into recovery, into a 12-step fellowship, and very slowly I started to learn that I suffered with a mental illness. When I am in the height of my alcoholism, no human power can stop me from those things that I would have regret about for the next day, the next month, the next year or for life.

Finally, I asked him about the moment when he knew things had changed, when he was able to gain trust back and when he knew things were on the mend:

> *I realised the relationship was mending with my mum when I was in her house. She left the front room and she left her handbag. When I was in her house [before], her handbag was always under her arm, she never put it down, there was no trust and I don't blame them. That was a moment for me. She did it again when I was giving her a lift somewhere – she'd got out the car to go in the shop and she left her handbag in the passenger footwell and I thought: 'Fuck, I don't like this. I don't want to be around it.' [But] when I realised that my own mum felt safe to leave her handbag, that's when I knew there was a change, there was hope, things were different. When we're in addiction, no one trusts you. That handbag made me realise that this stuff works, recovery works and it helped me right-size that shame.*

Hearing of the handbag and all that it represented, my eyes filled up on that bench in Archway. Beautiful. I got it. I really did. Because the day when my sister left my nephew with me for a few hours, that was my handbag moment.

Out of all the relationships I had to revisit, I never thought my sister and I would get back on track. I never thought she would like me, never mind trust me again. For her, I had stolen the show for a fair few years and rightly she felt neglected. We'd had family therapy in Clouds – for many people who are supporting someone early in recovery, there's a lot of pent-up anger. For the loved ones, they are usually so happy and desperate for you to stay on the right track that they suppress their harboured feelings. And, holy cow, we were no exception – what a can of worms. In one short session I accused Ange of using her 'phone voice' and being fake; I had me mum telling me that how I felt wasn't actually how I felt; our Becca admitted she battered me to knock sense into me; I turned into Kevin off Harry Enfield; and the counsellor gave our Becca a new label, one that she continues to dine out on to this day: 'The forgotten child.' But that term is bang on the money – I can never give back to Becca that time or attention I had from my mum. That pains me, but the truth often does.

Jade and I recorded an episode of *Hooked* that was on family and friends, which was a chance for my sister and one of Jade's besties to come on and share their experience. To open up in a recording studio about her feelings was the furthest away from my sister's comfort zone she could get, but she agreed. I was two years sober by this point and we were in a good place, but hearing her share how my addiction had impacted her life and watching her cry, I have never felt pride (for her, obviously) or pain like it.

Knowing that I went back to drinking after she had had to perform CPR on me because she thought I was dead is a shame like no other.

Inflicting that much trauma on your family and friends weighs heavily on the mind and soul. From the moment I walked into Clouds, I thought that my life's purpose was to 'make it up' to my family. I think I spent the first few months of sobriety agreeing with everything our Becca said just so that we wouldn't have any cross words; trying my best to avoid any situation whereby she could bring up examples of when I acted like a twat. But that in itself is people-pleasing. I was trying to do everything in my power to be perfectly serene and caring, but that's not what they were after and it wasn't good for me – it was neither honest nor healthy. Acting this way wasn't me living in the present: I was still living in the memories of active addiction. I'm sure if I had had money in those early days of sobriety, I would have thrown all kinds of material things into the mix, but again, that won't cut it and you can't compensate with material things.

My recovery is for me, but the more I look after my recovery and take responsibility for me, the more I am the sister, the daughter, the aunty, the cousin, the niece and the granddaughter people deserve. Here's another cliché for you (bloody hell, I'm full of them) – actions speak louder than words, and when it comes to recovery they bloody well do. My actions – being honest, being more thoughtful, helping others, taking responsibility, not being a selfish bitch – speak volumes and are worth more than a half-arsed 'I'm dead sorry' (Scouse voice needed). These actions turn into habits, which then lead to personality traits/qualities that allow people to see me as dependable and trustworthy. I'm not saying I'm some kind of saint, by the way – I can be a complete and utter arsehole at times, but I try my best to do things the right way these days.

There are, however, certain events from my past that can't be redeemed by something as 'simple' as a conversation, and hearing people out, and taking baby steps to rebuild trust. How do you seek forgiveness from a profession, for example? Teaching – and crashing out of it – was an area of my addiction and my life that would cause me profound distress. Even with Jo and my mates, talking about it would induce a lot of panting, tears and a real ache in my heart. I was convinced that I had achieved nothing in that role, that I didn't help a single child. My deep shame, which was again fuelled by self-loathing and some harmful comments from around that time, made teaching a part of my story that was off-limits. I never thought I would ever get over the feelings I had about it, and I had almost accepted that this would just be something that I had to keep that was painful.

Just before *Hooked* was released in October 2019, Jade and I were both sick with worry. We didn't want to be judged, trolled and – get on this – we didn't want people who knew us to hear our stories. I remember thinking to myself, 'I wonder if there is a way to stop the Merseyside region hearing it?' My concern was less about old friends and partners hearing it, than the parents of the children – and the children – who I had taught.

When the podcast dropped, it was a long wait. A local Liverpool paper (that I clearly still feel resentment for) did a write-up and posted it on social media. Google 'Melissa Rice Cereal'. Scroll down your search results and you will see a series of charming headlines that read, 'Raging Alcoholic Teacher Pours Jack Daniels on Cereal'. No mention of recovery, or the podcast I co-hosted, not a thought to the impact that the headline would have on my recovery or the trolling that would follow. My words and darkest hours that I was trying to put to some good use were twisted and reduced to clickbait. I couldn't believe it. One throwaway story from Glastonbury 2014 made out to be such a shameful scandal.

The paper later admitted they hadn't heard the podcast and accepted that they misrepresented the episode but it was too late – I had been thrown into the lion's den of Facebook. Well, that was it.

I had people calling me a disgrace, that I should be in prison, that I belonged in hell, that I should be on a register … Thankfully I'm not on Facebook, but I had friends that were. For twenty-four hours the shame I felt wasn't exaggerated or just a part of my low self-worth. This was real. I really was all those things I thought about myself. I really was a failure: it was there in black and white.

But here comes the beautiful part.

Parents of the children I had taught came to my defence, saying things that I never thought would be possible. They owed me nothing, but they put themselves on the line to challenge the 'alchy teacher is a disgrace' rhetoric spurting from the fingers of the Facebook busybodies (to put it lightly).

As traumatic as that experience was, I am grateful for it. The worst thing anyone could have said to me was said and I didn't drink.

From this experience, I have also been able to reconnect with a parent and their child who I taught. He is a brilliant, kind and intelligent boy – sorry, young man – who doesn't realise just how fantastic he really is. This relationship and continued support from the parent has allowed me to make peace with the shame, and whenever I feel that voice say, 'You are a failed teacher', I now know I am not.

I have a framed card that I keep up in my living room – it is the only evidence I need:

To Melissa (Miss R)

Even after all these years, you still influence me in my studies. This is because of the confidence you gave me in year 4 – to always do my best.

Even with all the teachers I've had, I still wish I had you.

Making peace with our past isn't an easy thing. Cleaning up the mess from the harmful drinking days was a great start for me. (Of course it was, I am co-dependent – if people have forgiven me it will do wonders for the old self-esteem.) But I never realised that *I* deserved to be forgiven, that *I* should have been on the list of people that I needed to forgive. It didn't even enter my mind. It was Jo who pointed this omission out. I had to forgive myself? That felt very American – you know what I mean by that. It felt very motivational-speaker-meets-yoga-enthusiast. It didn't feel right to forgive myself. I had aborted a baby, lied, cheated … you know the drill. After everything I had been through, and put my mind and body through, I didn't think that I owed myself forgiveness.

Well, fuck me sideways – this weren't on. If I was able to forgive and make peace with others, why wasn't I willing to forgive myself? To do this, I had to come to terms with, and believe that, throughout my life, I did my best with the shoddy tools I had at the time. I had significant mental health issues, unresolved trauma and a body that wasn't functioning right – I did what I did to survive, to manage. I had to stop beating myself up for not knowing what I know now. I talked to Michael about shame and self-forgiveness. He said:

> *I always remember working with a male client. He was young, good-looking, had the gift of the gab, he was successful, he was well liked in the community. I remember thinking, 'We are not getting anywhere.' So the counsellors and I discussed a way forward and it dawned on me – he had not forgiven himself. With that in mind, in our next session we sat in front of a whiteboard (you know I love my whiteboard and pens) and*

filled it with his treatment to date and his experiences in active addiction. He was able to be really negative about himself at every stage of his life. So I asked him, 'What would it take for you to forgive yourself?' Often as a practitioner, silence is really important. He sat there and he started to cry. At that moment he became vulnerable and what this enabled him to do was to accept his vulnerability and move one step closer to healing from his past.

Ever the counsellor, Michael stopped his retelling and shifted focus onto me. 'Melissa, it's terribly funny, you're doing that thing with your hair again … you're thinking about something, it's caused a feeling.'

So I opened up. I told him that my mind went to a BBC recording studio in Salford. Uma, our producer, asked me that very same question Michael asked a client in rehab. I had no answer to give to Uma. I don't think there is one event or a 'moment', but I know that with time and the more I am in recovery the more I am able to feel at ease with myself and my past.

When I do feel the condemning, critical voice pipe up and the mind wanders to the bad choices, I try my best to give a big imaginary cuddle to that nineteen-year-old girl in the hospital, the girl who was ravaged by addiction, the girl who was always in over her head in situations, the girl with emotions and thoughts that she was unable to navigate. How could I possibly resent someone who didn't have a bad heart, someone who had 'had a bad time', and didn't have a good way of coping?

If I see anyone acting in a way that is self-destructive and who is acting out in a harmful way – I just imagine them with a bandage around their head. They aren't well people; they are in pain. By doing this silly thing, I am able to have more compassion for others than if I were to go on their actions' face value.

To forgive myself is to accept that I was a sick person, not a bad person.

It's about truly accepting what has happened and giving myself a fucking break. Who hasn't got a past or a moment in time that we are not proud of? So why do some of us – myself included – treat ourselves like we are the only people in the world without a colourful past? One of the best bits of wisdom that Jo has ever given me: 'Accept or change.' Like most of the super-useful recovery tactics I have under my belt now, I use this in all areas of my life. If I can't change something, I have to accept it. Simple and effective.

I still live with some shame, however – and annoying flashbacks. You gotta remember I'm only three years into this game.

Just like my self-harming intrusive thoughts, I have no control over the thoughts from the dark days or even the 'glory days'. It's rather strange, and a bit like when you end up down a YouTube rabbit hole: you go on the site with the intention of learning how to put a door hinge on, and you find yourself looking at 'Bad renditions of Lady Gaga's "Shallow".' I can be doing something vanilla and mundane, minding my own business, and all of a sudden, a memory comes back – one that is the furthest flavour from vanilla. Yesterday, for example, I was watching vintage *Gogglebox*. It was a Christmas episode and there was Leon (god rest his soul) wrapping up a box of chocolates in Christmas paper. Before he wrapped it up, though, he took a sweet out of the tin and enjoyed every second of it. Immediately my mind took me back to me brazenly giving someone a half-drunk bottle of wine as a Christmas present, completely certain that they wouldn't noticed half of it had gone.

This happens frequently, but the majority of these memories don't hold the same power that they used to. When they do happen, I have a few little techniques to banish them:

- **I look at where my feet are and remind myself of what year it is – sounds stupid, I know, but the chances are that this shameful moment was more than three years ago, and probably as much as ten years ago. As much as I love a repeat, why am I giving airtime to an episode I don't want to watch?**

- **If it's a really painful flashback, one that really taps into who I am as a person, I remind myself of all the positive things and the achievements I have done since getting sober.**

- **And here's a good one – my friend Cat shared this nugget, which was given to her by her granddad: 'Have you killed anyone?' For the majority of us, the answer is no. So when I am reminded of pissing in an alley for all the world to see, for example, I just say to myself: 'Melissa, you haven't killed anyone.'**

One thing shame isn't helped by is people saying: 'Do you remember that time when you [insert shameful memory]?' Please, I beg of you, if you have a friend or know someone who has had a difficult time on the booze, then for fuck's sake, do not ask this unless you know that it is appropriate and you have their trust. As much as the past is important to learn from, ask yourself: 'Am I trying to be constructive or am I trying to be funny?' If it's the latter, once more, don't be a dick.

I was on a night out once and bumped into someone who hadn't seen #NewMelissa yet. I didn't particularly want to delve into the depths of addiction while out socialising and, out of the blue, I was hit with this type of question, complete with a memory I wasn't prepared for. This pissed me off no end; it wasn't funny or kind.

Sorry, rant over.

If you're anything like me, the whole self-love thing might feel a bit strong to begin with; self-like was a more attainable goal (it suited the martyrdom complex I had), so I started out with learning to like myself. I started this process with Shahroo in Amy's Place: she asked me to write down my 'assets', the qualities of myself that I liked. God, that was a painful exercise. Have you ever tried to write out the things you like about yourself? Prior to recovery, I always thought celebrating yourself and being able to list things you were good at was arrogant and unbecoming. I have always struggled with motivational speakers – watching *The Apprentice* or any type of situation whereby people are selling themselves ... I physically cannot bear it; it makes me want to flay myself. I suppose I struggle(d) with it because it goes against the grain: every part of me shrivels at the thought of believing in myself enough to 'put myself out there'. But being confident in my assets, however uncomfortable I feel, is an important piece of the 'Melissa, you're sound' puzzle. To this day I find it easier to write out a comprehensive list of the things I don't like about myself, but I have to refrain from this all-too-familiar, destructive habit of concentrating on the parts of me I dislike. Writing out the good stuff, or even saying it to myself, has got easier over time and it does help build on what self-esteem I have. Quietly, in a little journal or on the notes application on my iPhone, I have the evidence to disarm my inner-critic.

The thing about my past is that, without it, I wouldn't be who or where I am today. I reframe it now. I have a choice: I can either see myself as a villain and victim mash-up, or I can choose to see myself as someone who has overcome some serious life shit; as someone who is taking responsibility for the pain they caused and is willing to make it right.

I have to choose how I see myself daily, and if I choose the healthy, positive image ... well, I'm in for a good day; if I choose the first – I will be on the couch, binge-watching and binge-eating, feeling sorry for myself, the tiny violin playing, getting nothing done. (This is where the iPhone notes come in handy.)

Shahroo introduced me to a Japanese art called *kintsugi*. When a piece of pottery, for instance a bowl, is smashed, rather than discarding the fragments and assuming it's rubbish, time is taken to mend it, putting it back together once more. The pieces are refixed using gold, emphasising the breaks. As a result, the bowl – that you thought would never be fit for purpose again, never mind pleasing to the eye – is now a unique work of art. It is beautiful because it has been broken. That reference means a lot to me, and whenever I feel down about my past, I remind myself that each situation that chipped, cracked or broke me into a million pieces is what makes me the person I am today.

* * *

Accepting my past pushed me towards accepting who I am, and I suppose reaching that 'self-love' mush we see all over social media. For so long, I was ashamed by so many parts of who I was: my sensitivity, my disgusting sense of humour, my jazz hands, my Crohn's, my alcoholism, my dodgy mental health. I never wanted to accept the things that made me me. I was ashamed of them – and hated myself for being me. Blows my mind now that I was living my life, embarrassed of who I was, believing that I was not enough or 'too much'. Through accepting who I am and what I suffer from, I'm able to worry less about what others think of me. Self-acceptance has made life that bit easier.

Takeaways

- **Shame keeps us sick and holds us back**
- **Shame is 'I am bad'; guilt is 'I did something bad' (there's a difference)**
- **You are not the only person who has done things you deeply regret when drinking**
- **Holding on to resentments only harms us**
- **Take your time before you attempt to reach out and apologise**
- **As painful as it is for us, it's important we hear how our drinking affected our loved ones**
- **Not everyone will want to forgive us**
- **Flashbacks of our embarrassing moments will get easier with time, the more we clear the damage of the past**
- **You have to forgive yourself or at least try to**

- We aren't bad people – we (alcoholics) were very sick people
- Learn to love (or like) yourself
- You are not your past.

Chapter 9

Boundaries, boundaries, boundaries

Doesn't seem that long ago that I was telling you all about my chronic people-pleasing, perfectionism, caring too much about what people thought and never putting my needs first. Well, my friends, there's a name for that – co-dependency. Although I am not in a relationship, I have co-dependency traits. I don't mind reiterating for the nth time that the drink was the symptom, my thinking was the problem and – more to the point – a shocking inability at maintaining healthy relationships was the problem.

I wasn't completely oblivious to the fact that this was an area I had to work on: there were patterns of repeated behaviour in all of my relationships, and I don't just mean romantic ones.

When looking for these 'behaviours' of mine, I had to take the other parties involved in the relationship out of the equation and just look at me and my behaviour. I can only do me. It quickly became as clear as my booze-free, well-rested complexion that I gave the whole of myself in most relationships: I consistently ignored my own needs for the sake of keeping hold of people or things. Don't get me wrong, I'm as extra as they come and my sense of humour always remained on the dark side, but I can also be rather submissive with people who I care about – a bit of a doormat, and an exploding one at that. I've never been great at asserting myself, so I just avoided that, and if a person walked on that doormat one too many times, it would explode.

This had to change. People don't know how to treat you if you don't tell them.

I kept on hearing the word 'co-dependency' in my meetings, so I thought I would enquire. Ever the girl for a quick solution and a sucker for old habits, I hit Google search, clicking on 'Co-dependency for Dummies'. (I won't have a bad word said about that 'For Dummies' series.) I was about eight months sober when I started to research it, so the old brain function wasn't exactly firing on all cylinders.

On the Codependency for Dummies webpage I found a 'cheat sheet' that gave a list of common traits for co-dependency (the sheet should have been titled 'Melissa Rice's personal bio'). Off we pop:

- *Low self-esteem*
  - *Not liking or accepting yourself*
  - *Feeling you're inadequate in some way*
  - *Thinking you're not quite enough*
  - *Worrying you are or could be a failure*
  - *Concerned with what other people think about you*
- *Perfectionism*
- *Pleasing others and giving up your self*
- *Poor boundaries*

- *Boundaries that are too weak and with not enough separateness between you and your partner*
- *Boundaries that are too rigid and keep you from being close*
- *Boundaries that flip back and forth between too close and too rigid*
- *Reactivity*
- *Dysfunctional communication*
  - *Difficulty expressing thoughts and feelings*
  - *Difficulty setting boundaries – saying 'no' or stopping abuse*
  - *Abusive language*
  - *Lack of assertiveness about your needs*
- *Dependency*
  - *Afraid of being alone or out of a relationship*
  - *Feeling trapped in a bad relationship and unable to leave*
  - *Relying too much on others' opinions*
  - *Intimacy problems*
  - *Avoidance of closeness*
  - *Losing yourself*
  - *Trying to control or manipulate others*
  - *Feeling trapped in a dysfunctional relationship*
- *Denial*
  - *Denial of codependency*
  - *Denial about a painful reality in your relationship*
  - *Denial of your feelings*
  - *Denial of your needs*
- *Caretaking*

- *Control*
  - *Controlling your own feelings*
  - *Managing and controlling people in your life; telling them what to do*
  - *Manipulating others to feel or behave like you want (people-pleasing is a manipulation)*
- *Obsessions*
- *Addiction to a substance or process*
- *Painful emotions*
  - *Shame*
  - *Anxiety*
  - *Fear*
  - *Guilt*
  - *Hopelessness*
  - *Despair*
  - *Depression*

You know what, though? When I read this cheat sheet, I didn't feel ashamed and I didn't feel panicked – I laughed my head off and thought to myself: 'Great, another bloody thing on my list.' I felt seen. I felt heard. This was it. Eureka, I've found it! I was a co-dependent.

Recovery really is about discovery, and the longer we stick at it and keep learning, the more is revealed about ourselves, and *knowledge is power*. The more I know, the more I can put in some work to manage it. If you're feeling a little unsettled and this checklist has opened a can of worms for you, I get it. I had a lot of messages after the episode for *Hooked* that aired on this subject; messages that weren't just from drinking folk: they were messages from muggles (non-addict folk), friends and folk I've known for years, all relating to co-dependency. In the States, people talk openly about it – the comedian Whitney Cummings, the amazing writer Nina Renata Aron. Maybe in Britain it's been a bit of a step too far to talk so freely about how we are in relationships? Well, if that is the case, when has that ever stopped me? Co-dependency and alcoholism are good friends, so it's only right that I explore it. And, for the record, it doesn't mean that if you have these tendencies you are an alcoholic; it also doesn't mean that if you are an alcoholic then you are co-dependent, either.

There are always misconceptions that certain behavioural traits are 'female'. I confronted that head-on in the previous chapter and I am about to do it again. I reached out to resilience coach, NACOA (National Association for Children of Alcoholics) ambassador and friend of *Hooked* Josh Connolly. If you don't follow this guy already on social media, then I recommend you do; I'm yet to finish one of his videos without feeling enlightened or motivated in some way. Josh is in recovery and also has the lived experience of growing up in an alcoholic home. Throughout the whole chat, I was like one of those Churchill nodding dogs that people used to put in the back of their car in the late nineties. I burst out laughing a fair few times because I felt he was describing me. Identification really is so powerful and when those moments of 'Mate, you are literally describing me' happen I feel pumped. It's magic. So off he went:

> *I didn't know anything about co-dependency and I didn't recognise how much it was playing out in my life. The way I drank was an attempt to fix my co-dependency because alcohol allowed me to*

stop being so co-dependent. I had a false idea that I was able to live and be on my own. When I drank, I didn't need anyone else, and when I was sober, I couldn't live on my own at all.

My want for validation and wanting to be loved stemmed from the co-dependency role I played when I was growing up, in the family dynamic I grew up in. I have a level of sensitivity, I pick up on other people's emotions; I was born that way and my sensitivity was heightened by the environment I grew up in. I grew up with an alcoholic father and I was so in tune to my mum's feelings. Rather than being myself, I became the version of myself that I thought my mum needed for her to be OK. When you take that into adult relationships it really plays out, let's say romantic relationships first. Because I was emotionally inept, rather than thinking 'how do I feel about this person?' or 'is this the right fit?' I would work out very quickly what that person needed and I would become that. The relationship for the first three months would be incredible because I would meet every single emotional need of the person in the relationship but after a while it would fall apart. This would happen regularly throughout my adulthood.

Such was my need to tap into other people's emotion and what they needed that I neglected my own needs. Even when I stopped drinking and began working on myself, I was consistently abandoning my own needs in order to show up for yours.

If someone told me that they were unhappy with my choices and my behaviour, I would fix it and change. If someone behaved in a way that I was unhappy with, I wouldn't say a thing. I used to think that if I speak up, they won't love me anymore – so I wouldn't communicate my need. It's not like that today. I *remember at the beginning of the relationship with my wife now, we would have a fall out, a fall out that most couples would have, and it took me a year or two to stop saying 'are you going to leave me?' after each argument. My belief was that if we argue, people will leave.*

As a human being, my value exists because I exist, my value is based not on what I do in the world, it is based on the fact I exist. I gained this idea from lots of different reasons growing up, that I am not loveable just as I am, that I have to play a certain role for me to be loveable.

There may be many differences in mine and Josh's stories, lives, experience of addiction, but my responsibility is to tune into the similarities and boy oh boy are they there. Consistently abandoning my needs and not communicating how I felt was my thing. Josh and I aren't alone, we aren't the only people out there who have to manage co-dependency. My darling Mimi bought me a book by Melody Beatty (dare I say, the queen of co-dependency?) and it's one of those 'daily readings'-style books. Each day is a different reading on a different subject relating to co-dependency and boundaries, and it's still a book I rely on today. If you do feel like this is an area that you're after a bit of support with, I recommend this bit of kit.

As I have mentioned before, addiction is often referred to as a 'family disease' and for many people who have an addicted loved one, co-dependency is often evident in the relationship. If I look at the relationship with me mum, for instance, and everything she described from 2017, she was very much in the caretaker role, and although the lengths she went to did keep me alive, her life's purpose was reduced to making sure I was OK, and that came at a cost. If I was OK, she was OK. If I was having a decent night's sleep, so was me mum. Unknowingly, at the time me mum took on my addiction, the only thing she didn't experience was being drunk. My sprees were her sprees and they shouldn't have been, they were my actions and not her messes to clean up. When you're in this situation, this caretaker/dependent dynamic is very hard to spot. I know, for Ange, I was her responsibility. Guilt, and feeling like she would be letting me down or would not be 'a good mum' if she did contemplate kicking me out, prevented her from doing so. Her dogged, relentless and unwavering belief that she could fix me caused great harm to her and I can't take that back.

'Enabling' is a word that I know people struggle with. When you call someone an enabler is cuts deep, and backs go up. But there can be direct and indirect enabling that happens when there is a caretaker–addict relationship. Lying for someone, always picking them up from a drunken spree, giving money, keeping the peace, buying alcohol, telling people what they want to hear. I can't imagine how excruciating and exhausting that must have been. No one wants to watch their loved one suffer and for many people, my mum included, their efforts, however 'enabling' they may be, come from a place of fear and love, and I will never condemn that.

I relied on that level of rescuing and, as grubby as this makes me feel, I abused the privilege of knowing my mum was there to help me, house me, love me. My behaviour didn't change, it only got worse. If we try to prevent someone from falling, how will anyone learn how to get back up? I was as completely dependent on this relationship as I was on vodka, and I wasn't learning any valuable lessons from it.

Leaving Liverpool was the start of taking back control, of learning to stand on my own two feet. Moving to London gave me the chance to fall; sure, not to the depth of rock bottom again, but I was able to fall, and from those minor tumbles I learnt how to get back up.

As well as being the one who needed rescuing, I am also a rescuer. If I think someone is in bother and struggling, all I want to do is pick them up and put them in my pocket and make their problems go away. Even though I know that 'rescuing' or 'saving' someone hinders development, I can't bloody help myself. What's ridiculous about this is that I can't even fix my own life, but I am willing to try and save someone else's! The audacity! In sobriety, I had to learn (pretty bloody quickly) that I haven't got the power to fix anyone. I'll never forget when Jade and I were chatting and the subject of 'going back out' (recovery lingo for relapse) came up and I said to her, 'If you did, I would lock you in and not think twice about it.' She laughed and I laughed, but there was a part of me that meant it.

There are so many other experiences, aside from alcoholism, when I just want to fix someone. I'll take over and take charge, no problem – but there's a huge difference between being supportive and being a rescuer. Support is asking what I can do to help; fixing is taking on the person's problem as my own.

A situation involving a Bengal cat called Ettie comes to mind, which really illustrates my fixing nature. January 2020, and St Jade was off to South Africa to do some charity work (I call her St Jade because she is the most proactive missionary-type person I've met). She asked me to mind her kitten. I had never had a pet before; no one in my entire family has ever had a house pet – if you're wondering why, the answer you will get is: 'They make the house stink.' (A very Kirkby, and reasonable, response, if you ask me.) So, I took on the role of guardian to a kitten called Ettie.

I was given specific instructions to show this kitten affection. I had explained to Jade that I can't pick an animal up because I hate feeling their organs and rib cage. There is something really odd about the underbelly of an animal which makes me feel uneasy, but as a former teacher I knew the importance of stimulation in those early developing years, so I was determined to overcome my squeamishness. So there I was, one adult Kitten looking after an actual kitten.

For those four weeks I was, as we say in Liverpool, 'harrashed'. My nerves were gone over whether this kitten was OK or not. With Jade's parting words of 'I don't want to come back to a cold cat' ringing in my ears, I carried that kitten in my pocket. This is not a metaphor, I really was putting mammals in my pocket.

As the weeks went on, however, she had enough of the pocket of my Marksies housecoat. She was a Bengal cat, and they like height, so I came up with another idea that allowed me to get on with my jobs, go about my business – and frantically Febreze ...

When it was time to hand the kitten back, I was extremely relieved and very politely told Jade that, if she ever needed to go away again, in no way was she to ask me to mind it.

After about two days of being reunited with her mum, I had a phone call: 'Mate, what the fuck have you done to my cat? She is as needy as fuck!'

I was rather taken aback at first, and went on to tell her our daily routine. Jade was floored that for a good 70 per cent of the month she had been away, her kitten had been pandered to and spoiled rotten, carried around in the comfort of the hood of a Rosie Huntington-Whiteley-range M&S robe.

Although I would say that our Jade wasn't clear on the amount of time I was supposed to cuddle Ettie, it was this experience that showed me just how much of a rescuer I am and how much I can forget about my own needs. Message received. It was clear that I had had no boundaries with my feline counterpart, and that had been the bloody problem.

Whether you're co-dependant, trying to get sober or have difficulty saying 'no', boundaries are your friend. I never really had any and if I did, they were easily forgotten. I mean, I had zero boundaries with alcohol, every self-imposed rule was broken, erm – controlled drinking, remember that? In their crudest form, boundaries were drummed into me at Clouds in the form of time boundaries: if you were late, you had to explain why and had to hear from your fellow residents why your lateness was disrespectful. The counsellors explained that if we were unable to meet simple boundaries in rehab, then we didn't have much chance of not crossing more complex boundaries in the real world.

The time boundaries I could understand and adhered to no probs – I hate being late. However, I didn't really understand what personal boundaries were …

Personal boundaries

So what the hell are they? Personal boundaries are the invisible mental lines – a border – of where I end and you begin. These 'lines' are a bit like our rules: they allow people to know who I am and what I am OK with and, more importantly, what I am not OK with.

Boundaries are crucial for people to feel safe. For all human beings, we need to know where the boundary is.

Michael Rawlinson

Here's a very simple example for you. My name is Melissa. I used to hate being referred to as 'Mel'. My boundary *should* have been, 'Please don't call me Mel.' That way, people would have known how to address me and I wouldn't have been irritated. But I never put the boundary in place, and therefore many people dropped the two syllables that meant a lot to me. Each time I heard 'Mel', I would internally fume, but I didn't say anything. And by not acting early, it was hard to then go and put a boundary in because the 'Mel' had gone too far; it was entrenched, and how weird would it be to turn around and say, 'You've been calling me Mel for two years and it's not my name'?

(I'd just like to say that I don't mind being called Mel now, especially in the workplace. Kind of gives me the distance between personal and professional life – something which I wasn't able to have before.)

The thing about personal boundaries is that they are your responsibility, and you have to put them in. But that requires you to understand your values first, and decide what type of behaviour you are willing and not willing to accept.

Our personal boundaries are all different depending on our experiences and norms; for a lot of us, we don't know what our boundaries are until someone has crossed them.

Here are some examples of my early personal boundaries:

- **I have the right to put my recovery first**
- **I won't compromise my mental wellness for anyone or anything**
- **I do not apologise for taking some time for myself**
- **I am entitled to disagree with someone**
- **I am OK to cancel plans**
- **I don't have to respond straight away.**

When I got sober, I didn't know who I was any more. I won't say I didn't have any values – I did, but they were buried deep beneath emotional scar tissue and empty bottles. My values were often in accordance with what my mum's were, or what those close to me were. Which is probably why there was always a weird feeling of discord inside me: my values were always competing with others'. Essentially, I didn't even know the basics of who I was. What was my favourite colour? What was my favourite food? What did I enjoy? What did I think about fidelity? What was my opinion on, well, anything? As you've probably figured out by now, most of this recovery stuff is about exploring the past for answers and getting to know the real us. And we gain the clarity to figure out who we are when we ditch the booze.

First, I had to identify and reacquaint myself with my values, my principles – the bedrock of who I am. I started with privacy, compassion, understanding, loyalty and respect.

To do this, I began to think about those relationships and situations that had made me feel uncomfortable and I had to ask myself what it was about that person, that relationship, or that situation that made me feel unsafe, and why it had led to emotional reactions. I made a list. I suppose it's just like triggers, really: if I know that someone telling me how I am feeling causes me to get angry, then I know what my boundary is: 'Don't tell me how I am feeling.'

The list grew, and I soon realised that I was not OK with many things, which was a surprise to me because I was so used to acting unbothered. I think the most unusual one that surfaced was that I couldn't bear to be called dramatic. For so long, I was called dramatic when actually I wasn't (I was in bad shape mentally). Even if someone meant no malice and was just pointing out that I was an animated person whose reactions were rather theatrical, to call me dramatic crossed a fucking line.

I then started to look at the people in my life who I did feel safe to share with and with whom, when I left their company, I wouldn't start second-guessing myself or worrying. Once more, I made a list. For me, trust is a biggy, and I was always a very trusting person. I don't necessarily think being a trusting person is a bad thing – it's not. But as a trusting person who also loved an overshare – that ain't a good combination. Feeling exposed is something that causes me to panic, so to avoid that, I have a boundary of sharing my past (only) with people I trust.

The list of behaviours and boundaries kept growing and it became more clear that I wasn't willing to accept two-facedness, gossiping or dishonesty. (Funny, really – all the qualities I used to be. LOL.)

The thing with boundaries is that they can be rigid and they can be loose. Too rigid with my personal boundaries, and I imagine I would be in for a very lonely life: if I started to distance myself from every person who ever made me feel uncomfortable I would be stuck indoors watching *Shameless* again and afraid of ever being close to someone. But too loose with my boundaries, then the days of being a people-pleaser and being taken advantage of would return. I am a part of the loosey-goosey camp: my personal boundaries have always been loose because of my long-standing fear of letting others down and a remarkable inability to say no. I just had to get used to putting my needs first. I would feel so guilty for things like being off work sick, for wanting some time for myself after an intense day, for asking someone for money back (to name but three). I always thought that putting myself and the things that I need to stay right in the head first was a selfish act, and not a nice quality. Josh hit the nail on the head for me on this:

> *Look at the phrase that most people are used to, 'be the better person and hold your tongue'. There are times when that's a good thing to say, but we often use it in terms of 'stop communicating your needs and be who people want you to be'.*

For so long I had neglected myself physically and emotionally, until I was completely burnt out and spent, and then I'd be angry at others and feel taken advantage of. Now I know that you can't pour from an empty cup – I am no use to anyone or anything if I don't keep my cup full, and no one else can do that for me but me.

But even with all this new knowledge about boundaries, I didn't have a clue how to implement them. Do you just say to someone, 'Excuse me, this is a boundary!' and go all Gandalf-with-a-wooden-stick shouting, 'You shall not pass!'?

How you communicate them is just as important as the boundary you set. There's an Al-Anon (a group for loved ones of alcoholics) phrase: 'Say what you mean, mean what you say, just don't say it mean.' In the past, if I dared try to tell someone that their behaviour wasn't OK, I would go on the attack. It was always a long time coming and I would erupt: 'Don't take the piss out of me, you're making me feel like shit and I'm fucking sick of it.' (There probably would have been a really uber-Scouse accent to match, as I get more Scouse when I'm angry.)

There are a few things to take away about my old way of getting my point across. Firstly, it's hostile and accusatory – I am pointing out someone's behaviour but not explaining myself. Sometimes we do see red and there's no avoiding that but, in my experience, when I try to assert my boundary in this old way, the person in question can't hear what I am saying as all they hear is an attack, which leaves them backed in a corner, ready to go for the jugular. Another point to raise from that sentence is the 'you're making me feel' bit. I was bowled over when I heard this, but: 'No one has the power to make you feel anything.' I disputed this no end, but now I understand that only *I* can influence how *I* am feeling.

Here's another Cloud's nugget for you: 'I statements'. All the bloody time, we were reminded to 'talk from the I'. Let me break that down for you. Instead of: 'You always take the mickey out of me, you're making me feel stupid,' you say: 'I feel quite silly and small when I hear those things.'

What a revelation. Talking from the 'I' gives me the chance to speak 'my truth' without opening myself up to an argument. I use this technique quite a lot, to be honest – give it a go. It's worked wonders for me.

So, with some understanding of what my boundaries were and how best to communicate them, I started to ease myself into the process. I kicked off this new way of life with the classic: learning to say 'no'. Who knew that a two-letter word could cause that much bother to a human being? Usually, in the past, my 'no' would be followed by an essay of excuses and apologies as to why I didn't want to do the thing. Or I would say 'yes' and take part in whatever you asked me to do, even if it was inconvenient for me. Or if I really didn't want to be involved, I would tell a web of lies to get out of it when, actually, 'no' is enough. Jo tells me often that 'No' is a full sentence and, guess what, we all have the right to say no to something we don't want to do; in the same way that we have the right to put our recovery, our body, our time/schedule, our emotional needs, first.

The first few times of just plainly saying 'no' to something and someone was very difficult indeed. My mind immediately went to: 'They hate me', followed by intense guilt. It does get easier, especially when I remember that when someone tells me they don't want to do something I have asked, I don't hate them. There are times, though, when I slip back into people-pleasing. In 2019, I nearly went for a job in Kent. It wasn't even a job I was particularly interested in, but the person who had set it up meant a great deal to me and I felt obliged. What the hell was I doing? I even had to Google where Kent was (don't judge me). I cannot believe that I was deeply considering taking a job I didn't want and moving to a town I didn't know out of some weird form of social politeness. Ridiculous.

For the longest time, I wasn't just your 'yes' girl, I was your 'yes, no, three bags full' girl. This level of dishonesty doesn't go down well with people – we might think it does, but it really doesn't. My default setting is clearly people-pleasing, so to give myself a buffer between people-pleasing and being the queen of boundaries, I pause. I love the phrase 'I'll let you know'. You can take a minute, figure out if you want to do it. (Otherwise I'd be moving to Kent.) Owning your 'no' is different from just saying it; 'owning' for me means actually following through with it. How many of us say 'no' but know full well we will end up doing it anyway? By sticking to it, it starts to feel quite freeing and almost empowering … ever closer to being that girl who 'does what's best for her'.

When it came to implementing boundaries in close relationships, it was all the harder, particularly with my family. The status quo had been the same for so many years: I was the child who needed its nappy changing, and my mum and sister had the baby wipes and nappy bags ready and waiting. To change that dynamic and put some boundaries in place was difficult, and still is. It can feel alien to those you love; it can even feel like some kind of rejection or even coldness, and that's a lot for them and for the person putting in the new rule. But how someone reacts to us putting our needs first is not our responsibility, and not our burden to carry. Again, this is easier said than done, especially if we are trying to assert ourselves with a loved one – it can be really bloody hard not to take on their pain. One time, I told my mum that I was really busy with work and therefore it wouldn't be good if she came to visit. I didn't say it in a nasty way, but she cried and thought that I was distancing myself from the family. I promised myself I would never make my mum cry again, but it was a scenario where I really had to hold it together.

I spoke with Josh about his experiences of this – not just for the book, but for my own benefit. Having that peer support is a resource, a really wonderful, game-changing resource, so why not use it? Josh said:

I'm at the stage in my life where I find boundaries relatively easy with people who I am not seeking attachment from. But in relationships where I am seeking attachment, you best believe it's still a challenge.

I don't believe a functional family exists; there's obviously varying degrees of dysfunction but we all play a role. When we no longer play that role or that part, the status quo is changed in the family dynamic. There comes a sense of abandonment and instability. We have detached from the role we used to have – for example, the one who needs fixing – and our family members also feel abandoned and question what their role is. The thing about boundaries, the very reason I avoided them was fear of abandonment, and the very thing you are going to get is some level of abandonment, because we are putting our old self to bed.

I remember I used to be the crazy, loud one at parties – the one who is up for a laugh and the centre of attention – and my family all celebrated that. Now I am not that, I'm happy to be in the corner absorbing it all. I'm happy with that. I remember my little sister got a bit funny about it. She was looking to me to play the role, to make everyone laugh, and it didn't happen. It's important to have a certain amount of compassion for our family members, they have lost that version of us. Even though we were drunk and we were causing trouble, they had a part to play. When we get well, what is their role now?

I learnt about family roles in Clouds:

Everyone has a role to play, the lost child, the hero, the wall flower, the scapegoat, the mascot, and they can be interchangeable.

Michael Rawlinson

One thing's for sure, I was never the wallflower. But if we are in a family and we all have a role to play and then we change, there is a transitional period for everyone, which is why it's important that I have compassion for my family. And remember that I 'have a programme'. I have received support and gain insight on this stuff daily. They do not and it is not my place to force anyone into attending self-help groups or, worse, start pointing out every behaviour.

Starting to 'cut the cord' – as this was essentially what I was doing with me mum – can be extremely hard. For example, I've had to learn that if something is going on with me, the first thing I do is speak to another alcoholic – I talk it out with them, and *then* speak to my mum or my sister. If I don't, then it's just too easy to become 'the dependent' once more. I have to be responsible for me now.

Through these steps, I am beginning to figure out what I should be doing independently, and I do think our family has grown from it and is the healthiest we have ever been.

On the flip side, with a lot of people, the kindest thing someone can do is detach with love. Not all recovery stories include family reunions and mended hearts. This isn't always a sad or a tragic thing, but a kindness. I know many people who, due to the unpredictable nature of their relationship with their family member or friend, have decided the best thing to do is to detach. Or the family member has decided to detach from the person who is drinking/using. Having to put this stringent boundary in place doesn't make you a cruel person with no heart. Irrespective of what the history or relationship is, if you are drained, or your mental health and well-being is being impacted by someone's behaviour, it is more than OK to detach, to take some time, to look after yourself.

Personal boundaries help to keep me safe emotionally and make sure of the headspace I need to look after myself. They can prevent my recovery being put at risk, they can protect me from taking on someone else's drama, and they also give me this wonderful thing called integrity.

I never truly had integrity before recovery, and the constant shifting and changing of my opinions or statements must have made me appear flaky, disingenuous and unreliable. Making a stand or making a decision that is right by me and my beliefs and then sticking to my guns still isn't something I particularly enjoy; it can cause me a lot of distress, to be honest. Sometimes doing 'the right thing' is the hardest thing, and the easiest thing is to cave and give in to someone. I was in this position in the summer of 2019, when someone in my life was behaving in a way that had the potential to harm me and a project I was involved with. Each day was unpredictable and I couldn't read this person's intentions, and what should have been an amazing opportunity felt exhausting, laboured and chaotic. I knew that this person's behaviour wasn't right and so, with the help of others involved in the project, I came to the decision that it was best if this person was no longer involved. I was a mess and there was a lot at stake, but I knew it was right.

The old me would have put up with the behaviour, have made

excuses and justifications and learnt how to live with it (probably unleashing passive-aggressiveness from its case at the same time). #OldMelissa would have walked on eggshells and enabled this person, just so I could keep the job and project alive. But I couldn't do that now – I didn't get sober to do the same old shit. For the first time in my life I stood by the decision, trusted in my instincts, put my feelings and sanity first and backed up my own judgement. Those in charge tried to mediate the situation, but the rest of the team and I had already tried that. Parting ways was the only solution to a problem that was getting worse. It was a long and torturous four weeks of waiting to find out the outcome; my mind racing with self-doubt and thinking that I had over-reacted or I was being ridiculous. But, lo and behold, the project went ahead without said person.

As difficult as it had been, it was a character-building experience, to say the least. But now I know that I can do it; that I can put in place a really difficult boundary. I am the person who upholds their values even when every part of my body is telling me to give in. I know what's the right thing by me.

It can be really frigging hard to put yourself first, especially if you are worried you are going to upset someone. I have to remind myself, though, that I have no control over people. As a self-identified co-dependent, I know I like to be the one in control at all times. Before recovery, I never once considered that I was a control freak: how can someone who admits they don't speak up for themselves and struggles with assertiveness be controlling? I hear you, brother/sister. Look, telling people what they want to hear, playing the victim or wanting situations to have the outcome you want *is* kind of controlling. Being a perfectionist is wanting to be in control. I had to learn and accept that the only thing I have power over is my reaction and my behaviour. I don't have to insert myself in every situation these days and try my best not to be dragged into drama – I'm very much a 'not my circus, not my monkeys' kind of gal these days and I have to thank Jo for that useful way of life.

As a recovering alcoholic, it's important that I am able to see the things I can control and the things I cannot ... for my own sanity and for the sake of others. How I respond to events such as a cancelled train or a late delivery is my choice, and if I want a semi-serene kind of day I gotta let that shit go and just look at the things I am able to do and let the rest go. If it's out of my hands, then it should be out of my head too.

Boundaries with alcohol

Instilling personal boundaries was way more of a challenge to me than when it came to my boundaries with alcohol and protecting my recovery. But I wasn't trying to keep drink in my life, I wasn't trying to control the uncontrollable. This was life and death. I know that may sound a bit melodramatic to you, but I was and still am certain that I don't have another relapse in me. So with the firm belief that another drink would finish me off (either quickly or slowly), as far as I am concerned there is no such thing as being over the top with boundaries that protect sobriety.

In the beginning, my boundaries were things like:

- **Not going to boozy places**
- **Asking friends not to talk about 'funny' stories from the drinking days**
- **Not being around people or places that caused me stress**

- **Not going to house parties**
- **Speaking to someone in recovery every day**
- **Not talking to people about my alcoholism**
- **Not skipping an AA meeting for a social event.**

With time, and with my recovery more firmly embedded, I was able to ease up on these boundaries. Now, I tailor them to suit where I am at. If I am having a rough patch and I catch myself isolating, telling white lies and other telltale signs that I need a meeting, I go back to my original boundaries. They are there for me and not for anyone else, and I can do as I please with them. They are there to protect me, and not to appease others.

There are still things in my life that I need to be more boundaried with: my screen time on my phone is ridiculous, the number of times that Netflix asks, 'Are you still watching?' is embarrassing, and the way in which I have no control over Asda's chocolate-chip muffins all point towards a lack of boundaries. But it's a process, I'm aware of it and I know what actions I have to put into place. I'm outing it with you, which is a bloody good start.

Takeaways

- **Co-dependency is more common than you think**
- **You can have co-dependency traits without addiction, and vice versa**
- **Neglecting our own needs for the sake of others leads to resentment**
- **You can't pour from an empty cup**

- You can't fix anyone, you can only control your own reactions
- Boundaries are your friend, your best friend
- You may not know your boundaries and that's OK
- Practise saying no, practise getting your needs met
- Putting in boundaries can feel terrifying but they protect us
- Our boundaries can change to suit where we are at.

Chapter 10

Anything is possible in recovery,
so what the hell are you waiting for?

So here we are, the last chapter. First of all, thank you for putting up with me. If you are fed up with me by now, I don't blame you ... but just imagine being me – I am sick to the back teeth of myself all the bloody time, and writing about myself, at length, has taken that to a whole new level!

I'm not usually one for an ending – most endings in my life end in tears (shock), even the good ones. And if you're expecting some kind of 'And I lived happily ever after' rhetoric, you'll be waiting a while. Why? Firstly, I don't believe my recovery will ever be over; there's always going to be trying moments and, therefore, new learning – I'll never be a finished article and I don't want to be, because that would mean I am stagnating, and usually that means I go backwards instead of forwards. Secondly, I still have my moments of despair and unhappiness, so to tell you life's just perfect would be a bigger lie than the vodka-not-smelling one I dispelled earlier.

You may be rattled and somewhat frustrated by this harsh dose of reality, thinking to yourself: 'So after an entire book, she's still not happy – what's the point in this? I want a refund!' But before you do that, let me explain. Sure, I may still have bad days and bad weeks: I mean, I made a batch of scones at 10 p.m. the other night, and I didn't have the patience to wait for them to bake. So, with no fucks to give and a mantra of 'only god can judge me', I ate that raw scone dough with my bare hands, in my knickers and housecoat, sobbing my way through *Normal People*. But whatever pain I experience in sobriety, whatever life throws at me and however hopeless I may feel, today I know it will pass, today I know that I have the resilience and enough about me to overcome it. Even in those low moments, they are nothing compared to when I was drinking, and they never will be. I'll say it again: the problems I have in sobriety, the problems I have today, are the problems I would have wished for when I was drinking. My worst day sober is still a thousand times better than any day drinking. I genuinely believe that, and I have to believe it if I want to remain sober. There is no situation in my life today where drink would improve how I am feeling – it would only ever add to the problem. Every day sober is a good day. I repeat – every day sober is a good day. It certainly doesn't feel that way to me sometimes, but it is. Being sober is miraculous, particularly if you self-identify as an alcoholic. When I pause and say to myself that a sober day is a miracle I feel a sense of relief, a sense of perspective. Everything I feel today is real and authentic and not induced by a bottle of voddy, and to feel this 'realness' is a gift for me.

Keeping momentum going comes easier to some people. I'll call a spade a spade: I can be a right lazy bitch at times. Two weeks at the gym, on the cusp of 'feeling myself' as Beyoncé would say, and then three days later I am back to square one. Honestly, I am that person who buys a 'goal journal' only for it to be found covered with dust some six months later, and I wonder if I can carry it over into the next calendar year. There's no fad I haven't participated in, and every fad was short-lived. I would say that the only thing that has been consistent in my life is inconsistency, and that has always worried me in recovery. But I cannot afford to be that way.

For reasons unbeknown to me, I *have* managed to get three years of maintained sobriety under my belt. (Actually, I do think I'm being harsh on myself there, as I did everything suggested to stay sober.) I got to three years not by looking ahead but by taking it day by day. 'Keeping present' has always been a challenge, and I always thought living in the moment was what got me into this mess – if there was a drink involved I'd flip the bird to tomorrow and straddle the 'moment' that I was in. It took a good while to learn to live my life in twenty-four-hour blocks, to make good choices and concentrate on the day in hand. As far as I'm concerned, I am just as sober as the person with one day's sobriety as I am with the person who has twenty years' sobriety, because we are all sober for 'today'. Not everyone has that way of thinking but that is my way of keeping life in the day.

And when it comes to being present, I'm no Eckhart Tolle – I am the world's worst meditation expert. I totally understand the benefits to the mind and the body, but my ability to concentrate on the breath can sometimes make me more anxious than the reason I downloaded the Headspace app in the first place. I meditate through music and take some time to just sit and listen. A walk in the park is also my way of connecting with the still and reminding myself of where I am in that moment.

I remember I threw a right paddy in the second rehab I was in, when I was asked to set my goals for the future: 'You keep telling me to be present and now you're asking me to set goals for the future – make your bloody mind up!' I thought the two should never meet; that I was only expected to live in the here and now. But now I understand that I can have goals and that I can break things down and work on them day by day.

SMART goals are all the rage in rehab and CBT:

Small
Measurable
Attainable
Relevant
Time-boundaried

I use this approach to most things without even thinking about it now. Gone are the days when I thought I could do it all and set myself up for not meeting my own ridiculous to-do list. There's nothing more deflating than not doing everything you set out to do in one day. If I am trying to get to five meetings, redecorate my flat, get abs, eat well and get a dream job all in a week, then I am only going to feel like shit. I have to break it down into manageable tasks, figure out the milestones, determine what I am able to do and accept what I am not able to do. This doesn't mean I don't continue to push myself, I do – I have to push myself, otherwise I would become ... complacent.

I did think that after the first year it would get easier; that as time went on, it would all be plain sailing and up, up and away. Bollocks. Recovery isn't linear.

When we do finally look at our lives and think, 'Bloody hell, Ricey, you've smashed it', then can come the feeling of 'What's next?' You see, there is a risk of becoming complacent in recovery. I have had my moments when I thought, 'Nah, I don't need to go to that meeting, I feel all right.' But in those periods, when I haven't been as proactive or as 'on it' as I was in the beginning – boy, oh boy, have I felt it. My decisions and reactions aren't right, they are more off-key. It genuinely baffles me that I often don't do the things that I know and have proof of that they improve my life. But that is my self-sabotaging behaviour coming into play, and I have to be hyper-vigilant with that.

Complacency is rather dangerous, particularly in recovery. We have the potential to end up with a false sense of security and maybe get a bit too cocky … I have the job, I have the partner, I haven't drunk – I don't need to be worrying. The truth is, that stuff is easy come, easy go, and really, what is it all for? When I was drinking, I had my hair done in Toni and Guy (£150 a pop – fucking mental), I went on holiday, had a cute car, had the job, had the clothes – but as you've read, I was miserable, mental and lost. In Amy's Place, I was on benefits, had no job and I had no real interest in or means to be arsed about the material things, but I had more internally than I ever had before – I had freedom from drink, I had happiness and I had hope, and you can't put a price tag on that stuff. You'll probably call bullshit on that, but it's true. The gifts of recovery are way more than the stuff that is just that, stuff. I'm not saying I don't entertain nice things any more – I do. But if I start to chase those external things and put them on a pedestal, then I'm losing sight of what the gifts of recovery really are, of what's really important, and that behaviour would mean I am on dodgy ground, ground that would probably be outside the local offie. I have to remain teachable and I have to remind myself that I don't always know best – keeping close to recovery keeps me grounded, and around words like 'humility'.

I read on social media that 'recovery is never owned, it's rented, and the rent is due every day'. When I spotted this, I didn't roll my eyes or cringe my tits off: it really hit home – the importance of this stuff. My sobriety, recovery and mental health require daily action if I want to keep them in good shape. I remember Michael, at Clouds, explaining that recovery is like a muscle: if we don't exercise it, we will lose it and if we lose that muscle, that strength, then our defences against our vice are depleted. I've heard too many people say, 'After five years, I started drinking again' and it gives me the willies – but I have to hear that stuff, I have to hear about relapse. If I don't, then the old 'You're fine now' voice (Michael's Poison Parrot) will become louder and louder. It's not a risk I am willing to take.

For me, dropping off parts of my recovery routine and 'medicine' stinks of ungratefulness and arrogance – and I know that these traits are the part of my character that have caused mayhem in the past. Recovery has given me the chance to get to know myself well; enough so I can tell you what my default behaviours are. Through knowing these behavioural traits, I can spot 'em and change 'em.

Actually, before I go on the 'ungrateful' rant I was about to get into, I just want to highlight something remarkable about recovering addicts. We/they are some of the most self-aware folk about, and the champions of champions of self-efficacy. Gone are the days when I repeat the phrase, 'I don't know what the matter is, there's just something not right with me'; today it goes more like: 'I've been isolating the last few days, and I can feel myself projecting into the future and catastrophising. I can feel my self-doubt is on me.' That, my friends, is progress. This is what bloody happens when we throw ourselves into recovery – we become extremely tuned in to our emotions and what is going on for us – which is why I genuinely love recovering addicts: highly emotionally intelligent beings. Sorry, I went off-piste there, didn't I? Oh, well, you're used to that by now.

Back to being ungrateful. Like I said, when I start to put things before my recovery, cut a few corners here and there, and rest on my laurels, there is a lack of gratitude on my part. I was quite happy to reap the benefits of recovery when I was at my most desperate, but where's the 'giving back' in the ungrateful scenario? Where's the respect for recovery? Ricky (my wise guardian angel in London) once told me: 'A grateful alcoholic will never drink.' Like with most of this stuff, it took me a while to understand, but I get it now. Throughout my drinking, I never looked at what I had in life – it was always about what I didn't have. I couldn't count my blessings because as I far as I was concerned, there were none. What a brat. I had no gratitude for the cushty position I was in, for the family I had, the privilege I had – I had no real appreciation for anything, really. So today, when I get caught up in some trivial bullshit (that will have no effect on my life in a year's time), and I feel overwhelmed, and it is easy for gratitude to go out of the window, I know that keeping an attitude of gratitude is a godsend. A lot of people in recovery send each other their gratitude lists each day. So, if I am in a shitty mood and moaning about something insignificant, forcing myself to think about the things I am grateful for has the power to change how I am feeling and how I am probably thinking about the situation.

Negative thinking can spiral, seeping into your vision until every part of your life appears to be unbearable and awful – and that will not be the case. On the subject of gratitude, Michael added:

Wise people have, for centuries, understood that gratitude is strongly and consistently connected to a better sense of happiness and well-being. Twelve-step members, balanced and wise people, professionals, happy and hopeful people, say that having an 'attitude of gratitude' increases our optimism, relieves depression, improves immune function and lowers blood pressure. It also strengthens our relationships with those around us. Almost thirty years ago now I was given a little badge that said 'Attitude of Gratitude' on it. I wore that badge on lapels for ages. Believe me, it is true, and it works.

Michael Rawlinson

There is a major caveat to this having an 'attitude of gratitude', and that is that there is such a thing as toxic positivity. By now you will know that I am not in the die-hard 'PMA' (positive mental attitude) brigade and I really don't want to knock it if you are. But I think there has to be a balance – being 'good vibes only' in sobriety is just as unhealthy as the denial I was presenting when I was pretending that I didn't have a problem with my drinking. If you are sad – feel sad. If you are pissed off – fucking feel pissed off. We feel what we feel and shouldn't apologise for it. Jo has often ever-so-gently pulled me up when I say, 'I should be happy,' when, really, I *shouldn't* be feeling anything. What I *should* be doing is sitting with (and dealing with) the feelings that I've got and not beating myself up over not feeling happy. Truth be told, there are times when I simply cannot look on the bright side and actually all I need is for someone to hold my hand for a few moments in the dark. But when my sadness tips into 'My life is the worst and I have nothing to be grateful for', that is when the gratitude list sorts me out.

I *will* say that I am grateful every day that I am sober. When I put my head on the pillow at night, I say, 'Thank you.' I don't know who I am saying thank you to, but I say it. Actually that's a lie, sometimes I say, 'Cheers' or 'Nice one' rather than 'Thank you'. I still don't consider myself a religious person but I do think I am more spiritual. I have a faith that's personal to me – more of a belief, really – that 'Everything happens for a reason' and 'Everything will be OK as long as I don't pick up a drink'. I have faith in both those things; take from that what you will.

This whole 'being grateful' is just one new addition to my thinking since coming into recovery, and it's safe to say that my whole outlook on life has changed as a result. I appreciate the small things in life and I get my kicks out of living life simply – I don't mean that I am boring or live my life off-grid collecting rain water and making compost, but I do take great pleasure in things that most regular adults have been doing for years. I'll never forget when I was doing the first 'big shop' for my flat in Amy's Place, on the local high street. There was a Poundland and an Iceland, which was wonderful for me and my bank balance. I came home, unpacked the shopping, opened the carton of chicken breasts and separated them into freezer bags and popped them in the freezer (Ange-hack). After washing my hands (of course), I then went to the bathroom and took out my new cleaning items. I popped a toilet block in. When I pulled that first flush, I was filled with so much happiness and pride … I was finally the type of person who gave a fuck about a lemon-scented flush. That moment of contentment was the first of so many, and I never thought I would feel content with anything, never mind anything so small and simple.

I know I am not alone in this: when I chatted with my chum Marcus on that bench in Archway, we spoke about actually noticing life. He explained how he had never noticed autumn leaves before and how beautiful they were. I didn't laugh or think, 'Christ, have you had a toot of a spliff?' I understood it. For a large portion of my life I was trapped in my own head, in my past, in my future or just in my own thoughts; I didn't see the world. Well, not properly anyway. Since recovery, I can see it all, I can feel it all and I 'get' the simplicities. Before, nothing was ever simple in my life, and everything always had to be dramatic, risky, larger than life – I was never settled, nothing would fill the 'hole in the soul' unless it was destructive or brag-worthy.

This switch from the brash and the bold to easy and simple trickles into all facets of my life and I'm all right with that. As long as I'm sober, there's food in my belly, a roof over my head and I have a good night's sleep, I'm all right.

I always thought that being in sobriety would mean I would have a chronic case of FOMO, but that hasn't been the case for me – it's just another lie I told myself to avoid giving up drink. Being in recovery has taken *nothing* away from my life; it has only added to it, hugely. I've done more in three years than I did in the ten prior to recovery.

Taking booze and other drugs (because let's not forget, alcohol is a drug – it's just legal) out of the equation forces us to find other ways to find pleasure. Just because I don't have hangovers or rely on a drug to have fun doesn't mean I am not fun or don't have fun. I do. I have an absolute ball. I can do things that people do drunk, like gigs, drag bingo and raves, and enjoy every second of it. And I get to remember it all: the laughter, the music, the joy … and the only thing I wake up with in my head is the French song '*Non, je ne regrette rien*' going full blast.

One of the best times I've had in sobriety is going to a fright night at a theme park with a bunch of recovering addicts. I'm not one for horror – I mean, I can't even watch *Jaws* – but I went, and subjected myself to extreme terror. It was a new experience and I didn't have to worry about the impression I was making; I was in safe company and, let's face it, we've all seen worse than a Scouse girl frightened by a zombie. Walking around that maze was horrendous – it was worse than that feeling of being trapped in Ikea – I couldn't get out, I couldn't see a door. (In the words of Gemma Collins, 'I'm claustrophobic, Darren.') In this fake-blood-filled maze I screamed so much that a zombie broke character and asked if I wanted to be escorted out. I looked over at Jade who was also crying … with laughter. (Twat.) In those few hours of rollercoasters and being chased by first-year drama students covered in special-effect make-up, we were like kids again. Four women who, collectively, had more lives than a cat sanctuary, had a good thousand hours of therapy, had been through the depths of addiction and who had started again from the ground up – there we were, happy, laughing at my expense, free from it all. The only demons and monsters in our life were the pretend ones chasing us, and I never want to lose that.

Life does not get smaller when we give up drink – my life was at

its smallest when I was drinking. Our lives get bigger and better …
because we get better.

Knocking the drink on the head and working on ourselves gives us
the chance to revisit the things that we lost in addiction, or it allows
us to go after the things that we always thought were out of our
reach. There is nothing more beautiful and totally inspiring than
seeing someone who you know from their early days of sobriety
achieve great things. The transformation that occurs really is hard
to put into words. I've had the honour of witnessing close friends
return to their careers in nursing and social work. I've seen parents
reunited with their children. I've listened to stories of people going
abroad for the first time in years. I've watched someone sing on
stage who never thought they would sing again. Our dreams and
hopes are ours alone and I do believe that anything is possible in
recovery. Think of it this way: if we applied the same amount of
dedication to our goals as we did our drinking or drugging, we could
be millionaires.

I made the decision pretty early that I didn't want to return to
teaching. I was still pretty shell-shocked over how it ended and, quite
frankly, I didn't want to put myself at risk of burn out ever again. My
head and health has to come first, always.

I started to explore my options and thought I would be best
suited to the charity sector. Although I was always risk-happy in my
drinking and some of the situations I put myself in professionally, I
never used to be the type of person who would even consider taking
a stride of faith, never mind a leap of it. Not any more, though – I
was now the type of person who made long leaps of faith: my first

had been in going to rehab, and then to Amy's Place, and both of those things had turned out for the best. I think when you've been to rock bottom, and gone through treatment, you develop a 'Why the hell not?' attitude. I just started saying 'yes' to opportunities that came my way, but not because I was returning to being the people-pleaser; I was saying 'yes' to new experiences that I wanted to try. These were *my* yeses. *Real* yeses.

I was asked to speak at a few events on behalf of the Amy Winehouse Foundation, which led on to doing a few more things for them, like a Fred Perry article – the first piece I ever publicly shared about my addiction and recovery. I then spoke on a documentary called *Amy Winehouse: The Legacy*. This planted the seed that I wanted to talk about my experiences and raise awareness. Too long has addiction been in the shadows … well, not on my watch.

I also started to realise that the more open I was to these new experiences and getting out of my comfort zone, the more opportunities would present themselves. Each door I walked through led to another one opening.

In 2018, I was a woman on a mission to build my CV. I had this certainty that it was all going to be OK (again, part of my new outlook sponsored by recovery). At first, I had a plan to tell any future employers that I had done some travelling to explain away that gap in my employment timeline. (I mean, it wouldn't have been a lie: I travelled from Kirkby to Wiltshire and London, and while on my travels I did find myself. Granted, I didn't have an armful of wooden bracelets and a pair of harem pants, but I did do some soul-searching along the way.) But you'll be pleased to know I didn't do that. After all, how would I ever get in-work support or be myself if

I was going to keep my past to myself? That hair-brained idea was my shame talking.

In October 2018, I had an internship with the housing association linked to Amy's Place. Yes, you heard right – I was an intern at the age of thirty. Recovery had taught me that I had to work for anything good, that I couldn't just expect to get where I wanted to without humbling myself and putting in the leg work.

For about eight months I was immersed in charity fundraising; it came about because someone believed in giving me a chance. His name was John. A brilliant man, with a brilliant mind and love of ginger nut biscuits. He didn't treat me like a poor alcoholic who needed help; he pushed me to be my best, and raised the bar week by week. My alcoholism wasn't even in his remit. I'll never forget a time when I had made a few typos and he said, 'Oh, have you had a few?' He was mortified. But that misplaced joke was proof that he wasn't constantly aware that I had been through what I had been through. This was the first experience that helped me get over this weird belief I developed in recovery – that people feel sorry for me. I can't tell you how good it felt to go into a workplace each day, having input, proving myself, achieving small goals. I had thought I would never work again and yet here I was, producing decent work, showing up each day, looking at The Shard. My confidence grew tremendously.

During this internship I was on a bit of a roll of trying new things: I still didn't try fish, obviously, but I started to feel this pull towards my writing again. Writing had always been something I had threatened to do but hadn't had the guts, confidence or the headspace to get on with. I used to write all kinds of comedy scripts in university that were always well received. I have video footage of them somewhere, but I'm the type of person who can't listen or watch themselves back; I always end up asking people: 'That's not how I sound is it?' But not writing, whether that be comedy or Melissa's musings, was going to be my biggest regret that I told my kids on my deathbed. I actually have a journal entry from rehab that says, 'Need to start writing, don't know where to begin,' even though Joanne bought me a fancy Paperchase notebook to go into rehab with and urged me pursue it … but look where we are now, ay?

I never showed anyone my writing at first. Although I was more confident in most areas of life, I didn't want to show anyone my personal stuff: it was too exposing. I didn't want to make anyone feel uncomfortable, like when someone tells you they have written a song and then they play it and you're sitting there thinking, 'This is a heap of shit, good god, they aren't even in key, what the hell do I say?' Withholding my writing was a kindness to me and to the prospective reader.

It probably won't surprise you when I say that I have little faith in my writing; in fact, every chapter of this book that I sent to the editor was always accompanied by some sort of 'I realise a lot of work needs to be done on it.' This automatic response is my way of calling my work a load of rubbish before you do. I struggle with imposter syndrome: I am always waiting to be found out as the fraud that I am. Even with physical evidence of success, I can still find a way to make any kind of achievement luck or a fluke, or say things like, 'Bloody hell, don't know how I managed that, I'm useless!' with a laugh and a grimace. I know this is imposter syndrome and a bit of shame. It's time I stop doing this and celebrate my wins.

* * *

In January 2019, I had a key-worker session with Rachel, a member of staff at Amy's Place. By that stage, I didn't need much support but it was good to see them all now and again. An avid BBC Radio 5 Live listener, she told me about a competition called the 'Rachael Bland New Podcast Award', a podcast that builds on the legacy of Rachael Bland, the creator of a trailblazing cancer podcast: *You, Me and the Big C.* Steve Bland (Rachael's husband) and Uma (a BBC Radio 5 Live producer and close friend of Rachael) were looking for a podcast that would 'change the narrative, that had light and shade and would give a voice to a community that wouldn't get one otherwise'. I read the brief and I thought, 'That's addiction and recovery.' I had already been writing down tales of addictions past; what did I have to lose?

I took the printed-out brief up to my little flat and I read it at least fifteen times. They were after a five-hundred-word submission and, as I read, I realised it was one of those times about the chance moments of life, with every opportunity you say 'yes' to adding to your skills and confidence to move onto the next. You see, my internship as a bid writer with John had basically been a crash-course in concise persuasive writing. And so, with the skills I had acquired, I divided the BBC briefing points up into percentages and then I made sure that my five hundred words had the same weighting, and had a laugh along the way. I remember thinking to myself, 'So, you want light and shade? I'll give you light and shade.'

I threw everything at the pitch, because this is what I did now. I was the type of person who didn't do things half-arsed any more; I did things properly, and by giving it my all, I know I can go to sleep without any 'should-a, would-a, could-a' taunting me (or I try to, anyway).

On 10 February 2019, I got an email. I was sitting in hospital, awaiting a routine finger-up-the-back-passage examination, so it was perfect timing. I couldn't believe it. That little pitch had got through to the next round. Next, I dragged Jade in to record something on my cracked iPhone. My script-writing mode kicked in and we got it done. I downloaded some editing software and taught myself how to edit a sound bite. It was all very exciting but still, there was never any genuine belief from Jade or me that something would come of it: I firmly believed the BBC would never take on addiction and recovery in all its not-so-glorious glory. Even the night before the results, Jade and I were still convinced we had 'fucked it' (Jade's exact words). We had just had a telephone interview with a producer, Uma, and we believed our interview was so bad that the only thing to do was devour an emergency Nando's. Poor Jade had already had her tea (dinner), but out of respect for my feelings of failure, she made room for chicken thighs and a side of halloumi – now that's friendship.

The next day the phone rang. It was Uma, sounding very sombre and moody. I remember saying to her, and genuinely meaning it: 'We know we haven't won, but thanks, you've made my year.' She then said, 'Steve wants a chat.' Steve did the whole: 'I'm sorry to tell you this … but you've won.'

This was the first time they were introduced to Tiny Tears: I lost it.

You would think that such an opportunity would have had me jumping up and down and screaming for joy. This was a chance to help people who were in the same position I was in, a chance to put the record straight and to do my little bit to challenge the stigma of addiction and recovery. Wrong. I had never been so torn. You see, a job had come up in the company I had interned in. It wasn't a shoo-in that I would get the job, but I had been at the company for a fair few months and, as painful as it is for me to say it, I knew I had produced good work during my time there.

I had been presented with two paths: the sensible and stable path, or the creative and uncertain one. It may sound like a first world problem, but this was major for me. If you don't believe me, here's Joanne's take on it:

> *There has only really been one occasion where I have been really worried about you, and that was when you won the podcast award. You had worked so hard and put so much effort into it, and it was amazing (and fully deserved) that you won, but for some bizarre reason you were considering swerving it for a bog-standard 9–5 job. Your mum obviously wanted you to take the path which would offer you long-term security, but when these amazing chances come your way you absolutely have to take them. You will ALWAYS be able to get a job, always. That isn't going anywhere. I was really proud of you when you stuck to your guns and chose the thing that you were passionate about. You took total control of your own future and that is something that I think has terrified you in the past.*

As Joanne has alluded to, and as I'm sure you're aware, I went with the pod.

I went with my heart and my gut and doing what felt right.

There was a hell of a lot of learning on both sides: this was risky ground for the Beeb – trusting two non-broadcasters, and thrusting two recovering addicts in early sobriety into the spotlight. But they believed in the pitch, the audio submission and, most of all, they believed in Jade and me. The podcast was just as much the team's baby as it was ours, and they trusted us to choose our topics and gave us free rein to be Melissa and Jade.

At first, there was a lot of tiptoeing on their part: I don't think they were used to people being so matter of fact and nonchalant about their drug and alcohol addiction, and I don't think they knew how far they could go with the questions. Jade and I took for granted how open and honest people in recovery are: the looks on the team's faces, as if they were thinking: 'Is it OK that I'm laughing at this?' were priceless. Quickly, our dysfunctional podcast family adapted: the responsible grown-ups (producers) learnt about our gang, and the kids (Jade and me) learnt how to sit in front of a mic.

There was a lot on the line with *Hooked*. I didn't want to bring any further shame to my family. I didn't know if the world was ready for our gallows humour and I didn't want to be judged. But Jade and I knew that we had to do it, that the podcast wasn't about us: it was about giving back and reaching out to people. If my tales of a chemical detox and Jack Daniels on cereal and Jade's perfuming her back garden and battle with drug psychosis could help one person feel a sliver of hope, then our self-obsessed (but justified) fear had to be put to the side. This was the other 'bonus' to it, for me: my biggest fear in life at this stage, aside from a relapse, was being talked about. So what better way to confront that fear than to share my depths of addiction and poor mental health with the UK?

We had absolutely no idea that the podcast would go on to achieve what it did. I don't just mean the hundreds of thousands of downloads; Jade and I were inundated with messages from people who had never felt heard before. We were in such shock, it felt like a huge responsibility, to tackle a subject in this way that had never been done before in the UK. So throughout the entire experience we put our recovery first, our friendship second and everything else had to wait. If either of us wasn't right, the pod went on the back burner. That's one of the proudest takeaways I have from that experience: that throughout it all, the hype, the interviews and the many messages, we just stayed two mates in recovery who looked out for one another. It was no different to the time when we were appointed house leader and deputy house leader in Clouds. (Yes, you read right: Michael and the team thought it wise to give me the role as house leader and I appointed Jade as my deputy. I was crap at laying down the law and Jade was somewhat challenged in the pastoral/nicey-nicey side of leadership.)

Can you imagine trying to explain to us then that we'd end up with our own show on the BBC? Bananas. *Hooked* was only supposed to run for six episodes, and we ended up with twenty-six. We went on to win Broadcasting Press Guild Radio Programme of the Year and even won a Silver British Podcast award for Best Wellness podcast.

While that recognition was fantastic, more welcome still was the fact that those awards were evidence to Jade and me that people were waking up, that the penny was dropping and society was ready for honest chat about addiction and recovery. Each episode was filled with lived experience, real voices, relatable people. The podcast was more about our guests, more about accessibility and allowing people to feel heard than it was about us two. The biggest reward from the podcast? People went to treatment, people came into recovery, people told us they didn't feel alone, people were able to understand their addicted loved ones more, and people felt hope. Life made and job done.

Being visible in recovery isn't easy, and for a lot of people it's not for them. I totally get that and I respect it. I am not the poster girl for anything: it's way too much responsibility for me; I just have to do 'me' and what's right by me. I'm no role model. I have battled with myself quite often over being pigeonholed. My negative association of being known as 'Melissa the alcoholic in recovery' fed into stigma that I wanted to squash, so I embrace it. It's the truth – it happened, and I know that it is nothing to be ashamed of. If muggles don't get to hear or see someone thriving in recovery, how will we ever change their views or thinking?

I say I don't shout my recovery from the rooftops, but here I am writing a book about it, and you can hear me on BBC Sounds (see, Uma and Nicky? I told you I would plug the podcast). But in my day-to-day life, I don't make my recovery my only 'thing'. It's not the first thing that comes out of my mouth in conversations, but I don't crumble or stumble over my words regarding it any more – I don't shrink or deflect like I used to. It is a huge part of my life; addiction can happen to anyone and I'm proud of being sober, but there is more to me, more to all of us, than our pasts.

My current employer really helped me to see that 'overcoming adversity' is an asset and not something to shy away from. Her name is Carolyn Harris. Carolyn is an MP, and in her role as chair of the All-Party Parliamentary Group for Gambling-Related Harm, she has campaigned tirelessly for reform, with great success.

You're probably laughing now, or thinking to yourself, 'How and why is this girl working in an office in Westminster?' I want to be a part of change and use my experiences for good. I know I said not writing was going to be my biggest regret, but I had another: I always regretted not studying politics.

I met Carolyn when I was asked by the Amy Winehouse Foundation to share my story for an event at the Centre for Social Justice (yet another example of saying 'yes' and chance meetings …). I then had to decide what I was going to do: sit around and only *think* about asking Carolyn for some experience? Nope. I had to go for what I wanted, and politely *ask*. Which was daunting but, as always, necessary.

Carolyn is a champion of all things recovery and I respect her determination, story and heart. She uses her own experiences to fight for change and I hope to be able to do the same one day. As far as mentors go – I have the best in the business.

Long story short, I undertook some voluntary work experience in her office, an experience I never thought possible as a thirty-one-year-old recovering alcoholic. I am proud to say that I am now employed as part of her team. Each time I log on or walk into the building, I am in utter disbelief. I know nothing lasts for ever and who knows how long the role will last, but to know that I got there, that I have had experience of doing something that I thought would always be out of reach … well, it moves me to tears, every single time. In the same way as John did, I am never made to feel anything less than a former teacher who is finding a new career. (Despite this, when I was offered the chance to write this book, I did worry that revealing my past would hinder this relatively new career that means such a great deal to me. So I checked this with Carolyn, nervously, one day. In the most stunning South Wales accent, I was told that my past was 'something to be proud of' and 'the qualities of a person who has gone through darkness' and 'come out the other side shows strength.' Hearing such sentiments from anyone, never mind someone you admire, means a lot to a recovering addict.)

Me sharing the story of *Hooked* and getting a job with an MP isn't meant to be all 'Aren't I great? I'm just so wonderful' (gross). I hope it reiterates three key things:

1. **Anything is possible**
2. **There are good people who don't judge you and who support your recovery**
3. **Healthy risks are important.**

My endorsement of healthy risks doesn't mean that I take uninformed risks or go back to a 'sod the consequences' attitude, but if I don't push myself out of my comfort zone (but stay safe) there is more of a risk of me feeling quite resentful. There have been occasions when others around me, mainly my family, are terrified by my choices and I have to be really careful not to take on their anxieties and fears. This has taken a long time to conquer. Here's an example. When I was in active addiction, I booked a trip to Bali. As you can imagine, I was in no fit state to go – I would have come home in a body bag. I wouldn't have even managed to get out the door, let alone the airport. But I had made a decision in rehab that one day I would go to Bali. I was in one of Shahroo's sessions and I told her about my dream of going – and that I wanted to say a proper goodbye to my body as I knew it.

You see, my Crohn's did not get better after my drinking; it was as troublesome as ever, and the decision had been made to go ahead with the stoma surgery. Now, call me vain, but I wanted one last time in a bikini, and I hadn't been abroad for years. I had done my research and knew that Bali had an AA community, and I knew that my motives for going weren't rooted in escapism or running away. We spoke it out, and I told Shahroo that my family would be worried sick. She simply said, 'Why are you asking permission?'

I didn't know why I was asking permission. So I didn't ask: I knew my truth, and I booked the trip, and I told my family it was booked. It wasn't open for discussion, this was my choice. This was a major milestone for me.

I went to Bali for four weeks and I had the time of my life. I went straight to an AA meeting when I got there, and then stuck with the recovery community while I was there. I couldn't believe that this was my life. Granted, it was more 'shit pray love' than *Eat Pray Love*, thanks to a few street-food mishaps and Crohn's. But the fact that I was so far away from the UK, so far away from the girl I had been less than a year ago, was mind-blowing, and a real moment of 'You did it, kid.' If I had taken on the anxieties of others I wouldn't have gone. Just as, if I had taken on the anxieties of others with the podcast or even this book, I wouldn't have bothered. I have to go with my instincts, be in tune with my intentions, talk it out with like-minded people and believe in myself. Because even if that meant falling flat on my face and it all going tits up, it would be a mistake I had made – not one made for me. And I also now know I can pick myself up again, and that I have enough tools and a support network to help me.

I spent my whole life living in fear – my drinking was fuelled by fear, and where did that lead me? A wise owl (Michael, obviously) taught me a little acronym:

False
Evidence
Appearing
Real

By using this quick little prompt in my day-to-day life, I'm rapidly reminded that I have a mind that reports 'fake news' more than any conspiracy-theory bot account on social media. So if I take a minute to breathe and look at the evidence I have in front of me, I am able to stop that snowball. My anxiety has been at an all-time low since I stopped drinking – no surprise. But I don't think that's because I don't have the alcohol in my system any more – it has more to do with the fact that I have new ways of thinking and healthier ways to cope. I still have my moments, of course I do – I will have this head for life – but I can't think my way out of problems: I have to put in action. I've had many a conversation with Jo who tells me, 'Take your head out of it and just do it.' Taking my head out of a situation basically means that I need to stop thinking and start doing. How many times have you deliberated over something? (I'm trying to think of an example – hang on a sec ... Got it.) You know when you see an advertisement for a job, and you think it's the right job for you, so you download the application pack – and you do absolutely nothing with it. You talk yourself out of the job before you even put your name on the bloody form. Then you spend some days thinking about how you would go about your answers and how your experiences match the required specifications. You still don't fill the form in. It's two days before it's due in and you finally put fingers to the keyboard and then you start to realise it wasn't that difficult. That's the type of situation when I have to take my head out the way and just get on with the task in hand. And that's what I try to do these days: less thinking, more action. Sometimes I just need to stop myself. *Breathe, take a minute, sod it, take ten minutes and remember who the fuck you are.*

I can't avoid fear, I can't avoid pain and I can't avoid life. I tried that with vodka. There are experiences and challenges I have faced in recovery that I never would have thought I would be able to get through sober.

Ever since I was diagnosed with Crohn's in 2012, I never wanted a stoma bag. It was off limits; I was so terrified of what others would think of me (mainly men); I didn't want to be the girl with the bag; and even the thought of it would send me into a meltdown. The worst thing about Crohn's is that it's triggered by stress and, let me tell you, my bowel was stressed for years. It was flare up after flare up, admission after admission. And a point-blank refusal of an operation that would improve my life.

When I came into recovery and was practising acceptance, building myself up, putting myself first, I had another flare up. And Mr Arthur (my hero, my surgeon) said, 'Enough now,' and I agreed. Just like my drinking, I was done fighting. Just like my drinking, I wasn't willing to compromise my quality of life and mental health.

I had my operation in July 2018 (the NHS's birthday, in fact). I had mentally prepared for the op, I had done my farewell bikini tour of Bali, and I knew that once I woke up I was going to have a life free from accidents (and worrying myself over where the nearest toilet was, when the next flare up would be, and what food was going to cause me crippling pain). The one thing I was worried about? Pain relief. It won't come as any surprise to you, but I have always loved recovery from any surgery: I was given the good stuff (and that pain relief gives you the buzz you deserve when a nurse is poking a stick into a 3-inch-deep wound next to your vagina). I know full well how and why opiate pain relief addiction is a hidden and equally dangerous addiction. One of the worst detoxes I have seen was someone coming off codeine. This poor woman was blissfully unaware that she was addicted. She had arthritis, and it was only when she ran out of her prescription pain relief and panicked and started to go on the dark web that she realised she needed help. (If you want to hear more about prescription med addiction, we did an episode on it; it's well worth a listen.) So, yeah, I was a bit worried about the pain relief. I was having big surgery, so of course I was going to need it. But I decided I just had to be open, honest and clear with the doctors and with those around me.

Ironically, after all my worrying about going on a morphine drive and being on the super-wavy pain relief, I had a terrible time. I didn't enjoy it one bit: I was out of it and out of control and I couldn't bear it. My body didn't react too well, either: I was rolling around on the floor covered in vomit and thinking that I'd soiled myself. They even put me on an old friend, ketamine, and I still couldn't hack it. There was a little part of me that felt robbed but at the same time I wanted my marbles back – this was a revelation.

After twenty-four hours of being out of my nut and sending pictures of a commode with a smiley face on it to friends, I told the pain relief team I wanted out, at once. Although they were not too impressed with my decision, I explained to them that if I didn't have my mind then I wouldn't be able to get through it. We agreed that if the pain increased then I would go back on it.

As soon as I 'came to', I was able to get to work with the new way of life. The bag life.

As you know, I believe that everything happens when it's meant to happen. Don't get me wrong, I have my moments, particularly in changing rooms, when I hate the bag, or when I have eaten something rather fibrous, which can result in what I like to call a bag-cident. But I took to the bag straight away because I knew it was an act of self-love to do that, and I knew I could get through anything as long as I didn't pick up a drink. I'll be honest, I shocked myself (and everyone around me) at how well I took to it. So much so that a gorgeous nurse asked if I would have a chat with another stoma newbie. What the actual hell? Me? A positivity coach? Well, I never.

And you know what? The nearly seamless transition from bog to bag was all down to the work I undertook in recovery. I gained acceptance, I spoke to my support network, I took it a day at a time; I cried when I wanted to cry, I practised gratitude, I avoided self-pity and I saw it as a new life, not a death sentence.

See, this stuff works in all areas of life.

By working on my recovery, I am able to be the version of Melissa that I never thought possible. I have changed my outlook and I will always be working on rewiring my thinking, but I'm still me. I recently reconnected with an old friend from the past, one of the good guys. I hadn't heard from him or spoken to him for three years (for obvious reasons), but after a chance encounter on Instagram, initial communication was made and the awkward 'Yeah, a lot has happened in three years' conversation was covered. During it, I was thinking of a way to describe how I am still the same but also changed. I needed a simple way of explaining it, and I don't know why I compared myself to a software update, but to me, it makes sense. I am Rice 2.0. Just like a phone update, it can take a while for the update to complete, there is even that nervous feeling of 'Why is it taking so long? Help! My phone must be broken!' followed by the relief when it's finally rebooted. I like to think that I've had my bugs fixed, new software and features installed, and some new algorithms (coping strategies) put in place. However, I still have the fundamental properties of Melissa: the quirks, the sense of humour and the Melissaisms – all still there. There are people who prefer to describe themselves as a new person, and again, whatever you feel best with. But I don't feel a new person – I feel the most Melissa I have ever felt.

The thing about this 'update' – I don't really notice the changes too much; it's the world around me that sees these changes most. Sure, I feel different: from a youngster, up until recovery, I had that 'hole in the soul' and lived with the unholy trinity of being 'restless, irritable and discontent' (AA). Of course this threesome still rears its ugly head from time to time, but I have a handle on that now and it's this 'handle' that is what others see.

The effects of recovery ripple out, just like the damage of addiction. One of the biggest gifts of recovery is giving my family their peace of mind back. My mum goes to sleep knowing that her youngest daughter is sober, my dad no longer has to question if I am going to cause murder in the home, my sister has a sister and my nephew, Noah, has an auntie. As Ange put it:

> *Today our relationship is as strong as ever, our conversations are very different, we have time to laugh, time to do all the things we*

have missed out on and time to look forward to a much brighter future. That said, we don't take anything for granted – Melissa continues to work on her well-being and is living the happiest life – and that's all I could ever ask and wish for her – love Mum

(I don't think she really grasped how to format a quote for a book. I haven't got the heart to remove the 'love Mum' sign off.)

Today I am trusted, and I can be the friend/family member you call in a time of need. I've been there for friends who have been shat on by exes and helped friends move into their new home, and have been the person who will pick up the phone and listen to you when your mum isn't too well. I never thought anyone would come to me for support. Ever. I never thought anyone would want to share their stuff with me. I can be there for people and be relied upon today, and that was never possible when I had drink in my life. I am not a liability any more; I'd go so far as to say that I'm a bloody good person to have in your life (god, that was hard to type). To be there for people you love is an honour, and I don't take that for granted.

I want to keep on this discovering quest and keep finding out about me. I flooded myself for years to try and flush out and drown the pain, the thoughts and the real me. Each new phase in recovery reveals more than the last and as I peel back each layer and work on the part of me that's holding me back, I become more certain of who I am. I think I was always looking for answers and searching for a way to live and to feel accepted. I thought I would find it in a career, in partners, in the bottom of an empty bottle. But I found what I was always looking for in recovery, through AA – I know Rice 2.0 is who I am supposed to be and the person I always wanted to be. So why would I ever want to trade this in? For what? A few hours that I won't remember? Nah, you're all right. Keep your hangover, huns – been there, done that, got the podcast and now the book. My recovery is my most treasured possession, I protect it at all costs and I wouldn't give this away for anything or anyone. Period.

Throughout this writing experience I have always kept #OldMelissa in my head: her worries, her pain and her struggle. When I was in the green coat days, drinking in secret, chemically dependent, a tormented recluse, there was little that I could connect with. Now, there are so many things that I would want to tell 2017 Melissa to try and put her mind at rest and give her some hope. So here is what I want to say to her, and to anyone who identifies with even the tiniest bit of #OldMelissa, for that matter. I suppose what I'm about to do is a 'Jerry's Final Thoughts' (from *The Jerry Springer Show* for those of you under thirty …).

Melissa, you think recovery won't work for you: it will. If you don't believe it will, believe that it has worked for others – and hold on to that. If you don't have the strength to do it, let others hold you until you do. You've been through too much now and your self-esteem, self-worth, head and your heart are all in pieces. You are entitled to feel happiness. I know you feel hopeless and you have tried so many times before. But keep trying, even when it feels pointless, keep whatever shred of faith you have safe and don't let it go. You really are enough, and you are worth more than a life of worry and alcohol. I know you think you are the worst person on earth because of the things you have said and done, but please know you are not on you own, kid: everyone has their shame – you're human. You are not a bad person, Kitten, you are a person in pain and a person suffering. You're not well and you need some help. You aren't useless, you aren't a failure and you're not better off dead. You deserve compassion, you deserve a break.

People will understand and people will support you when you decide to let them know what's happened. And if they don't? Well, fuck them – they will be out of your life and aren't worthy of having you at your best. Recovery is painful, it's arduous but it is worth it, and you can do it. You will get out what you put in, and Melissa, you are going to go on to live a good life and you will do the things you thought you never would. You're going to have friends and you won't feel alone. You will be loved and you will start to realise that you were always loved – you just didn't love yourself.

For Christ's sake, shut up about work, as you *are* going to work again, and people will see in you what you can't see in yourself. You're going to move on from your past. Your experiences with drink and being batshit will be put to good use and you will be there for others in the same broken boat. You won't carry all that pain around any more, you'll get some help, you will forgive yourself and have moments of peace. You'll even be forgiven by most and through this will learn the human consequences of your drinking. You will go from Bring Your Own Bottle to Be Your Own Bestie, and you'll laugh your head off again. One day, you will be able look back at some of the stuff that made you want to drink bleach, and you will laugh until you wee – seriously, you will. You'll be grateful for life because you will know how precious it is. You're not 'nothing', Melissa, you never were, and you never will be.

Life's going to be tough; it won't all be fixed at once but bloody hell, as you've put yourself through years of drinking and lived with that head of yours, then you will get through anything. Things will begin to make sense and you will get the chance to unpick your past to stop it from repeating. You'll know how best to look after yourself and that head of yours. You'll know what's best for you, and you will *do* what's best for you. You'll even get a grip of your anxiety and your depression and have clever little ways to keep your 'Jean' at bay. All that 'compare and despair' routine will stop and you're going to value who you are and embrace it – you won't want to do or be like everybody else, you'll do you. You won't keep your harmful thoughts to yourself any more: you'll share them, and people won't leave you when life takes a turn. You have nothing to be ashamed of – addiction does not discriminate. You're going to be OK … Actually, who am I kidding? You're going to be *better* than OK. I just need you to go for it now and give yourself that chance to have a better life. All is not lost, kid; it's just you who is lost but you will be found, and you will come home and I promise you, you will make your mum proud.

I am not an anomaly. This isn't a fluke or even an extraordinary tale of overcoming addiction. I'm just a regular girl who is also an alcoholic and got sober and has fallen in love with recovery. I don't know if this book has been any use to you. I don't know if you feel inspired, or you may feel like I am chattering on with utter bollocks, but I hope you have been able to take something from my lessons. If you haven't, there are so many other books, so many different paths to take to achieve sobriety, and I hope you find your path, your freedom.

So, what's next?

Who knows.

Truthfully, I don't need to know. What my experience has taught me is that it's best to have no expectations: when I stopped trying to be a clairvoyant and master puppeteer the good stuff happened. As long as I'm sober, life's good. What I do know for certain about my future is that I won't be shutting up about addiction. I will do what I can to reduce the stigma about it, and use my experience to help others. Stigma is holding us back, holding the cause back and stopping so many of us from getting well. I will keep banging the recovery drum in the hope that people will realise that this is a mental health matter, and a genuine crisis that isn't going anywhere. I will keep reiterating that we need to improve services and we have to stop punishing people who are in desperate need of help. We have a long way to go, but there's hope.

One last thing: I want to thank every person who has supported me. It has taken a small village of people to get me to be the person that's sitting at this laptop, and I'll never forget that. Whether you were in the thick of it with me, a family member, a friend, a supporter of *Hooked* or have given me a kind smile when there were tears in my eyes, you'll never know how much I appreciate it. To Action on Addiction and the Amy Winehouse Foundation, thank you – without the work you do I wouldn't be alive today. My family and I will never be able to thank you enough for giving me that chance to get well, that chance for me, Melissa, to come home.

Right, I really am fucking off now. Wishing you all the happiness, freedom and blessings in the world. Sorry for all the swearing. Lots of love, Melissa x

(Get me the tissues.)

Takeaways

- Life still happens and getting sober doesn't mean we won't have problems
- My worst day sober is still one hundred times better than my best day drinking
- Be careful with complacency – recovery isn't owned, it's rented and the rent is due every day
- An attitude of gratitude can work wonders
- When we work on ourselves, we figure out who we are and what our dreams are
- There are good people out there who think recovery is awesome
- Healthy risks aren't a bad thing
- Recovery is about discovery
- We can handle anything life throws at us when we don't pick up a drink
- Life gets better because we get better.

Further support

NHS Alcohol support: https://www.nhs.uk/live-well/alcohol-support/

Alcohol Change UK: https://alcoholchange.org.uk

The National Association for Children of Alcoholics (Nacoa): https://nacoa.org.uk

Club Soda: https://joinclubsoda.com

Soberistas: https://soberistas.com

SMART Recovery: https://smartrecovery.org.uk

NHS Drug addiction – getting help: https://www.nhs.uk/live-well/healthy-body/drug-addiction-getting-help/

Action on Addiction: https://www.actiononaddiction.org.uk

Change Grow Live: https://www.changegrowlive.org

We Are With You: https://www.wearewithyou.org.uk

Amy Winehouse Foundation (for young people and young women aged 18–30): https://amywinehousefoundation.org

Frank: https://www.talktofrank.com

Mind: https://www.mind.org.uk

Samaritans: https://www.samaritans.org

Twelve-step groups

Alcoholics Anonymous: https://www.alcoholics-anonymous.org.uk

Narcotics Anonymous: https://ukna.org

Gamblers Anonymous: https://www.gamblersanonymous.org.uk

Sex and Love Addicts Anonymous: https://www.slaauk.org

Overeaters Anonymous: https://www.oagb.org.uk

Co-Dependents Anonymous (CoDA): https://codauk.org

Al-Anon (for family and friends of alcoholics): https://www.al-anonuk.org.uk

Acknowledgements

Family

Where do I begin? I think you know whose coming first …

Mum, I don't know if there will ever be a way to thank you for all you have done for me. You'll probably bat this of with a, 'I'm your mum, it's just what I had to do.' It wasn't. Without your faith and strength I wouldn't be who or where I am today. You must be relieved this book is finished, I know I've had you up the wall. Well here's my gift to you to say thanks: I'll never cook with the windows closed and make the clothes 'stink of dinners' again.

Becca – 'Oscar, Oscar' look where we are. I love you (there I said it, don't throw up too much now Biggy). I couldn't have written this book without you Bec – in the countless phone calls you've taken when I've been in tears or panicking I've said too much in chapters, you have listened and reminded me 'not to give a fuck'. For never giving up on me when most did, thank you.

Dad – Tozzer, the funniest pain in the arse I know, you have been proud from the off and knew that one day I would be sharing stories – don't think you meant my dirty washing though. Sorry Dad. Thank you for that constant stream of support throughout this writing ordeal, sorry – wonderful experience.

To my huge Wilson lot – as a family we have been through so much over the years and throughout it all we have had each other. Having your love and support from my darkest days to writing this book means so much.

Book people

September Publishing – you have championed this book from a couple of episodes into *Hooked*. You have given me the chance to be unapologetically me and that ambition I had from early in my life has now been fulfilled. I have you all to thank for that (I've got something in my eye here). Hannah, you have always prioritised my mental health and recovery and those breaks from writing you insisted on are a perfect example on how 'employers' should act. Charlotte and the rest of the team, thank you for answering my many, many, many emails. As a first-time writer, you have made this experience less intimidating through your support.

HHB – oh you guys! I don't know what I would have done without you throughout this experience. When it comes to this book stuff, clearly I don't know my arse from my elbow! Special thanks to Elly, my wonderful literary agent (wow, that still sounds so awkward, 'my agent', cringe). Thank you, Elly, for your friendship, insight, cheerleading and for always answering the rambling silly questions that I often have. We got there in the end ay, and I'm grateful to have you by my side.

BBC lot

The most special of thanks to Rachael Bland (broadcaster and creator of *You, Me and the Big C*). Although I never had the privilege of meeting this formidable broadcaster in person, *Hooked: The*

Unexpected Addicts would not exist if it were not for Rachael and her ground-breaking work. Without The Rachael Bland New Podcast Award, many people wouldn't have sought support with addiction, found identification and this book wouldn't certainly wouldn't be happening. To be a part of Rachael's legacy is a true honour.

How could I not mention our Jade? My friend, my co-host and the voice of reason. It doesn't seem that long ago we were rambling away in Clouds thinking our lives were over. I don't know how you cope with me to be honest, but I'm so thankful that you do. For trusting me to take part in *Hooked* (not that you had a choice), for being a rock during that crazy time, for reminding me that some things 'ain't that deep', for your saltiness and for having my back throughout the 'I've had it up to here' days, thank you. As much as I love you, I want it in black and white, please never ask me to mind Ettie again. 'Fack off.'

Steve Bland, Uma Doraiswamy, Nicky Edwards, Al Entwistle and Stewie Birch – #FORZAHOOKED family. Thank you for giving us two lunatics the chance to be just us (in all our glory). For always challenging me when my imposter syndrome is on me and for believing in me when I'm not able to. Podcast or book, you've forced me to feel proud and I need that.

Generous contributors

Thank you to every contributor to *Sobering*, your generosity and willingness to share your experiences shaped this book. I never wanted this to be, me myself and I – the more voices united in this cause the better. Our Zoom conversations have massively helped me in my own recovery and understanding. I just know that so many people will find identification from your contributions and give people the hope and courage they may need to make some changes. You're all incredible.

My mates

Whether you were privy to the madness or with me now in recovery. Thank you. I learnt that you cannot do this on your own, and I know now that I never have to be because we're in it for the long haul. To have you all in my life is one of the best gifts of recovery. You keep me going, pull me up on my shit, laugh with me (sometimes at me), support me, listen to me and above all else love me. All of you have heard me say (more than once) 'The book is a pile of shit, I can't do it', and all of you have encouraged me to ignore my negative head.

AA family

Jo, throughout recovery you have been a guiding light. You have shown me the ropes and the way, you always remind me of the tools of recovery: to stay calm; to keep life simple; to put things into perspective; and importantly to embrace (enjoy) this book. I'm still working on self-doubt but with you by my side I know I will get there.

To Ricky, Linda, Marcus, Laura – my North London lot. You make a lost Paddington feel found in the Big Smoke and throughout this process you have given me the hope and drive to keep going.

Organisations

The Amy Winehouse Foundation – Jane Winehouse, Mitch Winehouse, Rachel Geary, Shahroo Izadi. From January 2018 to the present day, you have been with me from funding rehab to relocating. You have provided me with opportunities and experiences that built my self-esteem and confidence. Your heart, passion and overall awesomeness has changed my life, and young women suffering with addiction are lucky to have you.

Action on Addiction – where it started. Whether it be The Brink, Clouds House or your ongoing support with *Hooked*, you guys have saved my life and had my back. I am not alone, you have given so many people and families the chance of happiness. A very, very, special thanks to Michael, for being more than a former counsellor, ally of *Hooked* and professional voice for this book – thank you for being a friend and for challenging that part of me that wants to shrink and bat off any achievement.

Alcohol Health Alliance – your work is invaluable to the UK and I hope more people will recognise just how urgent alcohol harm is and listen to your calls for action. Special thanks to Meg, Sarah, Professor Sir Ian Gilmore, Professor Julia Sinclair, Dr Tony Rao for your contributions and most importantly for the lengths you go to for all those suffering with alcohol.

About the author

Melissa Rice is one half of successful BBC Radio 5 Live podcast *Hooked: The Unexpected Addicts*, which won Broadcasting Press Guild Radio Programme of the Year 2020, Best Community Podcast 2020 and a Silver British Podcast Award. Melissa was, until 2016, a primary school teacher. After hospitalisation for her alcohol addiction and a period of rehabilitation at Clouds House she submitted a winning pitch for the podcast *Hooked: The Unexpected Addicts* with her friend from rehab, Jade Wye, for the Rachael Bland New Podcast Award. *Hooked*'s aim is to debunk the stereotypes of who and what an addict is, interviewing real people, with regular lives, whose voices are rarely heard. With help from the Amy Winehouse Foundation, Melissa now lives in London.